D1074048

ELIZABETHAN MILITARY SCIENCE

The Books and the Practice

Caliver just after firing.
From Jacob de Gheyn's *The Exercise of Armes*.
Reproduced by permission of
The Huntington Library, San Marino,
California.

ELIZABETHAN
MILITARY SCIENCE

The Books and

the Practice

by Henry J. Webb

====

The University of

Wisconsin Press

Madison, Milwaukee, &

London, 1965

Published by
The University of Wisconsin Press
Madison, Milwaukee, and London
P.O. Box 1379,
Madison, Wisconsin 53701
Copyright © 1965
by the Regents of the University
of Wisconsin
Printed in the
United States of America
by Kingsport Press, Inc., Kingsport,
Tennessee
Library of Congress Catalog
Card Number
65–24191

To
Ernest P. Kuhl
in affection
and
gratitude

Preface

The idea for this book came to me during my graduate days at the State University of Iowa and my interest in the project was strengthened by my experiences as combat historian with the Ninth United States Army in Europe. After the war, I began collecting microfilm copies of all the sixteenth-century and early seventeenth-century English military texts that I could locate in England and the United States, using Maurice J. D. Cockle's *A Bibliography of Military Books up to 1642* (London, 1900; reprinted 1957) as a guide, and supplementing it with various other bibliographies as well. The result was a compact library of microfilms of approximately two hundred Tudor and Stuart books and pamphlets on the art of war.

Most of these came from the Huntington Library, but others were found in the Bodleian Library, the British Museum, Cambridge University Library, Folger Shakespeare Library, the Library of Congress, Lambeth Palace Library,

Peterborough Cathedral, University of Chicago Library, University of Michigan Library, the John Crerar Library, and the Newberry Library. I wish to express my appreciation to the directors and staffs of these libraries for their helpful services.

Invaluable to this study were, of course, the numerous letters, ordinances, treasury accounts, army lists, and so forth, appearing in the *Calendar of State Papers,* the *Acts of the Privy Council,* the *Carew Manuscripts,* the *Manuscripts of Lord de L'Isle and Dudley,* and the *Salisbury Manuscripts.* The major secondary sources were C. G. Cruickshank's *Elizabeth's Army* (London, 1946), Sir John Fortescue's *A History of the British Army* (London, 1910), Cyril Falls' *Elizabeth's Irish Wars* (London, 1950), and Sir Charles Oman's *A History of the Art of War in the Sixteenth Century* (London, 1937). The interested student should also consult chapters on warfare by John R. Hale in Volumes I and II of the *New Cambridge History* (1957 and 1958) and his *The Art of War and Renaissance England* (Washington, 1961). Also valuable is the same author's edition of Sir John Smythe's *Certain Discourses Military* (Ithaca, New York, 1964). Further information concerning the military career of Barnabe Rich, who occupies a large portion of Chapter II in this volume, may be found in *Barnaby Rich, A Short Biography* (Austin, Texas, 1953) by Thomas M. Cranfill and Dorothy Hart Bruce.

A great deal of information concerning the Elizabethan art of war is located in articles—too numerous to list here—written about Elizabethan literature, such as those by John W. Draper, John Robert Moore, and Paul A. Jorgensen. For anyone who wishes to familiarize himself with what the sixteenth-century English reader of narrative verse and drama was likely to learn about military matters, two books are especially recommended: G. Geoffrey Langsam's *Martial Books and Tudor Verse* (New York, 1951) and Paul A. Jorgensen's *Shakespeare's Military World* (Berkeley and Los Angeles, 1956).

Material for five of these chapters has appeared in shortened and somewhat different form in the *Bulletin of the History of Medicine, Isis, Journal of English and Germanic Philology, Military Affairs, Modern Language Quarterly, Notes and Queries, Philological Quarterly,* and *Western Humanities Review.* I wish to thank the editors of these periodicals and the directors of the Johns Hopkins and Oxford University Presses for the privilege of using this material. Permission to reproduce the illustrations was kindly given by the Huntington Library, San Marino, California, and the Folger Shakespeare Library, Washington, D.C.

In quotations from sixteenth- and seventeenth-century sources, I have modernized spelling and punctuation and omitted meaningless capitals and italics. Titles of books and pamphlets I have generally given in as brief a form as seemed reasonable, retaining the spelling and the punctuation of the original, but standardizing the capitalization and disregarding certain typographical conventions of the time.

This work could not have been done at all had it not been for a generous grant from the University of Utah Research Fund.

I wish to take this opportunity to thank my wife for the encouragement she has given me through the years and for the stalwart manner in which she has weathered my changing moods. I am grateful also to Mrs. Sarah Nestor, Mrs. Ellen Krogh, Mrs. Sally Allen, and Miss Roselee Robinson, who spent long hours typing and re-typing my manuscript. If an occasional felicitous turn of phrase occurs, it is because my colleagues, Professors Kenneth Eble and Harold F. Folland, have leafed through these pages with red pencil in hand.

Henry J. Webb

University of Utah
June, 1965

Contents

Illustrations

ELIZABETHAN MILITARY SCIENCE
The Books and the Practice

I

Elizabethan Military Literature: Its Classical Background

Elizabeth's army appeared late on the battlefield of sixteenth-century Europe. It came in confusion and, for a while, fought in disorder. Before the era was over, however, its leaders had worked out a fairly sound theory of tactics and organization based upon classical as well as contemporary foreign models. Combining theory with experience obtained in the field, they helped it shed most of the medieval characteristics which had plagued the English army before the reign of Elizabeth—indeed, which had perniciously lingered on for some years after she had ascended the throne—so that by the turn of the century they had made it, with all its faults, a relatively efficient implement of war.

This transformation was caused in part by the spate of military books and pamphlets during the latter years of the reign of Elizabeth, a spate that was itself a natural result of warfare in an age rapidly discovering to what varied uses the printing press could be put. It is the purpose of the present work to trace the development of this military literature, to consider its effect on the English army, and to reflect upon the impact of warfare on English military textbooks published during the sixteenth century.

The origin of Elizabethan military literature lay in the study of the classics. That the writings of the ancient Greeks and Romans should have influenced Elizabethan military ideas is not surprising; among the Elizabethans, as numerous scholars have pointed out, all serious argument was supported by classical authority and illustration.[1] This was as true of war as it was of philosophy, or education, or medicine; and, of course, since the ancient historians dealt more fully with war than with any other subject, it was in their works that the answers to most tactical and strategical questions of the battlefields were sought. It is particularly significant in the light of later ideas that the very first classical history to be turned into English, Sallust's *Jugurtha* (*ca.* 1520), contains a preface by Alexander Barclay, the translator, acknowledging its value as a work of military instruction. "I remembered," he writes,

that a martial matter is most congruent unto a martial and victorious prince. Wherefore I have attempted to translate into our maternal language the ancient chronicle and famous history of the war and divers battles which the Romans did against the tyrant Jugurtha, usurper of the kingdom of Numidy . . . a right fruitful history, both pleasant, profitable, and right necessary unto every degree, but especially to gentlemen which covet to attain to clear fame and honor by glorious deeds of chivalry.[2]

From 1520 on, as more and more histories were translated and as the military activities of the Romans and the Greeks became better known, Barclay's estimate of the usefulness of history, especially classical history, was readily accepted by many authors and translators.

One of the fullest statements concerning the martial value of history can be found in the preface to Thomas Proctor's *Of the Knowledge and Conducte of Warres* (1578). Pointing out that individual experience in matters of arms does not always bring "knowledge and perfection" to a soldier, he advocates that "skill" be obtained by the study of "reports, histories, and chronicles written of wars." There were "sundry books," he reminds his readers, written "in the Latin tongue, and other languages, by great learned and expert men," which dealt with military "rules, stratagems, and instructions." These works, he says, should be consulted because

the knowledge of the ancient orders and government of war, with the sundry sorts and attire of battle, used among sundry nations, their manners and practices, the examples of the antiquity, the experience, policies, prudent counsels, most excellent experiments, instructions, behavior and discipline of the greatest chieftains, and most renowned conquerors that ever were, be requisite and needful unto a good captain. For what is the experience or opinion of one man, to the practice and judgment of a great number of such as have conquered in all countries, vanquished great armies, overthrown many mighty battles [*i.e.,* troops in battle formation], and honorably passed all dangers of war, whose doings be judicially, and perfectly noted of most learned and wise men in sundry great volumes and writings, for example and profit of the posterity, which the unlearned cannot taste or attain without some preparative by plain plot drawn, or introduction in apt order made, to lead them into the knowledge thereof.[3]

The sundry books which Proctor had in mind are listed in the indispensable *A Bibliography of Military Books up to 1642* by Maurice J. D. Cockle. The movement toward the recognition of classical histories as final authority for all things military was given impetus in England by the translation and publication, between 1539 and 1572, of four ancient books on the art of war: Frontinus, *The Strategemes, Sleyghtes and Policies of Warre* (1539); Onosander, *Of the Generall Captaine and of His Office* (1563); Caesar, *The Eyght Bookes of Caius Julius Caesar Conteyning His Martiall Exploytes in Gallia* (1565); and Vegetius, *The Foure Bookes of Martiall Policye* (1572).

The first of these, the *Strategemes* of Sextus Julius Frontinus, governor of Britain between 75 and 78 A.D., is no more than a culling from ancient histories of notable military exploits which could conveniently be grouped under general chapter headings. Thus, a reader interested in "the sleights and policies exercised in war," or the method of conducting an army "through places beset with enemies," could turn to the chapters dealing with those subjects and learn what various leaders of antiquity had done. Translated by Richard Morison to help English military men "increase and nourish their imagination, invention, and dexterity, in using like sleights, . . . [and] easily escape all traps, schemes, and ambushments laid for them," [4] it had appended to it five pages of the "general rules of war, taken out of Vegetius." The importance of the *Strategemes* here lies in the fact that it is one of the first books published in English in which the author attempted to organize and categorize the military experiences of the ancients into a truly useful body of knowledge.[5]

A more important work, because of its direct and far-reaching effect upon Elizabethan ideas of warfare, is Onosander's *Of the Generall Captaine,* written in the first century A.D. Onosander, like Frontinus, had obtained his material from Roman histories, but he went one step further and attempted to construct, from the military experiences of the Romans, a series of theorems or rules of warfare. His work was translated into Italian by Fabio Cotta,[6] and in that form attracted the attention of Peter Whitehorne as a treatise particularly practical and profitable for Englishmen. In his English translation, published in 1563, Whitehorne urged the application of the military rules set down by Onosander, so that "foreign countries" could be "brought in subjection" and England herself could be "kept from outrageous cruelty, and ravenous spoil of the enemies." [7]

The Eyght Bookes of Caius Julius Caesar is of course not a military textbook, but a history of particular campaigns by a soldier greatly revered in Elizabethan England. This was not the first English translation of the *Commentaries* to appear. Thirty-five years earlier a little book had been published with the title of *Julius Caesars Commentaryes, Newly Translated into Englyshe, as Much as Concernyth Thys Realm of England* (1530), a folio edition only thirty-six pages long, with the Latin printed in the margin of the text. As the title reveals, it covers only a portion of Book IV of the original. Although the translator—generally considered to be John Tiptoft, Earl of Worcester [8]—abbreviated the beginning somewhat, he faithfully reproduced and translated the whole account of the British campaign. Obviously he undertook this work as a contribution to English history, particularly since he considered Caesar to be "the eldest historian of all other . . . that ever wrote of this realm of England." [9] In doing so, he fathered the first English translation of Caesar and one of the earliest sixteenth-century histories of England, but he was not concerned with the lessons of warfare that might be gleaned from the pages of his work.

But when Arthur Golding published his translation, *The Eyght Bookes of Caius Julius Caesar,* in 1565, he showed that he recognized the military importance of the *Commentaries* by apologizing for his own inexperience in matters of war and by appending to the text "a description of certain engines of war used . . . by the Romans." [10] Not only does this appendix describe weapons like the battle ram, but it also gives details about such organizations as the legion and cohort, which correspond roughly to the modern infantry regiment and company. Something of the interest this book aroused among Elizabethans is indicated by the fact that it was republished in 1590. Since the *Commentaries* is an historical rather than an analytical approach to war, its usefulness, like that of the *Strategemes,* was limited; nevertheless it was much perused and highly recommended. According to Golding, for instance, Caesar "achieved his affairs with . . . felicity and valiantness." [11] Sir Roger Williams, a soldier and an acute military analyst, linked him with Alexander, Scipio, and Hannibal, "the worthiest and most famous warriors that ever were," and found him unusual in that "he imputed part of his honor unto his lieutenants and officers." [12] Louis le Roy considered him far superior to any other Roman general.[13] Matthew Sutcliffe, who had served under Leicester in the Low Countries as judge-advocate general, summed up Caesar's generalship for Englishmen by stating that Caesar "in his actions was the most considerative, in hazard and danger most resolute, in executions speedy . . . , painful in labor, in dangers watchful, in diet sober, a liberal rewarder of valiant men, a good judge." [14]

A shift in the presentation of the *Commentaries* from military history to an analysis of the art of war occurred in 1600, when Sir Clement Edmondes brought out a new translation supplied with voluminous comments upon military art as it was revealed in the text. The book is appropriately entitled *Observations, upon the Five First Bookes of Caesars Commentaries, Setting Fourth the Practice of the Art Military, in the Time of the Roman Empire.* Dedicated to Sir Francis Vere, who considered the *Commentaries* to be "the breviary of soldiers, and . . . worthy of as great regard, as ever M. Brutus attributed to Polybius, or Charles V to Philip de Commines," [15] it ran through five editions in ten years.[16] Only two other military works of the period approached the popularity of Edmondes' book: Peter Whitehorne's translation of Machiavelli's *Dell' arte della guerra* (as *The Arte of Warre,* 1560, 1573, 1588) and Thomas Styward's *The Pathwaie to Martiall Discipline* (1581, 1582, 1585).[17]

Edmondes begins his book by joining in the Renaissance controversy over experience versus precept and example in education. His conclusions, as applied to the soldier, are certainly sensible: "Reading and discourse are requisite to make a soldier perfect in the art military, how great soever his knowledge may be which long experience and much practice in arms has gained." [18] The reading which Edmondes requires of his military men is such as would gain them "the knowledge of the manifold accidents which arise from the variety of human actions"; and this knowledge, he believes, can only "be learned in the registers of antiquity and in histories recording the motions of former ages." [19] Caesar's *Commentaries* is one such history; and so his purpose in translating and commenting upon it is obvious. The form the book takes is typical of the thought, if not the general practice, of the Elizabethans: translated portions of the *Commentaries*— from a few sentences to several paragraphs—are followed by detailed "observations" which point out the moral or the general precept of war to be learned from the text. The result is a military book such as Shakespeare's Fluellen might have read.[20]

Edmondes attempts to teach Elizabethans four main rules:

(1) Officers should be exceptionally wise soldiers with flexible minds and the ability to inspire confidence in their men. They should be experienced in the field and well read in the battle experiences of others.[21]

(2) Modern tactics should conform generally to the tactics employed by the Romans, although the experience of later generals and the invention of new weapons should modify certain principles of action.[22]

(3) The severe but just discipline by which the "wise and prudent captain" in Roman times controlled the "vulgar conceit" and "false judgments" of the common soldiers should be applied to contemporary English forces.[23]

(4) Armies should be organized into units similar to those created by the Romans, who made each part fit into a whole and each man into his place.[24] With manifest chagrin, Edmondes complains that the lack of organization has "dishonored the martial government of this age," causing controversy among commanders and leaders. A notable exception (Sir John Smythe to the contrary, as we shall see later) was the organization of English companies in the Low Countries.[25]

Besides these four main precepts, the Elizabethans could learn a great deal from the *Commentaries* about fortifications, provisioning, weapons, intelligence reports, and especially about the tactics to be employed in certain types of actions. In short, Caesar's *Commentaries* became in Edmondes' hands a valuable guide for the contemporary military man.

The *Observations* was reprinted in 1604, with an important appendix entitled "The manner of our moderne training, or tacticke practice," which appears in all subsequent editions. Only ten pages long, it contains a wealth of information on the organizing and drilling of foot soldiers, and can be compared to our modern *Infantry Drill Regulations*. It demonstrates to what extent the *Commentaries* had become a text on the art of war during the Elizabethan and Jacobean periods.

Perhaps the most useful of the classical military treatises to be turned into the vernacular was *The Foure Bookes of Martiall Policye* by Flavius Vegetius Renatus, a fourth-century Roman. It deals with the selection of soldiers, the organization of troops, field tactics, and the besieging and defending of cities, in many instances going into the sort of detail which an Elizabethan student of the art of war might find of practical value. Thus Book One concerns mainly the procurement of soldiers; there is a discussion of their age, stature, "countenance and making of the body," the "sciences" they should be skillful in, and the training they should undergo. Book Two describes the elements in a legion, the duties of the various officers, and the method by which officers should be promoted. Book Three, which is something of a hodgepodge so far as organization is concerned, treats of engines of war, arrangement of troops on the battlefield, joining battle, disengaging, and the general rules of war which Morison had earlier tacked on to the *Strategemes* of Frontinus. The final book, on fortification, discusses the construction of walls and ditches, the provisioning of forts, the defense against assault, and the employment of siege weapons. As a kind of afterthought, this section ends with "Precepts to be observed in making war upon the sea." The work concludes with six excellent illustrations of siege weapons. (See Figures 1 and 2 for examples.)

Like *Of the Generall Captaine,* Vegetius' work was based upon Roman discipline and, also like the former text, it was turned into English for a practical purpose. John Sadler, the translator, points out that an understanding of Vegetius, together with a knowledge of "the best historical writers both in Greek and Latin" and "of such worthy authors as have . . . gathered out of the best histories the chiefest points and devices of wars," should be of value to English soldiers. This knowledge plus experience would enable them in time of war to "do high service to God, their Prince, and their country." [26]

These four ancient texts, then, with their emphasis on Greek and Roman tactics, did much to establish a framework upon which Elizabethans could build quasi-classical armies. The theories promulgated in these books were aided and abetted by Greek and Latin *belles lettres.*

Though classical *belles lettres* with which the Elizabethans were familiar do not particularly emphasize war, those that do were as avidly perused for military information as were the works of history. Such works as Vergil's *Aeneid,* which ran through numerous full and partial Latin and English editions during the century, and Homer's *Iliad* were read as much for profit as for pleasure; and though the profit was largely moral and political, the military lessons that one could presumably learn from them were not ignored.

The widely popular translation of Plutarch by Thomas North may have had something to do with the acceptance of Homer as a military authority, for therein Alexander—who was considered, along with Caesar, to be the greatest of ancient generals—is reported to have called the *Iliad* "the institution of martial discipline." [27] When Chapman translated Homer, he helped fix the idea that the epic was a military text by stating that "soldiers shall never spend their idle hours more profitably, than with studious and industrious perusal" of the *Iliad*.[28] This attitude toward the *Iliad* may have stimulated interest in the military aspects of the *Odyssey* and the *Aeneid,* for although Odysseus and Aeneas never had, for Elizabethans, the martial stature of Agamemnon, Achilles, and Hector, they were occasionally mentioned as military figures well worth emulation.[29]

Finally, foreign works on the art of war, some of which were translated into English, were frequently based upon Greek and Roman military science and tactics and stimulated further study of classical modes of warfare. Foremost among them was Machiavelli's *Dell' arte della guerra,* first translated, as we have noted earlier, by Peter Whitehorne in 1560 and reprinted in 1573 and 1588. But also of historical importance were Jacopo di Porcia's *The Preceptes of Warre* (1544) and the Sieur de Fourquevaux's *Instructions for the Warres* (1589).

Peter Whitehorne's translation of Machiavelli's famous work on the art of war, completed some ten years earlier while he was in the army of Charles V, was published in 1560 as a "gift" for his fellow "country men, not expert in the Italian tongue." His reason for such a publication was simply patriotic—or so he advised Queen Elizabeth—for he "thought (that for the defense, maintenance, and advancement of a kingdom, or commonwealth . . .) no one thing to be more profitable, necessary, or more honorable, than the knowledge of service in war, and deeds of arms." [30] Machiavelli, Whitehorne had learned from experience, could supply this knowledge.

With martial directness, Machiavelli presents his own case for such a book. "The end of him that will make war," he declares, "is to be able to fight with every enemy in the field, and to be able to overcome an army." In order to do this, he continues, "it is convenient to ordain an host. To ordain an host, there must be found men, armed, ordered, and as well in the small, as in the great orders exercised, to know how to keep array, and to encamp, so that after bringing them to the enemy, either standing or marching, they may know how to behave themselves valiantly." [31]

Sounding much like Vegetius, whose work he had obviously read with some care, Machiavelli devotes seven books to these matters. He gives advice about the type of men to procure, the arms they should bear, the training they should undergo, the tactics they should use, the encampments they should make, the discipline they should follow, and the fortifications they should throw up. This advice, presented in dialogue form, is followed by a number of figures illustrating the "order of the battles, . . . and of the armies, and lodgings in the camp." (See Figure 3.)

Neither Porcia's *The Preceptes of Warre* nor Fourquevaux's *Instructions for the Warres* is as impressive as Machiavelli's tome, although both were important in establishing the classical foundations of Elizabethan military science. *The Preceptes of Warre,* written in 1527 and dedicated to King Ferdinand of Hungary (afterwards Holy Roman Emperor),[32] was translated by Peter Betham so that it could be read side by side with Morison's English version of the *Strategemes* by Frontinus.[33] Porcia would supply the rules and precepts of warfare, and Frontinus would illustrate them with historical action. In his dedication to the Lord Chancellor of England, Betham implies that his work will be of great benefit to

English officers. At the same time, perhaps to keep from giving offense, he hastens to point out that "the youth of England do so flourish in warlike knowledge that they pass all other both Greeks and Romans to this day." [34]

The work consists of two books, the first composed of 206 general rules of warfare, and the second of a number of "laws of war" plus 84 additional rules. Not arranged in any particular order and often repetitious, these rules and laws cover everything from the choice of officers to the capture of cities; and although Betham insists that they are "precepts of chivalry" which can be proved by the deeds related in the *Strategemes,* it seems doubtful that Porcia had Frontinus in mind when penning his book.

Fourquevaux's *Instructions for the Warres* (1589) was translated into English by Paul Ive, who at the same time brought out his own military book, *The Practise of Fortification* (sometimes found bound with *Instructions for the Warres,* which does not cover the subject).[35] The *Instructions,* like Vegetius' *The Foure Bookes of Martiall Policye* and Machiavelli's *The Arte of Warre,* is a practical treatise on the procuring, training, and employment of soldiers. Indeed, with a few exceptions, the result of Fourquevaux's French background and the advance of military science since the days of the notorious Italian, the *Instructions* is in many places almost a verbatim rendering of *The Arte of Warre,* which Fourquevaux had read either in the original edition or in the French version entitled *L'Art de la guerre composé par Nicholas Machiavelli* (Paris, 1546). Presumably he had read other things, too, for in his preface he acknowledges his indebtedness to "the most renowned" military authors, stating that he had chosen for his "chief guide the uses and customs . . . of the ancient soldiers, after whose example I do

govern myself." [36] Realizing that the development of weapons had resulted in certain changes in tactics which made it
impossible to adhere strictly to Greek and Roman discipline,
Fourquevaux occasionally modifies, though with a great deal
of circumspection, some of the "fashions" employed by the
ancients: "And although I follow the ancient manner in most
part," he writes in his preface, ". . . it is without rejecting
our own fashions in any thing that I think them to be surer
than theirs." [37]

Many were the articulate military men, then, who fer-
vently believed that to be indoctrinated by the classical
principles of war was to be moulded in the form of a perfect
soldier. These men saw—or thought they saw—that tactics of
offense and defense on the battlefield had been "from the first
creation of the world until now the very same, the disposition
of the people only varying in the difference of weapons,
engines, and instruments, which have been invented." [38] The
Greeks and especially the Romans had brought these tactics
to maturity, teaching their soldiers, as Peter Whitehorne so
aptly put it, "the perfect knowledge of whatsoever thing
appertained to the war." [39] It is not only the translations of
classical works that attest to the popularity of this theory;
there were a great number of works by Englishmen who,
believing in the pre-eminence of ancient military art, undertook to urge English soldiers, as Thomas Styward did in his
Pathwaie to Martiall Discipline, "with most willing minds"
to "prosecute the ancient order of the Romans." [40]

II

English Military Writers

Foremost among English military authors who argued for an army based upon the military practices of the Greeks and Romans were Thomas Digges, Barnabe Rich, Sir John Smythe, and Thomas Styward. They did not always fully agree with one another, however, when it came to the application of Greek and Roman "discipline" to Elizabethan units; and frequently, because of their experiences in the field, their tactical theories were as modern as English muskets and harquebuses.

———

Little is known of the early life of Thomas Digges. He was born in Kent, possibly in 1530, and, according to his own account, spent his "youngest years . . . in the sciences liberal, and especially in searching the most difficult and curious demonstrations mathematical . . ."[1] In this pursuit he was undoubtedly aided by his father, Leonard Digges, a mathe-

17

matician and architect of some moment, who, though he had been a student at Oxford, sent his son to Cambridge in 1546. At Cambridge, Digges conceived the necessity of converting his theoretical knowledge into "sensible practical conclusions," and after devoting his "years of riper judgment" to this conversion,[2] he published in 1571 *A Geometrical Practise, Named Pantometria.*

This work, although not pre-eminently a military book, does have very definite military applications. It is divided into three parts, entitled Longimetra, Planimetra, and Stereometria. The first part, treating of lines, could be applied by "the ingenious practitioner . . . to topography, fortification, conducting of mines under the earth, and shooting of great ordnance." The second part, which considers the measurement of "superficies, plain, convex and concave," might "serve for disposing all manner of ground, plats of cities, towns, forts, castles, palaces or other edifices." The last part, which deals with the measurement of solids, would be of use to the architect, who might make it "serve his turn in preordinating and forecasting both of the charges, quantities and proportion of all parcels necessarily appertaining to any kind of buildings."[3]

That Digges had a classical turn of mind is immediately apparent in this first work of his. Realizing that the study of mathematics was not, in early Elizabethan times, ordinarily considered the pursuit of a gentleman, he defends his book by references to ancient authorities. Plato had said that those who were ignorant of geometry were unable to proceed into the higher secrets of philosophy, and Aristotle, in the fifth book of the *Nicomachean Ethics,* had used geometry to explain moral philosophy. This branch of mathematics, Digges points out, is also useful in the study of astronomy, music, perspective, cosmography, and navigation; moreover, as the deeds of Alexander, Quintus Fabius Maximus, and Cyrus amply prove, it is the proper subject for "a gentleman . . . that professes the wars."[4] In short, although Ascham and Elyot omit mention of mathematical sciences in *The Scholemaster* and *The Governour*, Digges tries to demonstrate that no useful and patriotic Elizabethan should be without the knowledge of such a science.

A year after the publication of *Pantometria*, Digges tried his hand at statecraft, sitting in Parliament for Wallingford. This brief excursion into politics apparently did not dampen his enthusiasm for mathematics and military science, for in 1579 he published his second work: *An Arithmeticall Militare Treatise, Named Stratioticos*. This book was dedicated to the Earl of Leicester, who, after the publication of *Pantometria*, had become the patron of the young mathematician. That this patronage was not merely the idle protection of a powerful name is indicated by Digges' avowal that he was indebted to Leicester for recommending him to Elizabeth's services and for bestowing other favors upon him, but unfortunately no information as to just what service Digges was permitted to perform can be gleaned from his writings. Leicester had at one time promised his protégé "the fame of an honorable enterprise," undoubtedly of a military nature, and the hope of going on an expedition under the leadership of his patron had moved Digges, as he says, "to employ my mathematical muses upon this military argument."[5] Before publishing his labors, he submitted them to Leicester for approval, and then in 1579, his first draft "in some points altered and augmented," he saw his work through the press.[6]

In *Stratioticos*, as in his first work, Digges draws upon his knowledge of antiquity to illustrate the value to Elizabethans of such a work on warfare. He points out that reading ancient history (as well as observing the discipline of modern armies) will show the necessity for military preparedness in a nation desirous of prospering:

And finding not only by the whole course of histories of all times and countries how kingdoms have flourished in all felicity, whereas this art has been embraced and duly practiced, and contrariwise, how most happy empires after warlike discipline have been corrupted, have fallen to ruin and miserable servitude, but also by experience even in these days seen what extreme disorders grow in those armies where military laws and ordinances have been neglected, [I] have thought this matter not unfit to be remembered in these flourishing and quiet times.[7]

Following the lead of the military classicists, ancient and modern, Digges praises the "ancient Roman discipline for the wars; their exquisite order of training the soldiery even from their infancy in sundry sorts of hardness, labor, and activity; their invincible order in marching, fighting, and encamping, together with their divine laws to keep their armies in obedience," and points out that it would be well for Englishmen to revert to the ancient discipline of arms in anticipation of a possible war. Nor does he admit that "the Roman orders of the field" are outmoded; on the contrary, he asserts, they are "more convenient, more serviceable, and more invincible . . . even in these our days, than they were for that age wherein they were used and practiced."[8]

Only in three areas does Digges feel that current methods of fighting and encamping are superior to classical methods. He notes that among the "infinite . . . forms of embattling [*i.e.,* the arranging of tactical units in battle formation]" used by generals of antiquity—for instance, the circular, the triangular, the "lunula" (*i.e.,* the crescent, "wherein the Turk especially delights") and the square—the square alone is practical in modern battle. Not only are the other figures difficult to form, they cannot be maintained in marching.[9] Secondly, he notes that since artillery had been invented recently and was therefore unknown to the Romans, "Roman precedents therein can nothing pleasure us." [10] Finally, he feels that the amount of camping space allowed by the Romans to cavalry and infantry is too small, and refers to his unpublished work on fortifications for amplification of this subject.[11] But in all other respects, Digges bows to the superior skill and judgment of the Romans.

It must be remembered at this point, however, that Digges is basing his remarks, not upon military experience—unless it were elementary training in the militia [12]—but upon his reading in ancient history. And, typical of the "book soldier," he apparently scorned those men who contested his point of view merely because "they had been in a few skirmishes, or taken any degree in field." [13] This attitude, which was certainly not a unique one, is particularly noteworthy in view of what Robert Barret was to write concerning works on the art of war which had appeared in England during his lifetime. In *The Theorike and Practike of Moderne Warres* (1598), Barret says: ". . . some have been penned by learned men, as politicians, geometricians, and mathematicians, which never saw any wars; some by men of small learning, but by their practice and long continuance in wars; some again have been penned by men both of good learning and long experience in wars; the last of these are to be best approved, as all men of judgment must confess." [14] Clearly Digges, at this point in his career, falls into the first category.

Such was the nature of the man, however, that, had the

opportunity offered itself, it is to be supposed that Digges would have tried to prove his theories on the battlefield (as if they had not already been proved by the Romans, who had put them into practice). When the practicality of his suppositions concerning navigation was called into doubt by mariners, Digges took to the sea and demonstrated that he had been correct and the mariners wrong:

> I spent fifteen weeks in continual sea services upon the ocean [he writes], where by proof I found, and those very masters themselves could not but confess, that experience did no less plainly discover the errors of their rules, than my demonstrations. Since which time, I have learned no more to be abused with the opinions of men, what office, or degree soever they have borne, or what fame soever go of them, if reason be repugnant to their opinions. . . .[15]

Some years later, after his experiences in the Low Countries had made it impossible for anyone to attack his theories as the impractical speculations of a book soldier, Digges reiterated his belief in the superiority of Roman training and discipline.

In spite of the fact that much theory and little practice went into the composition of *Stratioticos,* it was an excellent book for its period.[16] Like *Pantometria,* it is divided into three sections—Arithmetic; Algebra; and Military Laws, Offices, and Duties—but where the earlier book quite often leaves to the imagination or ingenuity of officers the application of geometry and trigonometry to warfare, the later one strives to present numerous problems actually dealing with field maneuvers. The section devoted to algebra, for instance, presents a method of computing the size of camping grounds necessary for various numbers of soldiers, a method of determining the range of artillery, and a method of computing the amounts of pay and provisions due organizations of different strengths. It also illustrates methods by which a captain of pioneers might solve engineering problems, such as the number of laborers needed to cast up a trench of a given size within a given time.

Between 1579 and 1582 Digges published nothing, but he was not idle. He probably visited the Low Countries during this period, observing the "sumptuous, rich, and beautiful cities," the "great number of ships and mariners," and the profitable "intercourse and traffic" which were the result of so many new and excellent Dutch harbors.[17] Upon his return home, he could not help comparing Flemish prosperity with the "beggary" to which "Winchelsea, Rye, Romney, Hythe, Dover, and many other poor towns" were reduced as a result of decaying harbors;[18] and when he learned of the interest which the Privy Council was showing in the repair of Dover Harbor, he concentrated his attention upon that particular port.

On his own initiative, Digges questioned the most skillful mariners and the oldest inhabitants of Dover concerning the alterations that had occurred in the harbor during the past forty years. Then he "sounded all the channels, shelves, and roads there, and set them down exactly in plat." Finally, after consulting English and foreign engineers as to the best method of constructing a "perfect haven," and comparing their opinions with those he had formed after observing "artificial" havens in the Low Countries, he resolved upon a plan of repair. This he submitted to the Queen early in 1582 under the title *A Briefe Discourse Declaringe How Honorable and Profitable to Youre Moste Excellent Majestie, and Howe Necessary and Commodiouse for Your Realme, the Making of Dover Haven Shalbe.* Two of his arguments, which may have seemed very persuasive to Elizabeth, were to the effect that the development of Dover Harbor would cause an increase in navigation that could prove a source of wealth in time of peace and strength in time of war and that an improved harbor would protect ships from both storms and enemies.[19]

Probably because of this tract, his *Pantometria,* and the patronage of Leicester, Digges was appointed, along with two others, to confer with the Commissioners of Dover Harbor on the choice of a plan for the repair of the harbor. In June 1584 he submitted to the Privy Council a long description of his proceedings at Dover, and in November of that year he made his last report, pointing out the services he had rendered by exposing the errors of others.

The next year, after another brief excursion into politics as a representative of Southampton in Parliament, Digges finally went on the military expedition which Leicester had promised him sometime before 1579. He was appointed muster-master general of all the Queen's forces in the Low Countries, and accompanied Leicester across the Channel. Once there, besides concerning himself with the musters, he examined the fortifications of Sluys, Ostend, Flushing and other fortified towns, reported their condition to Burghley and Walsingham, and made recommendations for their repair.[20] He also observed the military discipline of the troops under the command of the Earl of Leicester, coming to the conclusion that the army which Elizabeth had sent to the Low Countries in the late 1580's was probably the most unbridled and disorganized force ever mustered by the English nation.

His letters to Burghley and Walsingham are filled with recommendations for the improvement of military discipline, and he prepared three long papers on the subject, possibly with a view to submitting them to Elizabeth, as he had done earlier with his plans for Dover Harbor. One of these was published in 1587 as *A Briefe Report of the Militarie Services Done in the Low Countries by the Erle of Leicester.*[21] For some reason, the other two papers were not used until nine years after his death, when his son published them, with two essays of his own, under the title of *Foure Paradoxes* (1604).

To Digges the problem of discipline was really a simple one: choose men carefully, pay them adequately, and control them by a rigorously enforced set of rules and regulations based upon those used by the Greeks and Romans—views which were essentially the same as those he had earlier expressed in his *Stratioticos.* The "antique Roman and Grecian discipline martial," he declared, "does far exceed in excellence our modern . . . And . . . (unless we reform such corruptions as are grown into our modern militia, utterly repugnant to the ancient) we shall in time lose utterly the renown and honor of our nation . . ."[22] He hastens to add, however, that he did not mean "precisely to bind" the English army "to the same very rules or laws" of the ancients, because changing conditions might make it necessary to "mitigate or increase, alter or accommodate" these rules. But it was worth noting that the French attacked corruption in their army by forming camp laws "favoring altogether of the antique true martial discipline."[23] To those who argued that man's nature was not so angelic that it could follow laws and ordinances as strict as those promulgated by the great generals of old, Digges gives a simple answer. If the Greeks and Romans could keep the discipline, so could the English.[24]

On March 25, 1588, the office of muster-master was abolished, and Digges was free to take care of his estate at home, which had deteriorated in his absence.[25] Once home, he brought out two books, a new one entitled *A Breife and True Report of the Proceedings of the Earle of Leycester for the Reliefe of Sluce*[26] (1590) and a second edition of his *Stratioticos* (1590). The new edition of *Stratioticos* had a slightly different title from the first, being called a "Warlike Treatise" instead of a "Militare Treatise," and contained the laws and ordinances issued by Leicester in the Low Countries. These laws, standing as they did side by side with those "published and practiced among the Spaniards" and those issued by the Prince de Conde, indicate Leicester's indebtedness to the Spanish and the French for the discipline which he had attempted to establish in his army. They all, of course, bear a marked resemblance to Roman martial laws. The greater part of this second edition of *Stratioticos,* however, merely repeats what is in the first, and it is apparent that experience in the field had not changed Digges' opinion about the value of classical discipline.

The year following, a second edition of *Pantometria* appeared. The first edition had dealt obliquely with war; this one was given a thoroughly military cast by the addition of numerous theorems and definitions pertaining to ordnance.

These two books marked the end of Digges' career as a military author, although he had intended to publish two more military works. (Possibly written, but unpublished, were four other essays or books on navigation, nautical architecture, the revolutions of Copernicus, and surveying.) In both *Pantometria* and *Stratioticos,* he speaks of his unpublished "Treatize of Martiall Pyrotechnic and Great Artillery" in which he discusses

the weight, quantity, and number of powder, shot, and sundry sorts of pieces, to strike any mark at random [*i.e.,* the full range of a piece of ordnance]; the number of carriages [caissons], ladles, of ramrods, scourers, wads, tampions, cartridges, matches, barrels, or lasts [twenty-four barrels] of powder, etc. Also, the number of gunners, assistants, pioneers, smiths, carpenters, and other artificers, to attend on the artillery, what numbers of horses and oxen to draw them, their wheels and carriages. . . .[27]

He also mentions an unpublished work on fortifications, in which, among other things, he intended to give a fuller treatment of pitching camps than that in *Stratioticos.*[28] In 1592 he published two non-military works, an augmented edition of his father's *Boke Named Tectonicon* and the *Perfect Description of Celestial Orbs.* In August 1595 he died and was buried in the chancel of St. Mary, Aldermanbury, where on a monument erected to his memory he was described as a man "of rare knowledge in geometry, astrology, and other mathematical sciences."[29]

Barnabe Rich (1542–1617) was the most prolific military author in England during Elizabethan and early Jacobean times.[30] Five of the twenty-six works he composed between 1574 and 1617 were directly connected with army affairs:

1. *A Right Exelent and Pleasaunt Dialogue, betwene Mercury and an English Souldier* (1574)
2. *Allarme to England* (1578)
3. *A Path-way to Military Practise* (1587)
4. *A Martiall Conference* (except for the title page, not extant)
5. *The Fruites of Long Experience;* also published as *A Souldier's Wishe to Britons Welfare* (1604)

A sixth, *Faultes Faults, and Nothing Else but Faultes* (1606), was partially devoted to a criticism of certain types of officers—criticism, as we shall see, engaged in by a number of pamphleteers of the period.[31] To this list we might also add Rich's dedication in his *Farewell to Militarie Profession,* although the general contents of the book were anything but military. The only other writer who approached Rich's productivity in this particular line was Thomas Digges.

Rich was twelve years younger than Digges, having been born in 1542, but he began his military experiences earlier than Digges, and in a different manner. He first fought in 1562 as a soldier under the Earl of Warwick, then controller of Newhaven (Le Havre),[32] and saw action thereafter as a captain and as an "officer of the field" in Ireland and the Netherlands.[33] That he was at least company commander of combat troops is obvious from remarks he makes here and there throughout his various works; but the fact that he designated himself an officer of the field may indicate that he served in capacities other than that of company captain. In any event, his long sojourn with troops in action lends authority to what he was to say about English military affairs.

Apparently he did not have the formal schooling which Leonard Digges provided for his son Thomas, but he was certainly an educated man. He voraciously read the classics,[34] to which he turned when in need of authoritative support for his military arguments. It is interesting to note that when he lifted passages out of Machiavelli's *Art of War* for inclusion in the *Dialogue,* he frequently discarded Machiavelli's references to the ancients and supplied his own cullings in their place. Most of them are far too long to have appeared in commonplace books, and it is probable that he made long winters of inactivity in France, Holland, and Ireland less tedious by reading such works as Hieronymus Osorius' *Of*

Christian Nobility (which he quotes at length in his *Allarme to England*) and Amyot's translation of Plutarch. He also read the Scriptures, English chronicles, and—if one can credit the ease with which he drops their names—writings of Plato, Cicero, Demosthenes, Pliny, Augustine, Sallust, and many another classical author.[35] Chief among the classical military authors whom he revered was Vegetius.

Rich's first literary venture, *A Right Exelent and Pleasaunt Dialogue, betwene Mercury and an English Souldier*, displayed a method of writing which characterized all of the military works he produced—lack of organization, or such loose organization that long digressions do violence to any orderly presentation of ideas. The *Dialogue* follows the pattern of Old French love-visions which Chaucer had long ago copied when composing the *Hous of Fame.* The setting is the woods on a day in May. The author, falling asleep under a tree, hears "the sudden sound of trumpets, drums, and fifes" and is confronted by a company of soldiers who beseech him to be their ambassador to the court of Mars. Appealing to the gods for aid in his ambassadorship, Rich suddenly finds Mercury at his side, and is guided by him to the castle of Mars. As the Old French love-visions usually described the experience of a hero in the service of love, so Rich's *Dialogue* relates the experience of a man in the service of "unfortunate soldiers" whose names had become "odious" and "reproachful" to the people of England.

In content, the *Dialogue* bears a most remarkable resemblance to Machiavelli's *Art of War,* which Rich may have read in a Continental edition or in the 1560 or 1573 editions of Peter Whitehorne's translation. In many instances he borrows whole passages from Machiavelli, although he often condenses the rather verbose explanations of the Italian and he almost always uses original examples to illustrate his precepts. A great number of paragraphs dealing with the proper occasions to attack an enemy, military crimes punishable by death, the choice of soldiers and their training, orations to troops, propaganda, and tactics follow the phrasing of Machiavelli almost word for word.[36]

The *Dialogue* is more than a book on the art of war, however. It is a work condemning "the orders of the service," which he finds to be "corrupted" in modern wars, and a plea for the enlisting of experienced officers and the impressing of honest private soldiers,[37] ideas which the Romans had promulgated by precept and example.

At the beginning of his second military work, *Allarme to England,* Rich expresses the attitude toward war ordinarily held by authors in the sixteenth century,[38] calling it "a most grievous plague . . . so evil, so strange, and so pernicious, that it comprehends and surmounts all other kind of evils." Because of wars, he writes, "good laws are decayed, humanity is defaced, equity is suppressed, holy places are profaned, murders are committed, virgins are deflowered, chaste matrons are defiled, kingdoms be subdued, cities be ruinated . . ."[39] It is only natural, then, that the soldier's profession should be considered by some to be "a thing more fit for ruffians, roisterers, blasphemers, and people of the vilest condition, rather than an exercise for honest men."[40]

But Rich presents the thesis—by no means an original one—that war, fearful and devastating as it is, is not totally abhorrent. To establish this thesis, he quotes from the Scriptures and from classical and medieval authors with an ease more characteristic of a schoolmaster than a professional soldier, ending with the statement that "in the ancient time, there has been no glory thought so great, no renown esteemed so honorable, as that which has been gained by force or martial prowess." [41]

Rich then condemns pacifists, whom he terms "peace-mongers": people who hate war "not so much for any special love they have of peace, as for fear of taxes, payments, and other charges hanging upon wars." [42] In other words, he classes them with gross and selfish materialists, worrying about the changing weight of their moneybags, and with contemptible slackers who, he affirms, "would love the wars well enough, so themselves might be free from pressing." These he scornfully describes as people who, in time of peace, "enjoy the laws and liberties of their country," and in time of war, "when their country stands in need, do show themselves every way to aid and assistance, with as willing minds, as a bear comes to a stake; these be right bastards to their country, and are indeed worthy to enjoy no benefit of their country." [43]

Finally, Rich attacks those "whose consciences be so pure (so they say themselves) that they can allow of no wars, either to be good or godly, considering what murders, spoils and other outrages by them are committed." [44] If one were to follow the line of argument they pursue, he adds, one could prove that peace was detestable, because "in peace men grow to be slothful, idle, proud, covetous, dissolute, incontinent . . ." For authority to back up his statements, Rich goes not only to the Scriptures and to St. Augustine but to classical history, pointing out that Carthage was "more hurtful . . . to Rome after her destruction, than during the whole course and season of the wars . . . for that whilst they had enemies in Africa, they knew not what vices meant in Rome." [45] He hastens to assure his readers, however, that he does not mean to persuade them that wars are preferable to peace, but merely to show that war should not be condemned because of the "many disorders and sundry outrages committed" during broils and battles.[46]

Rich's third military work, *A Path-way to Military Practise,* though a product of his reading of contemporary authors and of his experience in the field, was also based upon his knowledge of classical military history. It is a short, valuable, and comprehensive description of Elizabethan army officers and the peculiarities of their command, penned (so he states in a bold dedication to Queen Elizabeth) after the Crown had received his previous works "so favorably." [47]

He begins by echoing what he had already said in his *Allarme to England* and in the *Dialogue:* A country should always be prepared for war, and, to that end, should be provided with sufficient, and expert, soldiers, and proper armaments. He then launches upon a description of the duties of officers and men, and discusses battle formations and the tactical employment of troops. When he writes of the necessity of preparing in time of peace for war, Rich takes a paragraph from Digges' *Stratioticos,* reworking it much after the manner in which he had earlier reworked Machiavelli.[48] Similarly, when he writes of officers and men, he leafs through Digges and paraphrases what he finds there. When he delves into the problem of embattling troops, however, he deviates from the firm stand taken by Digges on the necessity of imitating the Romans, a deviation that shows itself even more strongly later in *The Fruites of Long Experience.*

Rich's quarrel with Digges is essentially the result of a misreading of *Stratioticos.* There, it will be remembered, Digges says that the Roman orders of the field are even "more convenient . . . in these our days, than they were for that age wherein they were used and practiced." [49] But at the same time Digges also rejects certain bizarre formations (such as the circular, the triangular, and the crescent) in favor of the square. Rich does likewise in *The Path-way,* throwing out the triangular, the crescent, and a few other "proportions" which, he avers, "are not worth the figuring forth as the service now stands." Today, he insists, "there is no form of embattling to be preferred before the just square, or . . . 2, 3, or 4 squadrons . . . ," [50] which is about what Digges believes.

Later, however, in *The Fruites of Long Experience,* Rich's break with Digges is sharp and final. In 1604, nine years after Digges' death, Rich finds Digges' *Paradoxes* (published earlier the same year with some material by his son) full of ridiculous statements. The formations which Digges admires are "fitter for the encounters . . . in Alexander's time" than for Elizabethan times, Rich insists with sarcasm, and the discipline Digges admires belongs to the age of King Arthur. Yet, as a matter of fact, although Rich does set out to refute the classical stand taken by Digges, he never comes to grips with any specific and concrete situation, contenting himself by stating that certain classical "forms and proportions" have been outdated by "the fury of shot." [51] It is quite probable that Rich's distaste for Digges stemmed not so much from the latter's Roman orientation as from his contemptuous reference to corruption among contemporary captains, although Rich himself felt very much at ease when pointing out their imperfections. At the beginning of *The Fruites* Rich proudly refers to his "40 years training in the wars"; [52] and Digges, like a whole host of Elizabethans, set no great store by experience in the field.

In any event, whatever Rich may have thought of Digges' ideas, or whatever the barbs he cast at him after his death, *Fruites* was classically oriented. No soldiers were better, according to Rich, than the "Romans in the prime of their greatness." [53] Their discipline "was much to be wondered at, yet more to be honored." [54] Their method of electing captains and choosing soldiers was commendable,[55] and their martial camps were schools of "honor, justice, obedience, duty, and loyalty." [56]

If we omit *Faultes,* which has scattered comments about such subjects as officers, warmongers, and peace-lovers, *Fruites* brings us to the end of Rich's career as a military analyst and critic.

In the five books just considered, Rich discusses a number of important ideas or precepts dear to the hearts of classicists, ancient or modern. He makes clear his conviction that a country should always be prepared for war, and to that end, should be provided with "sufficient and expert soldiers, if it be but to defend the rigors of such as would invade." [57] To answer those who might respond that England was filled with men willing to spring to arms overnight in defense of their country, he recalls the spoil of Antwerp which Gascoigne had so vividly described in 1576: "If you think your great numbers of untrained men are sufficient to defend you, do but remember what happened to Antwerp, where they wanted neither men nor any other provision for the wars. But they wanted soldiers to direct them, and men of understanding to encourage them." [58] And if the thought of Antwerp could not startle Englishmen out of their complacency, history could offer proof of what happened when men "neglected the feats of war" and laid aside their weapons. Assyria, Persia, Athens, Macedonia, and Rome "came . . . to calamity" as a result of unpreparedness.[59]

It was not enough that the Tower of London was stocked with "ordnance, shot, powder, pike, caliver, armor" and that at Rochester rested "so worthy a fleet of royal ships, as no prince in Europe may make comparison with the like." [60] What could be done, Rich wanted to know, with such armaments "when you have not men of experience to use them"? [61] Preparation for war, he insists, "consists as well in training men, and making them skillful and ready in military knowledge, as in preparing all other equipment and necessaries appertaining to the wars." [62]

An army, he points out, should be diligently trained, since a "few men well practiced, more avails, than great numbers imperfect." [63] There were men, Rich was aware, who, even though they realized that a man could not master the lowliest occupation without serving seven years as an apprentice, believed that soldiers could be adequately trained within a month. [64] Soldiering, Rich maintained, was not a trade to be learned in a month, or even in seven years, but was an art which could not be thoroughly understood even by men who had followed the wars all their lives.

As Vegetius and Machiavelli had already stipulated, men selected for the army should be those who showed "quickness, nimbleness and readiness" [65] and had the virtues of "silence, obedience and truth." [66] Shiftless men who were accustomed to spending all their time "dicing, drinking and swearing" were not proper material for the army. [67] Nor should anyone who was a husbandman or a laborer be recruited, for such men could not endure hunger and privation and would not keep their equipment and clothes in condition. [68] The men should be given as much experience in the field as possible. They should also, like Shakespeare's Fluellen, read the "martial feats" of the ancients. It was out of books, Rich notes, that "Alphonso King of Aragon . . . learned both arms, and the order of arms: and did not Lucullus by the study of his books, become one of the noblest captains of all the Romans?" [69] But field experience, in the last analysis, was more important than reading of the experience of others. [70]

In order to have good soldiers, an army must be provided with well-trained leaders, for "through the default of one ignorant captain a whole army may sometime be overthrown." [71] Rich takes the four qualities which Cicero prescribed for a captain—experience, valor, authority, and "felicity"—and to them adds four of his own—justice, fortitude, prudence, and temperance. [72] Soldiers serving under such leaders should receive all the wages allowed them by their prince and nothing should be held back by dishonest captains. [73] Unpaid soldiers, says Rich, will not only steal from their friends and stir up mutinies; they will, because of weak bodies and feeble courage, bring disaster upon the army on the day of battle. [74]

Soldiers should be honored, not disdained. In direct opposition to Erasmus and his followers, who scorned all members of the military profession, Rich, like the Romans, commends soldiers for willingly enduring hardships in the defense of their country. [75] Well aware that ex-soldiers were frequently ill-treated by Crown and citizen alike, he urges that some provision be made for the care of veterans, for "a soldier is worth his keeping in the time of peace who has honestly served his prince in the time of war." [76] As an example of what might be done for ex-soldiers, Rich quotes Dionysius' oration to his troops:

I will have you to carry the name of old soldiers and to be called heroes. Your office shall be to govern the commonwealth, to reprove the evil, to praise the good, and from all other labors you shall be free. To what people or country soever you come to, the king shall find you meat, drink and clothes. You shall be most honorable with all men. Princes shall offer you presents and shall give their own garments. Whatsoever you say shall be allowed for truth. . . . The whole land shall be free for you to have safe traveling, and safe dwelling. If any man shall offend or grieve you with word or deed, he shall die by the sword.[77]

But Rich was a realist and used Dionysius' speech only to show the contrast between the ancient (and ideal) method of dealing with old soldiers and the English method. He did believe that a general tax should be levied on the people for the support of veterans, using the very logical argument that since "the soldier must fight in defense of all, why should he not be maintained by the help of all?"[78] He also suggested the taxing of law papers to support soldiers, much as beer and wine were taxed in the Low Countries.[79]

Like Digges, he believed that an efficient army must be well disciplined. The laws, disciplines, and orders should be established by the general with the advice of his counsel and should then be openly published to the soldiers "by sound of trumpet"; once proclaimed, they should be severely maintained.[80] Rich recommended the Roman discipline, which provided the death penalty for a multitude of crimes, from open cowardice to petty thievery.[81]

Finally, Rich believed that the nobility should supply the army with leaders, and he therefore condemned gentlemen "descended of honorable families" for their lack of interest in military affairs.[82] With evident bitterness, he remarked that the nobility had become "a servant to pleasure, and . . . idleness" and were "haunted by flatterers," while the nobility of old had been "followed by soldiers."[83]

These ideas show Rich's singleness of purpose during a long military and literary career. Uppermost in his mind for a period of thirty-two years was the desire to see England strong and mighty, able to withstand the onslaughts of any enemy secretly preparing an invasion of the isle. By means of his books he hoped to hammer complacent minds into wakefulness, clear out corruption, and instigate the building of an efficient fighting force under the direction of properly chosen and trained officers. Although he was only one of many who sought to do the same thing, his voice was perhaps the most eloquent and authoritative of them all; no other Elizabethan could claim a military record as long and steady as his own. He died in 1617 at the age of seventy-five, having served five English monarchs.

―――――

Perhaps the most interesting among this group of English military classicists is Sir John Smythe (1534–1607). Cousin to Edward VI,[84] he was a choleric individual whose long life saw him as diplomat, traveler, courtier, soldier, military critic, prisoner in the Tower, and eventually enforced recluse at Little Baddow in Essex. After fighting for twenty years as a mercenary soldier in various foreign armies—with the Hungarians against the Turks, with the Spanish against the Netherlanders, and possibly with the French during the reign of Henry II[85]—and at last returning to England to "live almost continually retired in [his] house," he decided "to compose four or five little books, all treating more or less of matters of arms . . . with intent . . . the same might someways profit the Crown and realm."[86]

His first attempt at composition was entitled *Certain Discourses Concerning the Formes and Effects of Divers Sorts of Weapons* (1590). A bellicose book, written in the defense of archery but also attacking contemporary English military discipline with great vehemence, it was suppressed by warrant on May 14, 1590,[87] probably not so much because it found fault with existing military conditions as because it cast doubt upon the honor and reputation of Elizabeth's army officers.

It did not pretend to be a eulogy of the ancient art of war, but, as a kind of diatribe against "modern" practices which were at variance with those advocated by older soldiers, it fell into the camp set up by Machiavelli, Fourquevaux, Porcia, and others writing on the Continent. That Smythe was influenced by his reading of the classics can be inferred from a list of twenty-five works he consulted—or said he consulted—in preparing his treatise. Included in the list, which is composed for the most part of ancient histories and biographies, are Livy, Tacitus, and Vegetius, all mainstays of classical military scientists.[88]

In *Certain Discourses,* after citing the ancient Egyptians, Macedonians, Greeks, Romans, and Arabs as peoples who had "the art military in great perfection" and who "did after, by living in long peace, . . . so forget all their orders and exercises military, that they came to be conquered," [89] Smythe advocates returning to the old order of things. In the proem to his book, he describes the pre-eminence of the old order as the result of a number of actions undertaken by successful generals of the past. These leaders, he points out, who had sagaciously formed counsels of "men of great sufficiency both in war and peace" for assistance, instigated regular and rigorous training among their soldiers. In order to win the affection of their men, they had them adequately appareled, armed, provisioned, and paid, and took all tactical precautions for preserving and saving their lives. In order to gain the respect of their men, essential if they were to win battles, these leaders also acquired the knowledge of "how to command, govern, and

order their armies, . . ." Finally, and most germane to the
main argument of the book, they developed archery as the
foundation of the infantry.[90] None of these things, he insists,
was being done in the English army.[91]

One great difference will immediately be noticed between
Smythe and his predecessors, both foreign and English, and
that was his insistence on bows and arrows as the primary
weapons for footmen. Here, it would appear, Smythe's great
love for bowmen, particularly English bowmen, and his
antipathy to calivermen, harquebusiers, and musketeers, sent
him leafing through histories in an attempt to find proof of
the military value of archery. As a result, although he certainly went to the past for examples, he went sometimes to a
different past from that to which most of his contemporaries
and predecessors turned. The bow had indeed been used by
Roman legionaries, but only as an auxiliary weapon; swordsmen rather than archers formed the strength of the Roman
army. But Smythe emphasizes that "the Egyptians . . . did
conquer a great part of Asia, Europe and Africa by their
notable militia, which did consist most of archery and bows,"
and the Macedonians, Turks, and Arabs achieved their successes with armies composed mainly of bowmen.[92]

Although this book marks the terminus of Smythe's tumultuous career—at least, he soldiered no more nor did he
engage in diplomatic activities—it did not stem his urge to
write. Not all the four or five books which he had in mind
got as far as the printers—indeed, it is doubtful if they
reached a perfected manuscript stage[93]—but in 1595 he
brought out another military text entitled *Instructions, Observations, and Orders Mylitarie.* It had been composed in 1591
and contains much that had already appeared in his first
work,[94] but it is more temperate in tone. Moreover, it deals at

length with subjects he never got around to treating in his *Certain Discourses:* ". . . the reducing of single bands of horsemen and footmen into their simple and single order of ranks . . . , and how to draw out many troops, and societies of shot to enter into skirmish, . . . as also divers different ways how to reduce many bands and troops into squadrons and battles formed, as well as march in the field, as to give battle with the most advantages . . ." [95]

Although Smythe writes less vehemently here, he handles these matters with criticism of the military profession in mind. Leo V of Constantinople, Smythe points out, when faced with danger from the Saracens "did compose a book in the Greek tongue, of late years translated into Latin by Sir John Cheeke, . . . entitled *Leonis Imperatoris de bellico apparatu liber, &c.* In which book the emperor does reform the disorders grown in the militia . . . and does procure to restore the same to the ancient orders and exercises military . . ." [96] As in his earlier work, Smythe intends to do likewise, for he is still perturbed by "the new fashions, and fancies of the disordered and corrupted militia that of very late years in divers civil wars have crept into Christendom." [97]

Touches of his old belligerence crop up from time to time in this work, for he was obviously still smarting from the suppression of his first work and the attacks made on him by "some three or four of our nation" in their "lewd and false pamphlets." These detractors, he insists, are "far wide . . . from the understanding of all true discipline," as "all men of right consideration may evidently see by their writings, speakings, vain opinions and actions." [98]

But Smythe does not end his work on this note. After delving into a problem that had concerned his predecessors and continued to concern his contemporaries—the selection and arming of men—he proposes that his instructions and military orders should be established by act of Parliament, "with certain different penalties for the reforming of the neglecters of such requisite matters military, as also certain . . . rewards for . . . such as do best." [99]

Smythe's subsequent actions show him to have been a rash man. On June 12, 1596, he rode to Windmill Field, where the Colchester militia was being trained, and made such statements as convinced the Privy Council that he should be apprehended and examined before the Star Chamber, possibly for treason. [100] He was taken up on open warrant, examined, confined in the Tower (although no formal charge was ever brought against him) and finally released in February 1598. He then retired to his home at Little Baddow, where he remained in relative seclusion until his death.

———

Thomas Styward (fl. 1580) was neither as vehemently classical as the other military writers we have been considering in this chapter nor so prolific. He wrote only one book, but a book whose popularity was attested to by the three editions in five years—1581, 1582, 1585. It was entitled *The Pathwaie to Martiall Discipline.* As he suggests in his dedication to Charles, Lord Howard, although many learned men before him had published books for the advantage of their countries, he could spend his time in no better way, for the sake of the commonwealth, than to imitate their industry. Therefore, besides drawing upon his own experience, he had gone to the works and opinions of the best soldiers, Italian, German, Swiss, French, and English, to assemble his collections of military laws and constitutions. [101] Like many of his contemporaries, he believed that a military treatise would be of value to his country, for, considering "the ambition of the world, it is a thing impossible for any realm or dominion always to live in peace without the use of the sword." [102]

At first glance, the reader might think Styward a modernist rather than a classicist. But it becomes apparent that not only did he urge his countrymen to "prosecute the ancient order of the Romans," [103] but also that the modern battle formations and tactics that pleased him most were those derived from the Romans. For instance, when discussing the composition and arrangement of a quadrant of 900 men (a unit comparable to a modern regiment), he states that the "proportion is after the German manner of embattling, much after the order of the Romans, who divided their legions into divers cohorts, to this intent, that when the fronts were wearied, the mainward and rearward [elsewhere sometimes termed "main battle" and "rear battle"] succeeded . . ." [104] Again, when discussing the "ordering of battles lately used," which seemed unsatisfactory to him and which he did not commend, he refers to the "prosperous success of the Romans," who "only through their good orders . . . became conquerors of many countries." [105] In two minor points, at least, he seems even more classical-minded than Digges. The latter revered cavalry more than the Romans did; but Styward goes out of his way to state that "horsemen are to be accounted as second, and not as superior or principal of the field . . . ," [106] a point of view which, as we shall see, may have determined the organization of troops Elizabeth put into the field as late as the turn of the century. Again, while Digges rejected some odd battle formations employed by generals of antiquity, Styward seems to have had a certain admiration for formations called wedges, saws, shears, and crosses, which were used by the Romans and which he considered "very profitable if they might be ordered and disposed in place convenient." [107] He agrees with Digges, however, that such formations would be difficult to maintain in marching.

The Pathwaie to Martiall Discipline is divided into two books. The first deals with the various duties of officers, military discipline, and the method of arming, mustering, training, and embattling soldiers. The second book is devoted mainly to infantry tactics, orders of march, and methods of encampment. Here and there throughout his work are inserted small sections on other aspects of war, such as despoiling the enemy, taking prisoners, and maintaining discipline. In other words, it is much like Digges' *Stratioticos* without chapters on arithmetic and algebra; and in some respects, at least, it is a better book in that it is replete with pictures and diagrams illustrating the tactical deployment of troops.

━━━

Not all Elizabethan soldiers, of course, accepted classical works as valid texts on strategy and tactics. Nor did they accept contemporary works, foreign or English, that based their art of war upon antiquity. This may have been so partly because a few of the very early Elizabethan advocates of Greek and Roman modes of warfare were not themselves military leaders. Some of them were scholars and educators and were, therefore, likely to be isolated from the military world. Consequently they were looked upon with suspicion by men who had first-hand knowledge of the "foughten field."

But the classicists put forward other reasons. For instance, there were, according to Sir John Smythe at any rate, a number of Elizabethan soldiers who attributed to themselves "greater wisdom and sufficiency in all arts and sciences, and specially in the art military, than . . . the notable men and great captains of former ages and greater antiquity." [108] There were also young, relatively uneducated men who had engaged, as Thomas Digges suggests, in only a few skirmishes. These men, he says, thought it a great "disgrace that anything should be desired in a soldier that wanted in themselves," justifying their position by arguing that "the time was changed, the wars were altered, and the fury of ordnances, such as all those Roman orders were mere toys." [109]

Not every man who adhered to the point of view of the modernist, however, was a young, unread "fresh water soldier." [110] Morison, in his translation of Frontinus, remarks that "the noble captains of England have oft declared that they little need any instructions, any books, to teach them to use their enemies." [111] The arguments of such men were no different from those of the men who lacked experience, who probably borrowed their own statements from them in the first place. William Garrard, author of *The Arte of Warre* (1591) and erstwhile soldier in the Spanish army, noted that "at this day we are constrained to vary our order from that of the Romans, considering our arms be varied, which do now fetch and wound much more and further off, and are more piercing than those of ancient time." [112] Even such a man as Sir Roger Williams, who, as we have seen, was not at all insensible to what could be gained from the study of antiquity, nevertheless pointed out that the ancients, "had they known artillery . . . would never have battered towns with rams, nor have conquered countries so easily, had they been fortified as Germany, France, and the Low Countries, with others, have been since their days." [113] Other experienced soldiers expressed similar opinions, but their statements seldom got into print except as theories to be attacked.

There were also a great many soldiers, experienced or not, who were opposed to an English army built upon Greek and Roman models, perhaps not so much because they considered ancient armies to be outmoded—which was the argument they used—as because they felt that an injection of ancient discipline would place irksome restrictions upon their activities.[114] The military classicists discussed above, for instance, stressed five lessons soldiers were expected to learn from ancient histories: the moral and physical qualities requisite in officers and private soldiers, the training necessary to achieve expertness in battle, the regulations most useful for governing and disciplining troops, the sorts of organizations best suited for different kinds of exploits, and the kinds of tactics most serviceable on the battlefield. Had the first three lessons (those concerning personnel, training, and discipline) been turned into practice, many officers in Elizabeth's army—particularly in the early stages of its development but much later, too—would have been demoted or cashiered, or would have suffered cuts in pay. For the ancients had demanded that recruits be of the finest material, officers be experienced and honest, and training be rigorous and just. In the Elizabethan army recruits were frequently notorious rogues and vagabonds; the officers, seeking their positions for wealth instead of honor, were as often appointed for favoritism as for experience; the training program was such that it produced soldiers "who," as Essex complained, "know nothing of the wars and little of the use of the arms they carry"; [115] and the discipline was as lax as poor pay and an uncertain military philosophy could make it.[116]

The practical application of the last two lessons, involving organization and battle tactics, might have met less opposition had incompetent officers and men not feared the entering wedge of Roman and Greek discipline. But even some rather respectable soldiers rejected Roman organization on the ground that modern artillery made it obsolete. Others sneered at the Roman method of fighting in depth, with support and reserves, believing that "a battle is won and lost in the twinkling of an eye at the first joining." [117]

It is well-nigh impossible to find a military work published in Elizabethan England that adheres completely to the "modern" point of view, except for several works on artillery discussed in a later chapter. Educated Englishmen, we know, were too well grounded in classicism to throw off the yoke of Greek and Roman discipline completely. On the other hand, even the classicists, with their general awareness of experiments being carried out on the battlefield and their own experiences in various armies, realized that they could not sit in taprooms and thump the table in behalf of Caesar's legions. What resulted was a sort of compromise: Roman tactics as modified by musket, harquebuse, and the "great" artillery.

We see this compromise in Digges. While advocating a return to Roman discipline in his *Stratioticos* and succeeding works, he nevertheless spends a good deal of time describing tactics which involve shot and artillery and delineating the duties of personnel unknown to antiquity. Similarly, Rich, Smythe, and Styward leaven their antique theories with modern practices.

A variation on what these men do, so that the effect is more modern and less classical, is the work of William Garrard and Robert Hitchcock in their *Arte of Warre* (1591). This, the title page declares, is ". . . the only rare book of military profession: drawn out of all our late and foreign services, by William Garrard Gentleman, who served the King of Spain in his wars fourteen years, . . . Which may be called, the true steps of war, the perfect path of knowledge, and the plain plot of warlike exercises." Captain Hitchcock, who corrected and finished the work (Garrard having died in 1587), added his commendation to the book, stressing its modernity. In it, he asserts,

a number of rare and probable matters are set down with great study, diligence, and experience, as well as foreign and familiar examples and proofs drawn out from fatherly counsel and their grave admonition, as also enlarged by new policies and practices of the greatest soldiers in Christendom in these our present days, and compounded with the long experience, toiling after the cannonwheel, and sharp services, penury, hunger, cold lying on the ground, and a hundred sorrows, hazards, dangers, and hard adventures, the which he himself has sustained being the author hereof.[118]

This work is divided into six books. The first book describes how good soldiers "ought to behave themselves in wars: together with the martial laws of the field, and other necessary notes and offices." [119] The second sets down the duties of sergeants, ensigns, and lieutenants in disciplining and training their men. The third deals with the duties of higher officers—up to sergeant major general—and goes into great detail about the tactical use of troops in the field. The last three books consider such various matters as the duties of general officers, the use of artillery, procedures in establishing camps and throwing up fortifications, siege-craft, and administration. Appended to the work is Hitchcock's "general proportion and order of provision . . . to victual a garrison of one thousand soldiers." [120]

Although the title page of *The Arte of Warre* and Hitchcock's recommendation would lead one to believe that this work reflects Garrard's experience with the Spanish army—and, indeed, Garrard does occasionally mention his observations of what was put into practice by Don John of Austria and the Prince of Parma [121]—it consists mainly of wholesale borrowing from Digges' *Stratioticos,* Styward's *Pathwaie to Martiall Discipline,* and Fourquevaux's *Instructions for the Warres.*[122] Garrard, however, does not place the emphasis on classical antiquity that these latter works do. At one point he mentions Cyrus, Cambyses, Marcus Cato, and Marc Antony, but only to note that they were loved by their men because they were just.[123] At another point, when emphasizing the need for constantly exercising troops, he cannot resist remarking that the Romans, because of their insistence upon training, "knew perfectly what were to be accomplished in a particular band." [124] Again, going along with Digges' theory that Elizabethan armies should break up their battles into squadrons and battalions, he backs up his statement by noting that this division would be in imitation of the Roman practice.[125] But by and large, in his insistence upon the tactical use of musketeer and harquebusier and in his description of the employment of artillery in the field and at sieges, Garrard is more modern than the authors from whom he borrows.

Even more modern are the contents of Humphrey Barwick's *A Breefe Discourse Concerning the Force and Effect of All Manuall Weapons of Fire* (1594?). Barwick, like Smythe and Williams, was an old soldier. He began his career at the age of eighteen, "which was the second year of that good and godly King Edward VI [*i.e.,* 1548], at which time our English archers were in force and greatly used, and harquebusiers not as then common." [126] And though he could not claim experience in the Low Countries, or in the civil wars in France, he had served in England, France, and Scotland, and also in Spain.[127] He himself is quick to point out that his "entertainment in the French king's service was such as none of our nation for a footman ever had, only Captain Lampton excepted" and that for his military services he had been promised a pension of two hundred crowns by the King of Spain [128]—which, like many another kingly promise in those days, resulted in nothing.

His book, which was written mainly as an attack on Sir John Smythe's *Certain Discourses* and to a lesser degree on Sir Roger Williams' *A Briefe Discourse of Warre,* immediately takes an anti-classical stand. In his introductory remarks "To all skillful captains and soldiers," he satirically asks, "shall we refuse the cannon and fall to the ram again?" [129] Later, he heartily condemns that foreign classicist Machiavelli, stating that although the Italian had "set forth his whole knowledge, as touching fortification, and other sundry policies," he would never have held such ideas had he been a soldier. Then, witheringly, he adds: "It is a sport to hear how he does by himself fight a battle in words and says that if he had been a soldier in his youth, he would either have won the field with valor, or at least have lost it without shame. Who did let [*i.e.,* prevent] him to become a soldier in his youth?" [130]

The work contains eighteen chapters or "discourses"—he perhaps uses this term because Smythe and Williams do—on the use and value of the caliver and musket, being particularly enthusiastic about the former. He has numerous scathing remarks to make about the inefficiency of the long bow, a weapon which, he says, he himself had used until he was seventeen and, therefore, knew something about,[131] and, as we shall see later, he has a good deal to say about the armor and arming of infantrymen and cavalrymen and the defense of the realm.

III

Military Personnel

Most works on the art of war known to Elizabethans dwell at some length upon the ideal soldier. For instance, in Onosander one finds that the general should be a man of position, though not necessarily of noble birth, a man who is "temperate, continent, sober, abstinent, and not excessive in eating and drinking, patient in travail, of wit prompt, not covetous, neither young, nor old, and that he have children, if such a one may be had, and to be a fair speaker, of good name and fame, and of much reputation." [1] Elizabethans would have accepted these qualities blindly. Not only were they derived from ancient histories by an author of antiquity, they were subscribed to by the translator, Peter Whitehorne, who had himself been, as we have seen, a soldier of some experience.

Caesar expands the picture presented by Onosander. Although Caesar does not undertake to describe the perfect general, his own actions, reported with "indifferency and faithfulness" in the *Commentaries,* were repeatedly seized

51

upon by Elizabethans as ideal examples of what their contemporaries should do. A perusal of this work will give one the picture of a leader who is a man of good character and moral stability.

Vegetius, in *The Foure Bookes of Martiall Policye,* shows more interest in the civil occupation and physical characteristics of the soldier than in his moral fiber. He says that although countrymen should be preferred to city dwellers, any man coming from proper trades or professions should be accepted: "Smiths, carpenters, butchers, hunters of the hare and wild boars, may most conveniently be called to war," but "fishers, fowlers, shepherds, linen weavers, and whosoever that deals with any thing that betokens a womanish niceness, should be utterly banished the camp." [2] The physical characteristics of the soldier should be those indicative of strength, endurance, and vitality. That is, he should not "look drowsily," but he should be "straight necked, broad breasted," and have "shoulders . . . well fleshed, . . . strong fingers, long arms, a gaunt belly, slender legs." Concerning his moral virtues, emphasized so strongly by Onosander, Vegetius merely states that a soldier should be honest.[3]

The three most important Continental military books translated into English during the sixteenth century—those by Porcia, Machiavelli, and Fourquevaux—all deal directly with the ideal general and the private soldier. The ideal general as described by Porcia does not differ materially from that described by Onosander, although Porcia emphasizes military ability more than does Onosander. According to Porcia, the general or "captain of your army" should be one who "is born of a noble and valiant stock, and fearing nothing more than shame and reproach, . . . is without all evil doings" [*i.e.,* "lechery and covetousness"]. He should be "lucky" and should have "from his youth . . . been in warfare, under a good captain." He should be expert in "keeping his array," and "always highly taken and regarded of the whole army." Finally, he should be "stout and valiant." [4]

Neither Machiavelli nor Fourquevaux says much about the general. But both are convinced that a leader of troops should be experienced in wars and acquainted with the tactics of the ancients. Fourquevaux adds that the ideal general should imitate "Scipio the chaste and Caesar the just," [5] thereby confirming what Onosander and Porcia had said earlier.

But if they say little about the general, they are articulate enough about the common soldier. Machiavelli argues that soldiers should be non-professional and native born. Countrymen, he feels, make the best infantry; urbanites, the best cavalry. Men chosen for soldiers should be between the ages of seventeen and forty, and they should be selected from among farmers, smiths, carpenters, ironmongers, and masons, not because such men are better fitted than others for warfare, but because they will bring useful abilities to an army. In this respect he differs from Vegetius, whom he dismisses in a phrase or two. [6] In another respect—that of physical characteristics—he agrees with Vegetius, stating that the soldier should be chosen "by the lustiness of the body, as Caesar did," to wit, "eyes lively and cheerful, the neck full of sinews, the breast large, the arms full of muscles, the fingers long, little belly, the flanks round, the legs and feet dry. . . ." [7] He ends the description by stating that the soldier should exhibit "honesty" and "shame"; that is, besides being no rogue, he should be modest or virtuous in behavior and character.

Obviously, Fourquevaux had read Machiavelli and had

agreed with most of his conclusions, for the qualities requisite in the ideal soldier are essentially the same in the works of both men. Fourquevaux agrees fully with the physical characteristics delineated by Machiavelli, modifies the age requirements slightly, and increases the number of occupations which best fit a man for the army. Like Machiavelli and Vegetius before him, Fourquevaux feels that soldiers should be selected from among honest men.[8]

It will be noticed that although classical and Continental thought on the subject of the ideal soldier is substantially the same, one idea is in conflict—that of the nobility of the general. Porcia, who wrote later than Onosander but whose views appeared in England first, believed that the general of an army should be of noble birth. This idea, of course, is consistent with what had been the practice in the medieval and Renaissance armies in England and on the Continent. But Onosander clearly states a revolutionary view: the appointment of a general should be based, not upon what his ancestors were or had done, but upon what he himself might be capable of doing.[9] This difference is an important one, for, as the century progressed, Porcia's concept that nobility of birth was a necessary qualification for a general, although it never totally disappeared from the literature, and in actual practice— at least where full generals were concerned—was never really displaced, eventually gave way to the view expressed by Onosander.

Most native English military books likewise deal with an ideal soldiery, although occasionally they differ from their classical and Continental predecessors. The classical and Continental works translated into English emphasize the moral, spiritual, and fatherly qualities of the general, usually dismissing his tactical and strategical knowledge with such phrases as "of much reputation" or expert in "keeping his array." But Digges, in his *Stratioticos,* began a new vogue in military analysis. Although insisting that a good general must be "religious, temperate, sober, wise, valiant, liberal, courteous, eloquent, of good fame, and reputation," Digges stresses the necessity of securing a man who is "learned in histories, and in those sciences and arts that may enable him of himself without direction from others, readily to conceive and judge of military actions." [10] Chief among the sciences the general should know are those dealing with mathematics. *Stratioticos* and *Pantometria* were works by which Digges gave point to this theory. This stress on learning is all the more interesting because Digges professed to believe thoroughly in Roman military discipline; it is clear that he was not a blind follower of the classical writers.

In the 1590's, we begin to find further elaboration on the purely military skills of the general. Sir John Smythe, for instance, while pointing out that generals should "win the love of their soldiers by taking great care of their health and safeties" and by treating them as if they were their own children, argues that the really important job of all military leaders is to train their men, to keep them well appareled, armed, and fed, to know "how to command, govern and order their armies, regiments, bands and companies," and to lead them in person against the enemy.[11]

The greatest swing from the fatherly and moral general to the purely military one may be found in the writings of William Garrard and Matthew Sutcliffe, authors of *The Arte of Warre* (1591) and *The Practice, Proceedings, and Lawes of Armes* (1593), respectively. Garrard, as we know, was in the Spanish army for fourteen years,[12] and Sutcliffe was judge-advocate general under Leicester in the Low Countries.[13]

Garrard's picture of the ideal general is that of a "prudent person" who is able to choose the correct subordinates to get the job done well and to see that "the soldiers' honors and military orders be not defrauded." Although morally and spiritually he may "be accounted most vicious, yet if he know how to govern and guide his charge, a soldier must obey him, and neither calumniously reprehend him, nor corruptly imitate and observe his vices, but duly and directly fulfill his precepts." Interestingly enough, authority for this statement was obtained from classical example, for Garrard notes that "Caesar was ambitious, great Alexander a drunkard, Hannibal unfaithful, cruel, and without religion, Fabius Maximus by lingering esteemed a coward, Marcellus rash and unadvised." [14]

Although Sutcliffe remarks that the first requirement of a general is religious faith, he writes in the same vein as Garrard does, stating that a general "ought not to be ignorant of any stratagem of war." [15] Almost as an afterthought, however, Sutcliffe adds the qualities which so many earlier writers had emphasized: "There are also other virtues required in a general which, although they be not so necessary as the former, yet for the execution of matters, are very requisite and profitable, as namely justice, liberality, courtesy, clemency, temperance, and loyalty." [16]

Of these authors, only Digges feels that the general should be of noble birth. But Digges, it should be remembered, enjoyed the patronage of the Earl of Leicester. Even Garrard, who saw all his action with Spanish soldiery, states that "neither high titles . . . [nor] favors of the Prince, can make a man wise that is not"; [17] and Sutcliffe elaborates upon this point of view by enumerating French generals, appointed "in respect of nobility, rather than sufficiency," who brought disaster to their armies.[18] A staunch supporter of these theories can be found in Robert Barret, who, in *The Theorike and Practike of Moderne Warres* (1598), refutes the idea that nobility is a necessary qualification for a general by enumerating famous generals of antiquity who had origins among the lower classes.[19]

As one might surmise from the quantity of military literature published in England during the sixteenth century, the ideal officer was also a well-read man, acquainted with the science and tactics of both the ancients and the moderns. As more and more books were written, however, it began to be suspected by a number of military men—particularly those who were long on experience and short on learning—that too much emphasis was being placed upon "bookish theory" and not enough upon actual combat. Military authors countered sarcastically that it took more than a short journey across the Channel to make a soldier. And the fray was joined. It was long and bitter, and it proved to be one-sided. Few opponents of the book-soldier were as articulate as Iago, who disposes of Cassio so witheringly in the first scene of *Othello;* and by the end of the century, in theory at least, the book-soldier won. Some of the most earnest advocates of learning turned out themselves to be soldiers of no little repute.

It is in the writings of Digges, Garrard, Sutcliffe, and their contemporaries that we begin to see a careful distinction made among all ranks of soldiers, from the private through the captain and colonel to the general. With this distinction there comes a difference in the emphasis on the importance of the various officers, and this shift in emphasis is based upon a very real Elizabethan situation. The core of English military organization, as we shall see in the following chapter, was the company or band of 150 men, led by a captain. Armies were thought of in terms of companies, not regiments. Men were levied by companies, trained by companies, paid by companies. This concept was strengthened during the war between the Dutch and the Spanish in the Low Countries, where Dutch armies were supported, from 1572 onwards, by companies of volunteers or pressed men levied in England. Information about the activities of English soldiers—and the Elizabethans were apparently eager for news of them—quite naturally stressed the activities of English companies and their leaders. Even when high-ranking Englishmen made names for themselves, it was often in the dual role of regimental colonel and company commander. So it is not surprising to find the captain becoming the officer best known to Englishmen and most critically examined by them.

There was not a great deal of difference between the qualifications recommended for a general and those for a captain. But there was one difference: from the very beginning all authors agreed on what qualities the company commander should possess. As Giles Clayton wrote in 1591, "The place of a captain is not lightly to be considered of, for that upon his skill and knowledge depends the safety or loss of many men's lives." [20] In general, it was argued that the captain should be "of notable capacity, experience, and exemplary in all his actions and enterprises." [21] Specifically, he should have risen from rank to rank, "none to be captains except first a lieutenant. None lieutenant but first an ensign. None ensign but first a sergeant"; [22] he should have obtained these various ranks through merit and not through "affection and favor"; [23] he should be morally impeccable; [24] he should train his men frequently; he should "have special regard that such provision be made for . . . [his] soldiers . . . as well for victuals as for armor, and munitions"; [25] he should "always lodge himself among his company, and endeavor himself to tolerate pains and hardness"; [26] and, as Digges so expertly sums up, "a captain ought so to behave himself as he be both loved and obeyed of his soldiers, . . . and that he endeavor himself by all means to annoy the enemy, and painfully to execute, with all diligence, such matter as he is enjoined by his superiors, and to fear nothing but infamy." [27]

The concept of the ideal private soldier underwent substantially the same change as did that of the general. Classical and foreign authors had been content to describe him—without much elaboration—as honest, strong, skilled in a useful trade, and, once in the army, well trained. And several of the English authors wrote much in the same vein. Digges, for instance, who represents a decided advance in the concept of the perfect general, sounds like Machiavelli or Vegetius when describing the private. Chosen from among men between the ages of nineteen and forty-five, skilled in "some occupation, not trained up in idleness," the soldier, says Digges, should be "of a strong composition of body to abide both heat and cold, hunger and thirst, travail and watching." He adds, however, that he should be "in expenses moderate" and temperate in the use of "meat and drink." [28]

Although Matthew Sutcliffe has much to say about the general, he, like Digges, neglects the common soldier. To be sure, he uses more space than either Machiavelli or Vegetius to comment on the requirements for a soldier, but he adds little to the descriptions they give. His greatest contribution is in requiring that the common soldier have high ethical standards similar to those which earlier writers had expected of the general. Realizing—as so many of his compatriots did not—that "if princes mean to have their honor and country defended, or their estate maintained, or service done upon the enemy," they must choose their soldiers carefully, he enumerates three points to be considered in levying troops: "first, the strength of the body; secondly, the vigor and virtues of the mind; and thirdly, the manner and trade of the parties' living." [29] When he goes on to expand these points, as he soon does, there is only one—the second—to which he gives more detail than his predecessors had done. Sutcliffe insists that "that which specially commends soldiers, is the vigor of the mind, and good conditions, conjectured by the visage and outward behavior, but known only by their conversation." [30] In other words, greater emphasis is laid upon the moral make-up of the common soldier than heretofore.

Similarly, the only important addition which Robert Barret makes to the already existing theories is in the realm of morality. After stating that the soldier should "ground his valorous determination upon four principles . . . defense of true religion . . . the honor of his prince . . . the safety of his country . . . [and] the art he professes," he cautions commanders to levy the "diligent, careful, vigilant, and obedient . . . sober, quiet, friendly" individual who is "no blasphemer, nor swearer" and who abstains from "dice, cards, and idle games." [31]

But some writers give greater attention to all details concerning the private soldier than do Digges, Sutcliffe, or Barret. William Garrard, for instance, spends a number of closely packed pages on the special requirements and duties of the soldier, based upon seven important points of conduct: obedience, silence, secretiveness, sobriety, valor, truthfulness, and loyalty. [32] After briefly describing the soldier's age and physical characteristics (he should be from eighteen to forty-six with "a strong body, sound, free from sickness, and of a good complexion"),[33] he carefully notes the type of training he should have, the care he should take with his clothes, armor, and weapons, the attitude he should have toward his comrades and superiors, and the way he should conduct himself in camp, on guard, and in battle.[34]

By the end of the century, the soldier had become—in the hands of perfectionists—a model of the finest ethical instincts, skilled in the most difficult aspects of military science. Thomas Smith, author of *The Arte of Gunnerie* (1600), describes him in the following formidable paragraph:

He may well be called a trained soldier that knows by the sound of drum and trumpet, without any voice, when to march, fight, retire, etc.; that is able in marching, embattling, encamping, and fighting, and such like, to perform, execute, and obey the laws and orders of the field; that has some sight in the mathematicals and in geometrical instruments, for the conveying of mines under the ground, to plant and manage great ordnance, to batter or beat down the walls of any town or castle; that can measure altitudes, latitudes, and longitudes, etc. Such a one may be termed in my opinion an expert soldier, though he never buckled with the enemies in the field.[35]

A soldier who might fit this description would be, in any age, nothing short of astounding.

———

To find a close correlation between the ideal and the real among soldiers of any period in any country would, of course, be too much to expect. The goal has always been inaccessible, although some ages apparently have been more successful than others in approaching it. Among sixteenth-century writers the armies of ancient Greece and Rome had acquired an enviable record for approximating their ideal, in contrast to the Elizabethan army, which came woefully short of the goal, particularly where captains and common soldiers were concerned.

Elizabethans were fortunate in one respect. For the most part, they had good generals. The Earl of Essex, Sir Francis Vere, Sir John Norris, and the Earl of Leicester are four big names, and only the last of these was not a competent general. Although much has been written about these men, a brief description of their careers as seen through the eyes of contemporary military writers—who, for some reason or other, have been generally neglected in the matter—may put them in proper perspective for this study.

Essex was everywhere regarded as valiant, and, in spite of his youth, fatherly toward his soldiers. As one writer put it in a dedication to Essex, "the skillful and expert captain took as good occasion to wonder at your singular valor, as the sick, maimed and poor simple soldier to commend your liberal bounty." [36] Elizabethan dedications, of course, must be taken with a grain of salt, but when such serious and reforming works as Garrard's *The Arte of Warre* and Sutcliffe's *The Practice, Proceedings, and Lawes of Armes* are addressed to Essex, one must accept something of what their authors say. Thomas Garrard, in his dedication to William Garrard's text, was surely speaking what he considered simple truth when he said that Essex' "humors and honors of mind . . . well suits with the honorable matter" of *The Arte of Warre*.[37] And the appeal made by Sutcliffe to Essex goes well with the earnest tone of his book:

The only hope [he writes concerning his desire for martial reform in England] that sustains me, and has thus far in these my endeavors advanced me, is grounded upon that expectation which all this nation has of your heroical actions. . . . As others choose ease, so Your Lordship has followed the weari-some travails of wars. By your own experience in the service of the Low Countries, of Portugal, and France, you both under-stand the practice of arms, and the wants of the soldiers. The general hope of all soldiers, nay of all that love their country, is that Your Lordship, which so well understands the common disorders of the wars and the great importance of them, and has so great favor and means by reason of your authority to correct them, will one day be a means to see them in some part re-dressed. All those parts which are required of a sufficient general, do seem to flourish and show forth themselves in your doings, and promise these things in your behalf.[38]

But Essex, for all his popularity with his soldiers, was rash, impetuous, and often unable to follow orders; and it has yet to be shown that he really understood all the aspects of military science set forth by contemporary writers on the subject.

Sir Francis Vere, though less spectacular than Essex, was certainly the better general. One anonymous author of a military newsbook referred to Vere as the possessor of a "great heart that scorns to stoop" and as a man of sound understanding, trained in holding fortified cities.[39] Another praised his great force and resolution in attacking the en-emy.[40] Sir Robert Naunton, writing about twenty years after Vere's death, stated that he was "inferior to none; but supe-rior to many";[41] and a perusal of Vere's *Commentaries* tends to substantiate this claim. Not only did Vere possess the two cardinal virtues of Essex—courage and a fatherly interest in his soldiers—he had as well a true understanding of military tactics. This understanding was combined with a feeling for what his opponent might do in a given situation—perhaps the quality which Porcia was referring to when he said that a general should be lucky—and the combination brought him many successes. Since Vere was also acquainted with mathematics and problems of intrenching and fortification and since he was probably well-read—at least well enough read, it may be remembered, to call Caesar's *Commentaries* "the breviary of soldiers"—he may be said to have approximated the Elizabethan ideal as well as any man then living.

If the same cannot be said for Sir John Norris, it must be admitted that he established an enviable record for himself in the Low Countries, Portugal, France, and Ireland. The fullest account of his exploits may be found in *A True Discourse Historicall of the Succeeding Governours in the Netherlands* (1602). There he is first mentioned as being "a gentleman of great courage and dexterity," and later as "a new Hector, another Alexander, or rather a second Caesar." [42] Through this film of praise one gets a glimpse of an officer who was at least valiant and energetic. He was also reasonably successful. But whether or not he was interested in his men is problematical, for it is known that Thomas Digges incurred his enmity by attempting to institute much-needed reforms in the Low Countries. Since these reforms would have benefited the common soldier at the expense of peculating officers, one may well wonder at the basis of Sir John's anger. [43] As a tactician, he would seem to have been inferior to Vere, but the latter has the historical advantage inasmuch as he wrote his own memoirs, while Norris' reputation depends upon the words of authors who were more interested in results than methods.

With Leicester, we can be more definite. Several interesting contemporary military accounts of his activities as governor-general in the Low Countries are available. Only two, both by Thomas Digges, whose patron the Earl was, attempt to describe him as anything but incompetent. The others show him as a man more interested in power than in destroying the enemy. As Edward Grimestone recorded in *A Generall Histo-*

rie of the Netherlands (1608, 1609), Leicester seldom held general musters of the English troops, and so, unaware of what men he actually had on hand, could not conduct an offensive war. He permitted officers who were negligent in their duties and careless of their men to enjoy command of troops. He appointed incompetent favorites as governors of cities, and he "put men into the admiralties at his own devotion, who had no knowledge of navigation, . . . [and were] nothing acquainted with sea causes and much less with war by sea and provision for fleets." [44] He neglected to see that his men were paid on time. [45] He was a blundering tactician, as even Digges, his admirer, inadvertently proves when describing his exploits for the relief of Sluys. [46] To his advantage it may be said that apparently he had personal courage and was more interested in the welfare of his men than most of his detractors realized. [47] But he was certainly not a military leader of whom Englishmen could be proud.

In the Elizabethan army, appointments all along the line were made on the basis of favoritism, and if the generals turned out for the most part to be competent, the same cannot be said for the company grade officers of the period. In 1570, Roger Ascham had been inspired to write that, "praise be God, England hath at this time, many worthy captains and good soldiers, which be indeed, so honest of behavior, so comely of conditions, so mild of manners, as they may be examples of good order, to a good sort of others which never came in war." [48] If Ascham spoke the truth then, things had changed greatly within a few short years. The last quarter of the sixteenth century saw so many corrupt and incompetent captains that numerous dramas, poems, and prose pieces were loaded with tales of their misconduct. [49] Their crimes ranged from petty thievery to mass murder. Immorality, cowardice, absenteeism, disgraceful neglect of men and provisions, disregard for even a modicum of military discipline, ignorance of training procedures and tactics—these were but some of their faults, so that the name of captain became odious to soldier and citizen alike.

Apparently most captains went to the wars to line their purses. They used any method which would work, but the most common was simply not to pay their men. When the outcry became too great or the unpaid men unmanageable, captains sent their companies on dangerous missions, collecting the salaries of those men who did not return.[50] The dead men had to be replaced, of course, since at least a skeleton company had to be maintained in order for the captain to fill his pockets. It may be imagined what sort of service such leaders rendered prince and country. And what could be done with pay could be done with food, apparel, and bedding.[51]

These abuses were violently condemned by honest soldiers in letter and pamphlet. Sir John Smythe and Thomas Digges led the attack, and they were echoed by many others in high and low places in both the Netherlands and Ireland. From time to time, the government attempted to rectify the abuses. For instance, in 1586 an Act of the Privy Council took payment of troops out of the hands of the captains and turned it over to the treasurer and the muster-master.[52] But the effort at reform was not successful. Captains attempted to bribe muster-masters, and, failing that, to hound them out of the service. Thomas Digges was glad to quit his post in the Netherlands, where he had been alternately cajoled and threatened. Reynolds, in Ireland, was told that he "must either wink at the abuses in the musters, or else . . .";[53] when he refused, he was imprisoned on a trumped-up charge of attempted rape.[54]

Many captains acquired the habit of being absent from their companies. The worst of these did not even bother to go overseas to join their charges, but, leaving their men to whatever subordinates happened to be on hand, remained safely in England. If they did not make as much money as their brothers-in-arms who loaded their coffers with dead pays, they escaped the rigors of a campaign and the dangers of the field.

This habit seems to have been most peculiar to officers employed in the Irish wars, particularly in 1599 and 1600, and men of responsibility in Ireland became frantic at the sight of so many leaderless soldiers assembled to fight the Irish rebels. Lord Justices Carey and Loftus bombarded the Privy Council with letters deploring the situation and warning their lordships that continued absences would result in "no small maim to the service." [55] Querulously, Carey wrote to Sir Robert Cecil that if captains "will or shall receive Her Majesty's pay, it is fit they should forthwith be commanded to their charge." [56]

Commanding was one thing; making the officers obey was something else. In the fall of 1599, the Privy Council dutifully attempted reform, warning "all such captains and commanders, as are now in Her Majesty's pay and absent from their charge, to return presently." The Council members were not overly sanguine about the effect of this order for immediate return, however, for they told Loftus and Carey that "because we know not how they may delay it, it is Her Majesty's pleasure that you do forbear to pay any man that is absent from his charge until he return again." [57] For some reason, even the withholding of money did not work the desired effect—perhaps the reports of rebel activities were sufficiently gory to outweigh the love of money—because by the summer of the next year captains still remained at home, and the Privy Council continued to receive indignant letters, not only from the Lord Justices of Ireland, but from those sincere officers who were anxious to see the enemy whipped.

Other captains, who went overseas, committed errors as grave by remaining "in great towns feasting, banqueting, and carousing with their dames" while their soldiers were, at the least, lodged "dispersed and straggling in villages" or, at the worst, sent out on some "dangerous enterprise." [58] Even when they went into combat with their men, these officers showed less interest in the objective and the troops who were to obtain it than in themselves. Sir John Smythe indignantly reports how some leaders saved themselves when the going was hot:

some of our . . . chief men of war in the Low Countries . . . have mounted upon horses . . . and either have accompanied their footmen upon the flanks or rearward . . . or else have put themselves into some bands of horsemen as though it were against their reputation to serve on foot amongst their soldiers; or rather . . . that upon any hard accident they might be ready (leaving their soldiers to the slaughter) to save themselves rather with the force of their heels and spurs, than with any dint of sword, which among many other, has been one special cause that there have been so great number of soldiers at divers times consumed and slain, and never any chieftain, . . . [59]

To these gross faults of murder, cowardice, thievery, and absenteeism must be added that of immorality. Sir Henry Knyvett, lumping all officers in one black pot, wrote that

it is known by long experience that the corruption of the army . . . springs only from the rash and evil choice which has been most commonly made of needy, riotous, licentious, ignorant and base colonels, captains, lieutenants, ensigns, sergeants, and such like officers, who have made merchandise of their places and without regard of their duty or respect of conscience have made port sale of their soldiers' blood and lives to maintain their unthriftiness and disorders.[60]

This was an exaggeration. Yet immorality and its results were certainly major causes for what authors liked to term "the decay of martial discipline." Smythe, as we have noticed, complained that captains spent overmuch time feasting and carousing with their women. Digges added that they provided for their "ease and commodity like petty princes, . . . where they may take their pleasure, and carouse lustily."[61] Such officers he called "bawdyhouse captains."[62] The name of captain was such a byword of incontinence that Thomas Nashe, writing on a different subject in *Pierce Penilesse His Supplication to the Divell,* could not keep captains out of his sly list.[63] And Thomas Dekker, in *The Devils Answer to Pierce Pennylesse,* remarks of the devil that "all the vacation you may . . . meet him at dicing ordinaries, like a captain."[64]

Even when captains meant well, they were often, through inexperience and lack of training, incompetent. Barnaby Googe, in a dedication to Barnabe Rich's *Allarme to England* (1578), bewails the lack of military knowledge found in so many company commanders:

We have a number of captains, such as never came yet under ensign [*i.e.,* company banner] in their life. Happy shall that realm be that shall have need of such expert soldiers, but most unhappy and unjust men that dare challenge to themselves the place of so great a charge. Soldiers enough we have that in time of peace can range their battles, cast out their skirmishes, assault towns, and conquer kingdoms, that a man would judge them at the first sight for very Hectors and Hannibals. But these be they (I know not how it happens) that are the first that will be gone when they come to it.[65]

All of these faults, as most military writers recognized, could be laid to two causes. First, the men given commission to select captains appointed their favorites, whether or not those favorites had training, experience, or ability. Second, the officers thus appointed, often having no knowledge of military discipline, conducted their army affairs as they might have conducted their civilian lives—not according to the laws and ordinances of war but according to their own desires. Writing in 1590 about the ineffective campaigns in the Low Countries, Sir Roger Williams asks: "What corrupted the discipline of the Netherlands? Chiefly placing their ignorant cousins and favorites to command. Who could have won Ghent, Antwerp, Bruges, Ypres, with an 100 other towns, that wanted no necessaries for wars, if there had been expert commanders in them?" [66] Eight years later, Robert Barret said much the same thing, indicating that neither the Queen, the Council, nor superior commanders heeded the lessons which many failures on the battlefields should have taught them. The "great disorders committed by some professors and followers of wars" were caused, Barret wrote, by "the bad choice of some captains, soldiers and officers, made at the first by those who had commission or authority for the same; next, by reason of the little discipline used among those so chosen, for many have been chosen by favor, friendship, or affection, little respecting their experience, virtues, or vices, whereby most commonly, the fawning flatterer, the audacious prater, the subtle make-shift is preferred before the silent man, the approved person, or the plain-dealing fellow." [67] And he adds the pertinent comment: "Then such being chosen and preferred, how do you think the conduction should be good?" [68]

The Queen could not have been ignorant of this situation. Captain John Baynard wrote directly to Elizabeth in December 1599, advising her to rectify the abuses in officer appointments if she wished to be successful in war:

It is most necessary that there should be no commander employed to have command of men in the wars, but such as are of experience and honest conversation; as that either he has risen by degrees of a soldier, or at least has been of long continuance; for there have been many that have and do thrust themselves forward to have command that neither know what belongs to preserve a soldier, much less to instruct or marshal him. For the wars are carried by judgment, experience, and well ordering, when it comes to the substance of battling and fighting. [69]

Elizabeth's Council was similarly warned. Sir Geoffrey Fenton wrote to Cecil in February of the next year, emphasizing a point professional military men have hammered home ever since. "Young men (being preferred to be captains before they had learned what was the office of a captain, or were touched with the true feeling of the honor and reputation of that calling) have little regarded the service, neither could they, being ignorant in the true points thereof." [70] But during the Elizabethan era nothing really effective was ever done to cure the ills resulting from poor appointments. The great breach between the ideal and the real was never closed.

One may well wonder what type of common soldier filled up the ranks commanded by such captains. If possible, the privates were worse than their company officers, although for different reasons. Geoffrey Gates, who was a soldier of experience and therefore an admirer of men-at-arms, noted that the common people of England "condemn soldiership, and . . . despise the profession of arms as a vile and damnable occupation." [71] As might be expected from a man of his position, he placed part of the blame on the "servile and unnoble hearts" of "the vulgar multitude." Nevertheless, he admitted that the immorality of soldiers justified the opprobrium cast upon them:

The common sort of our countrymen that go to war, of purpose more to spoil than to serve, and as under color of pursuit of arms, they put themselves to the liberty and use of swearing, drunkenness, shameless fornication, dicing, and thievery, in slow wars and under loose government in the tumultuous state of a foreign nation, where they think it foolish scrupulousness to use either tenderness of conscience, or yet any honest manners, so do they return into their country, so much corrupted with all manner of evils that they seem rather to come from hell than from the exercise of warlike arms or from the regiment of military discipline, and therefore so venomous a brood to their native country . . . that they are rather to be vomited out of the bulk of the commonwealth than to be nourished in the same. [72]

Those are exceedingly harsh words, made the more forceful because of the profession of the man who uttered them. But they are not exceptional. Barnabe Rich, also an old soldier, quoted Agrippa as saying "that if you would call a tyrant, a blasphemer, a murderer, a robber, a spoiler, a deflowerer, an oppressor, with many other such like, if you would . . . include all these in one short name, you may call him by the name of soldier." [73] This is a statement one might expect from the great humanist Erasmus, not from an army captain.

However well deserved, such epithets are merely indicative of corruption in high places. The cause for the evil lay with Elizabeth's military organization—and, therefore, ultimately with Elizabeth herself. In the first place, troops were generally levied by captains with the aid of justices of the peace and petty constables. The latter officials would assemble the men; the former would make their choice. From *Henry IV, Parts I and II,* we know what bad choices might be made by some officers. But justices of the peace and their helpers could be equally corrupt. There is a passage by Matthew Sutcliffe in *The Practice, Proceedings, and Lawes of Armes* which describes the poor selection that might be offered even the most careful captains:

For when occasion is offered of service, then for the most part order is given either to the officers of every parish to take up rogues or masterless men or inhabitants of prisons, such as if they had their deserts they were to be sent rather to the gallows than to the wars . . . or if a greater number must be taken, to the officers in the country, men for the most part ignorant of warlike actions and such as have no other respect most commonly than to disburden the parish of rogues, loiterers, pickers [petty thieves], and drunkards, and such as no other way can live.[74]

There is something of the same statement, with equally cynical phrasing, in *The Theorike and Practike of Moderne Warres* and *A Right Exelent and Pleasaunt Dialogue betwene Mercury and an English Souldier.*[75] Sutcliffe, however, adds: ". . . when I consider how in foreign nations men are sent to the slaughter, few in number, unprovided, unfurnished, unpaid, despoiled by their governors, contrary to all order of service, I must needs say, these men are the fittest to be sent."[76]

The justices of the peace were aided in their practice of supplying poor material for the army by the good yeomen of the country and citizens of the town, who, like many of their brethren of a later year, were not always eager to serve their country. Gates describes the shifts used by them to escape impressment: ". . . the rural man, by bribes, by a livery coat, by frank labored friendship, by counterfeit sickness, or by starting from his house under color of far business, does shift himself from the ordinances of the prince . . . the citizen or townsman does in likewise put forth his apprentice, his servant, or poor hireling, to supply his place, and to withdraw his own person from the royal ordinances." [77] Actually, this sort of behavior was to be expected from both justice and citizen, for the Queen herself, early in her reign, had given signal evidence of what sort of men she thought fit to be her soldiers. Writing to Sir Arthur Champernowne, Vice-Admiral of Devon, in 1563, she requested him to "deliver up to the bearer certain persons arrested on suspicion of offenses at sea, in order to be employed in the Queen's service," and the same year she requested the "names of as many prisoners as be in Newgate fit to be pardoned, and that be able to serve." [78] These statements are reminiscent of Falstaff's assertion that he had most of his men out of prison.[79]

But not all soldiers were of this sort. Sir John Smythe, who condemned much of what he found in the army at home and overseas, was moved to write to Burghley in 1590 that many of the men—indeed, "the whole Essex regiment" in 1588—were honest and exemplary soldiers. There have been, he points out, "thousands of the brave English people . . . consumed by sea and land within these few years, who have not been rogues, cutpurses, horsestealers, committers of burglary, nor other sorts of thieves (as some of our captains and men of war, to excuse themselves, do report). But, in truth, they were young gentlemen, yeomen, and yeomen's sons and artificers of the most brave sort, such as did disdain to pilfer and steal." [80] This change in the 1590's—if indeed there was a change, for Smythe and the anonymous authors of military newsbooks are alone in expressing this sentiment—may have been brought about by the astute Burghley. In the "Orders for the Musters" of March 1589/90, signed by Burghley, one may find the deputy lieutenants of the shires being ordered to see that captains select "able and meet men to serve under them as soldiers." [81]

When honest men were enrolled in the bands, however, they were often turned into dishonest men by the life they were forced to lead. Even if they were lucky enough to be placed in an outfit commanded by a competent captain, they were often forced to go without pay, adequate clothing, or shelter; and when enrolled under a corrupt officer, their life was horrible indeed. Thomas Digges, writing to Walsingham from the Low Countries in the spring of 1585, reported that "of the bands that came over in August and September, more than half are wasted, dead and gone, and many of the rest sick and feeble, fitter to be at home in hospitals than to take pay as soldiers." [82] Even the Earl of Leicester, who, as we have noted, was generally considered an incompetent commander, wrote to Walsingham at about the same time, requesting "leave to speak for the poor soldiers." "If they be not better maintained," he said, ". . . there will neither be good service done. . . . There was no soldier yet able to buy himself a pair of hose, and it is a great shame to see how they go, and it kills their hearts to show themselves among men." [83] Two months later, he described his men as "ragged and torn, and like rogues." [84] By mid-summer he was forced to admit that five hundred of his troops had run away in two days and that "our old ragged rogues here have so discouraged our new men as, I protest to you, they look like dead men." [85]

Added to the misery caused by being improperly clothed was that of being supplied with inadequate food. Many men were wounded or fell sick in the Low Countries, and as Leicester's master of artillery remarked, "It is impossible for sickness or a hurt of danger to be healed with no diet but hard cheese." Perhaps even such food, had it been good, would have been acceptable; but for every pound of sweet cheese, the soldiers were provided with six pounds that were "fusty and unwholesome." [86]

Nor were their quarters conducive to high morale or sound health. While many of the officers lived in private homes, the soldiers—"two or three hundred of them together"—were quartered "in some one church, and so in divers churches, upon the bare pavements." [87] Eventually, desperately sick for want of proper food, clothing, and lodging, the men were no longer of use to Leicester, who shipped them back to England, "of which foresaid great numbers of miserable and pitiful ghosts, or rather shadows of men, the Essex and Kentish carts and carters (that carried them) can testify." [88]

The same situation was repeated in Ireland later on. Among the many letters that were written in an attempt to change things for the better, the following, from William Jones, Commissary in Munster, to Cecil, succinctly sums up the Irish case:

I am sure . . . the most of them [soldiers] are as poor in apparel as the common beggar in England, and now grown to that mutiny for want thereof that I had much ado to free myself from them without outrage.

They have not yet received their winter suits, nor many of

them their summer, . . . And the most of the packs [of clothes] was so rotten that of 67 suits, which was proportioned for a company of 100, some found 20, some more, few less, that were not serviceable. . . .

The victuals heretofore were very bad, and great want of them.[89]

It is perfectly understandable that such men did not fight everywhere and at all times as their Queen might have wished. They lost many engagements and suffered great casualties. Yet, in spite of the sort of men some of them were and the miserable conditions under which they lived, Elizabeth's troops often performed magnificently. They fought the wild Irish rebels to a standstill and made glorious names for themselves at Turnhout, Nieuport, and Ostend. Surely Shakespeare had in mind such soldiers as these, as well as their famous ancestors, when he depicted the Duke of Alençon as saying of the English:

> Froissart, a countryman of ours, records
> England all Olivers and Rolands bred
> During the time Edward the Third did reign.
> More truly now may this be verified,
> For none but Samsons and Goliases
> It sendeth forth to skirmish. One to ten!
> Lean raw-bon'd rascals! who would e're suppose
> They had such courage and audacity?
> (*Henry the Sixth, Part I,* I, ii, 29–36)

IV

Infantry

In the Elizabethan army, as in modern armies, the infantry was an arm of close combat whose primary mission was to engage the enemy and destroy or capture him, effecting its purpose by combining fire, movement, and shock action. Its command was vested in a colonel general.[1] Below him came two groups of officers, one being the "head officers of the field," which today we would call field grade officers, the other being company grade officers. Ideally, the field grade officers, in order of rank, were the lieutenant general (often called the lieutenant colonel), the sergeant major general, the colonels of the various regiments with their lieutenants, and the regimental sergeant major. In practice, however, some of these ranks were not always filled. The company grade officers were the captains of companies into which the regiments were divided and their lieutenants and ensigns (or ancients), the latter being the color-bearers.[2] Besides noncommissioned officers roughly corresponding to our present-day ranks, there were priests, clerks, harbingers, surgeons, drummers, and fifers.[3] These ranks were essentially the same as in Continental armies in which a great many Elizabethan officers—a number of them authors of military books—had served their apprenticeships as mercenaries.

The colonel general in Elizabethan times normally had the responsibilities that would fall to a modern division commander were that division comprised of infantry only, except that he did not have charge of military intelligence. Besides being in charge of personnel, operations, and training, he was also chief councilor in the marshal's court or council (equivalent to the general's staff), where he was expected to speak his mind in all cases concerning the infantry.[4] However, according to theory and presumably occasionally in practice, he delegated most of his authority to the sergeant major general; so we can pass him by and consider the duties of this latter officer.

The sergeant major general, sometimes called the sergeant major or sergeant general, was the most important tactical officer in the field, occasionally taking over the complete command. He it was who had "the due government" of the army's marching, encamping, and embattling and, as most of his actions were "to be handled in the face and view of the enemy, and in place of greatest peril," he was expected, besides being experienced, "to be valiant, learned, quick witted, and ready conceited [*i.e.,* imaginative], wise, discreet, and ready both to see, and foresee, as well their own, as the enemy's orders or disorders."[5] Since he had to be able to form the men into different sorts of squadrons and "battles" he was also expected, as we have noted in Chapter III, to be well grounded in arithmetic.[6] It was also the duty of this officer, both in camp and in towns, to appoint the bodies of the watch (*i.e.,* the guard detail, sometimes called "corps de gardes" by Elizabethans) and to assign them to their posts.[7] During periods of inactivity, he was to assemble the bands for intensive training periods because, as Digges puts it in his *Stratioticos,* if the soldiers could be taught to maneuver perfectly according to the stroke of the drum, they could hold their own in battle against experienced troops who had never been so trained.[8]

Finally, the sergeant major general had certain administrative duties to perform, receiving from the muster-master general an accurate roll of the bands, which included the numbers of men carrying the various kinds of weapons employed by Elizabethans. When he found himself in short supply, he was to "admonish the muster-master thereof, that either they . . . be supplied, or his roll reformed."[9]

The regimental sergeant major, whose office was "of much higher degree, than any ordinary captain,"[10] and who did for the regiment what the sergeant major general did for the army, was supposed to possess similar characteristics. All of the regimental sergeant majors were entitled to have assigned to them "certain expert gentlemen" called corporals of the field, who were to be "men of such perfection" that they could "conceive, and lively . . . express anything sudden to be done"—which is to say that they ought to be able to make quick decisions about changes in tactics.[11] Styward states that the corporals of the field should be four in number, two for the ordering and placing of the shot and two for the embattling of the pikes and bills, adding that the most worthy of them should succeed to the rank of the regimental sergeant major upon the death of that officer.[12] But army lists in the *Calendar of State Papers, Foreign* and *Ireland,* indicate that corporals of the field were not as numerous as military theory would have had them to be.

Interestingly enough, Digges—first in 1579 and again in 1590 after his experience as muster-master general in the Low Countries—sees no particular reason for the inclusion of a sergeant major general or regimental sergeant majors in an Elizabethan army, remarking that the Romans didn't use them; the Roman equivalents of the commanding general and the regimental colonels had been able to perform the tasks assigned to sergeant majors.[13]

Like the captain, the Elizabethan colonel—appointed to his regiment by either Elizabeth, her Privy Council, or the commanding general of the army—was not always as experienced and capable as military authors would have liked. Favoritism often governed the appointment and if it was made hurriedly, on the field, the colonel might do no more than lead his troops into battle. Sir Roger Williams complains that "these colonels of three days mars all the armies of the world"; [14] and Matthew Sutcliffe, after observing the English army in the Low Countries in his capacity of judge-martial, contrasts the Elizabethan colonel with his Roman equivalent, belittling the function of the former. "Now," he writes, "this only belongs unto colonels, that they have their regiment and the captains and soldiers thereof in order, that they lead the same in service, and do such special services as are committed unto them." [15] Ideally, the colonel's immediate job was to levy his men, divide them into companies, and appoint the captains, his own lieutenant, a regimental sergeant major, the chief harbinger, chief drummer, and his own ensign-bearer. Having received money for the levying and paying of his men, he was expected to divide it among the captains, who, in turn, would obtain the proper provisions for their soldiers and (with the help of justices of the peace of the various shires in England) do the actual impressing.[16]

The colonel was to look to his men's equipment—a job that was done by the sergeant major general when regiments were combined but was generally left to the colonel when isolated regiments went into operation—and make sure that there was a sufficient quantity of "corselets, morions, brigandines, halberds, black bills, pikes, bows, harquebuses, lead, match, powder, and victuals."[17] Just as the sergeant majors had assigned to them certain corporals of the field, so the colonel was to have lieutenants extraordinary. These lieutenants were of two sorts: youths of noble parentage who after due trial had shown especial merit; and officers and noncommissioned officers temporarily without command. While waiting for commands of their own they were to serve the colonel in such capacity as he required, presumably being capable of handling any rank under the degree of colonel.[18] Garrard, looking back over his war experiences in the Low Countries, calls these lieutenants "gentlemen of the company" or "lance spezzate"; but out of patriotism ("in the memory of the ancient valor of our nation") would have them termed "the Cavaliers of St. George's Squad."[19] He adds the interesting comment that "the colonel must not only use and treat them well with an advantage in their pay, but also feast them, cherish them, and set them oftentimes by course at his own table, and always show them a courteous countenance, with which show of friendly courtesy, soldiers be incredibly fed, and contrary-wise marvelous displeased with the haughty looks of proud disdain."[20] It is unlikely that Garrard's exotic title for these men ever caught on in Elizabethan times, since only the terms "corporals of the field" and "corporals of the camp" appear in any army lists that I have seen. As Digges sums up the office of the colonel in *Stratioticos,* "above all things he ought to carry such a love to his soldiers and regard of his honor, that he should rather choose to die with them in fight, than shamefully to abandon them in the day of battle, or by horse to save himself while they are cut in pieces." [21]

While the rank of lieutenant colonel was granted in Elizabethan times, it was not always used to distinguish an officer second in command to the colonel of a regiment, quite possibly because military authors do not so designate him. Neither Digges as early as 1579 nor Styward in 1581 nor Garrard in 1591 nor Barret as late as 1598 discusses this rank. It is therefore not surprising to find it employed for the second in command to the colonel general only, the position which Sir Roger Williams held in the fall of 1585 under Colonel General John Norris. By the end of the century—probably because of the need to replace fallen regimental commanders—lieutenant colonels of regiments were appointed from among available senior captains, but on a temporary basis. Thus, at the battle of Armagh in Ireland, August 1598, Captains Willis and Parker were both lieutenant colonels and second in command of regiments. [22]

In a way, the captain of an infantry company (or band, as it was frequently termed) was the most important officer in Elizabeth's army because he was—or at least was supposed to be—the officer closest to the men. As Digges puts it, "A captain ought to consider that he has charge of the lives of men committed to his hands, and that if any quail under his conduct, either by rashness or want of knowledge, he is to render account thereof before the great Judge." [23] Like his colonel, the captain was to appoint the officers and noncommissioned officers under him.[24] These appointments were subject to the review of the colonel [25] and were to include, besides his lieutenant, two or three lieutenants extraordinary.[26] It was the captain's duty to train his men by "making them sometime shoot for wagers with harquebuse, sometime to wrestle, to run and to leap in their armor, to march in array, to cast themselves in a ring, to retire in order, and marching suddenly to stand, and such like." [27] Every night that the guard was posted, he was to send his sergeant to the sergeant major general to obtain the watchword ("the same to keep very secretly and use it warily"); and he himself was to walk the rounds to see to it that all inferior officers were tending to their duties.[28] He had the further (and probably onerous) task of inspecting the baggage of his soldiers "to see that they have as little superfluity as may be possible." [29] Although he was not expected to know tactics—the sergeant majors took care of operations—he was to have some knowledge concerning the making of trenches and ramparts and, of course, he led his men (or a portion of them, since an infantry band seldom fought as a unit) in battle. Finally, as we know, it was he who paid the men [30] (until misuse of funds led Elizabeth to put this job into the hands of muster-masters).

The lieutenant of a company was second in command of that company, but his major tasks were to keep peace among the men, see that the noncommissioned officers performed their duties, post the guard, and, like the captain, make the rounds of the sentinels.[31] The ensign had no command or administrative function. His job was simply to carry the colors (in the middle of his band in a set battle, at the head of his band during a charge or assault) and to conduct himself in such a way as to bring honor to his person. He was supposed to have two or three assistants, a drum or two, and a guard.[32]

Except when the captain was absent, the sergeant of a company had more things to do and keep track of than did the lieutenant, being in charge of personnel, training, and supply,[33] but his main concern was to accompany the guard to their posts and keep discipline among the men.[34] Finally, the corporal, who was in charge of a squad of twenty to twenty-five men, helped the sergeant keep discipline, stayed on guard with the sentinels, trained them in skirmishing and marksmanship, and appointed the scouts.[35]

The unit to which these officers and noncommissioned officers were assigned was a regiment divided, as has already been suggested, into companies of various strengths—usually 150 or 200 men—each of which was composed of shot (musketeers, calivers, harquebusiers, and in early Elizabethan days, bowmen) and pikemen, with varying numbers of halberdiers and men carrying bills.[36] A company of 250 men raised in Lancashire in 1584 was to include 120 shot (80 firearms, 40 bows), 40 halberds, and 80 pikes.[37] From the *Calendar of State Papers* it is apparent that, whatever the ideal may have been, bands were armed with whatever weapons were available, so that proportions varied from time to time and from place to place. In any event, after 1588 bows were generally replaced by firearms.[38]

The number of companies in a regiment also varied from time to time. For instance, Sir John Norris had seven companies in his regiment during his attack upon Grave in 1581.[39] The account of Richard Huddleston, treasurer of the army in the Low Countries (August 12, 1585, to May 31, 1586), shows that by the middle of December 1585 the entire contingent of footmen—4,091 strong—was organized into only one regiment of 27 companies. Four of these companies, totaling 600 men, were detached from the field army and sent to Ostend as garrison troops; but later on in the month, when Leicester took command of the troops, the footmen in the field were increased to 30 companies, still under one colonel.[40] These men had not yet been sent into the field to fight, and probably the intention was that once action was imminent, other colonels could be appointed from among available captains, and the captains' bands could be taken over by their lieutenants. An Elizabethan practice which supports this view was that of conferring a company of men upon an officer who had other commands or responsibilities. Thus Sir Roger Williams, lieutenant general under Colonel General Norris in 1585, and John Price, who was sergeant major general, both had foot companies assigned to them (probably for the purpose of increasing their pay); and Norris himself had both a foot company and a horse band under his nominal command.[41] At Tilbury in the summer of 1588 the Earl of Leicester was persuaded to divide the Essex regiment of 4,000 footmen into what Smythe sarcastically and disapprovingly calls "little regiments of one thousand under every colonel." [42] Whatever Smythe's personal opinion may have been, however, it seems to have had little effect on the make-up of Elizabeth's armies. The army under Sir Conyers Clifford, at the Curlews in Ireland almost ten years later, was composed of 1,496 men divided into three regiments, the largest of which had but 571 soldiers (186 armed men, 385 shot).[43]

======

The arms and equipment with which infantry men were supplied varied but little during Elizabeth's long reign. The pike, which was much like the spear used in ancient Greek phalanxes, seems to have been the favorite weapon. It varied in length from twenty feet, the length preferred by Machiavelli and Sutcliffe,[44] to fifteen feet, as Garrard favors.[45] Barwick mentions eighteen feet.[46] Smythe writes that the pike should be seventeen or eighteen feet long, adding that he would like to see "all the pikes throughout England (that are for the field) . . . reduced into one uniformity of length," not only for the sake of looks but for better tactical usage.[47] He states that pikes should be "light, and of very good wood [so] that they should be both portable and manageable, which many of our pikes at this present [*i.e.,* 1588 to 1590] are not."[48]

The method of manipulating the pike was more complicated than might be imagined, although there were only two main positions of handling it in a fight: one for the offense against footmen, one for the defense against horsemen. At the command "Charge your pike" in preparation for shock tactics against opposing footmen, a pikeman would stand sideways, feet planted solidly about two to two and a half feet apart, face held over his left shoulder in the direction of the enemy, pike held shoulder high and parallel to the ground, right arm extended straight back as if about ready to cast a javelin, and left arm bent at the elbow with left hand just under the chin. (See Figure 4.) An eighteen-foot pike would thus extend approximately fifteen feet out from the left side of the pikeman's body. Standing in such a position, a pikeman was ready to advance sidewise to "the push of the pike," jabbing his long weapon in the face of the opposing soldier.[49]

At the command "Charge your pike against the right foot and draw your sword"—which was given when pikemen were assaulted by enemy horse—the pikeman would plant himself as described above, except that his feet might be a little farther apart and his body twisted a bit more to the front, or to the left or right oblique if he were to cross pikes with one or the other of his "shoulder companions." The butt of the pike would be on the ground against the right foot (to give the weapon staying power) and the pikeman, leaning forward and bending his left knee, would grasp the pike with his left hand just at the bend of the knee.[50] Held in this manner, the pike would extend forward toward the enemy horse at about a forty-degree angle. The pikeman would then draw his sword with his right hand and hold it at the ready. Supported by his fellows in back and on the flanks, such a pikeman would be "as hard to be pierced with horsemen as an angry porcupine or hedgehog with the end of a bare finger."[51] (See Figure 5.)

Interestingly enough, Garrard, who was an experienced soldier, believes that "pikes among all other weapons that belong to soldiers, is of greatest honor and credit," a point of view with which Robert Barret and Sir Roger Williams heartily agree,[52] and this in spite of the fact that hand guns were coming more and more into use. Sutcliffe dissents from this praise of the pike, however, except as defense against cavalry, remarking that "execution is seldom done by pikes." He adds, "Sometime I grant pikes do charge other pikes, but it is not the pikeman that makes the slaughter." And then he lists a number of faults generally ignored by those who armed English regiments: Pikemen find their long weapons unwieldy in woods and shrubby ground; they are too heavily armored to pursue others; they cannot guard themselves against shot or targets if they themselves are not backed by shot; once their ranks are broken, they throw down their pikes, and take to their other weapons.[53]

Pikemen, of course, carried either a rapier or sword, depending on what they could get or what they had a predilection for. Sir John Smythe, looking around him between 1588 and 1590, notes scornfully that men of war "do nowadays prefer and allow that . . . pikers should rather wear rapiers of a yard and a quarter long . . . , or more, than strong short arming swords." He himself thinks that swords should be supplied, with blades three-quarters of a yard "or a little more" in length.[54] This point of view was enthusiastically endorsed almost a decade later by George Silver, London fencing-master and author of *Paradoxes of Defence,* who sneeringly refers to long swords and rapiers as "birdspits . . . fit for children not for men, for straggling boys of the camp to murder poultry, not for men of honor to try the battle with their foes." At the same time, he implies that times were looking up, because now "in the wars we use few rapiers or none at all, but short swords," complaining, nevertheless, that "these are insufficient also, for that they have no hilts." [55]

Pikemen also often carried daggers, some of them being, as Smythe describes them, "long heavy daggers . . . , with great brawling alehouse hilts." Smythe dislikes these as much as the rapiers, stating that they "were never used but for private frays and brawls." In their stead he would have pikemen wear "short arming daggers of convenient form and substance without hilts, or with little short crosses of nine or ten inches the blades." [56]

Occasionally they may have carried a small shield or buckler—termed a "target"—but Fourquevaux points out as early as 1548 that "there is but little account made of it, except it be for some assault, neither is there almost any man that will burden himself with it except captains." [57] By Eliz-

abethan times the target had been almost completely discarded, although Sir Roger Williams is able to persuade
himself that among ten thousand armed men, two hundred or
so might be targeteers. At the same time, he admits that
targets "are very cumbersome" and "their weights are such
that few men will endure to carry them . . . one hour."
Were the corselets of "reasonable proof," he continues, "and
the targets light," targeteers would be useful in small numbers "to discover breaches . . . ; to discover trenches or the
enemies' works; and for to cover shot that skirmishes in
straits." [58] Captain Nicholas Dawtrey, writing from Ireland
ten years later, puts this small number at fifteen for a
company of one hundred men.[59]

As for armor, Elizabethan soldiers were apparently not
fond of it. Early in the sixteenth century, pikemen were
covered with a corselet or with a shirt of mail, tasses (steel
skirts) down to the knee, hose of mail, a codpiece of iron,
vambraces (armor for the forearm) and gauntlets, or gloves
of mail, and a headpiece with a sight almost covered.[60] But
Smythe notes in 1590 that pikemen thought themselves well
armed when they wore their burgonets (light open helmets),
their cuirasses (breastplates) and their backs, without either
pouldrons (shoulder pieces), vambraces, gauntlets, or
tasses.[61] Gheyn, picturing the Low Country warrior at the
beginning of the seventeenth century, shows the pikeman
with burgonet or morion, corselet (composed of breastplate,
backpiece, and tasses), and leather gloves—no more; [62] but in
Ireland at the same time, even the breastplates and morions
were discarded, so that they lay "almost buried in the soil of
every quarter." [63] What went for pikemen presumably went
for billmen and halberdmen. Digges, in 1579 and again in
1590, states that the "halberdier may arm either with a sure

brigandine [coat of mail] or corselet." [64] He does not mention billmen, but Sir Roger Williams remarks that both "bills and halberds ought to have corselets . . . of the proof of the caliver discharged 10 or 12 score [200 to 240 yards] off." [65]

Apparently used less and less in the field during the Elizabethan period was the black or brown bill, a long-handled weapon (although a good deal shorter than the pike) with a hooked blade containing one or two spikes. As late as 1584, out of 7,400 infantry mustered on the Scottish border, 2,500 were billmen; [66] but by 1590 Sir George Carew, Master of Ordnance in Ireland, could write plaintively to the Lord Treasurer in London that he wished he had not received a consignment of brown bills. "Here," he says, "they are held in such scorn that unless I should sell them to the farmers of the Pale, . . . I am in despair to utter them." [67] Sir Roger Williams explains why this was so: the "common brown bills" are "lightly for the most part all iron with a little steel or none at all." [68] Such weapons he holds in contempt, but he thinks that if they were "made of good iron and steel, with long strong pikes [*i.e.,* spikes] at the least of 12 inches long, armed with iron to the middle of the staff," they would, like the halberd, be serviceable "to guard ensigns in the field, trenches or towns." But he would have only 200 billmen for every 1,000 pikemen. [69]

The least-used weapon was the halberd, a bill-like instrument approximately two yards and a quarter long, [70] with an ax-head (often ornately devised) affixed just below the point. With such a weapon a soldier could thrust and cut, but in Elizabethan times it was used more to distinguish or identify the sergeants of a band than as an offensive or defensive instrument—although some halberdiers were grouped around the ensign. Once again we can turn to Sir Roger Williams, for an explanation of the unpopularity of the halberds:

Because the Frenchmen make their halberds with long-necked pikes and of naughty stuff like our common brown bills, divers of our nation condemns the halberds. But let the halberds be of good stuff and strongly made, after the Milan fashion, with large heads to cut and broad strong pikes both to cut and to thrust, then without doubt the halberd is nothing behind the bill for all manner of service and arms a soldier fairer than the bill.[71]

Among the firearms supplied infantrymen in the Elizabethan period, the harquebuse was the lightest weapon, the caliver next in weight, and the musket the heaviest. All were matchlocks; that is to say, they fired by mechanically touching a burning match-cord to the flash pan, thus igniting the powder in the pan which, in turn, ignited the powder in the barrel. The method for doing what here has been simply described was very complicated: if done by the numbers, at least seventeen distinct commands were used for the harquebuse and caliver and twenty-eight for the musket; [72] for it must be remembered that besides loading powder and shot in the barrel, ramming these home with a ramrod and priming the flashpan, the match (really a long cord lighted at both ends) had to be affixed anew to the serpentine (the forked holder on the weapon) after each firing. (See the Frontispiece, which shows the caliver after firing, with the match held in the serpentine.) And with the musket, which was so heavy that it could not be aimed without help, the rest had to be set up and taken down.[73]

There was some argument among military men during the period as to which of the firearms were most useful in battle. As a matter of fact, there was, as Smythe points out, a certain amount of confusion over terminology, harquebuses being sometimes called calivers and calivers, harquebuses.[74] In England in the late eighties and early nineties, the harquebuse had a barrel "not above a yard in length"; the calivers were "of a greater length and height of bullet, and more reinforced than harquebuses."[75] According to Smythe, the former weapon, being lighter, was a better one to skirmish with.[76] But others, Smythe knew, thought differently, pointing out that "calivers will carry further point and blank, and also give a greater blow than harquebuses."[77] Smythe's reply enters the realm of tactics: caliver advocates, he states

> do very little consider that neither calivers nor harquebuses (considering their uncertainty) are to be used by any skillful soldiers with any volleys of shot against enemy in the field above three or four scores at the farthest, and that the harquebuses within that distance will wound and kill as well as calivers; besides that, through the lightness and shortness of them, they are so manageable that the harquebusiers may skirmish a great deal longer and with more dexterity and certainty than the caliverers . . . , as also that upon a hasty retreat, they may very well save and keep their pieces being so light, to the intent to make head again, whereas the caliverers in such action, through an over-much heaviness of their pieces, do most commonly cast them away and trust to their heels.[78]

While what Smythe says here about the lightness, short-ness, and usefulness of the harquebuse may have been true enough, his statement about the effective range of both caliver and harquebuse is far short of the mark. Rich, Wil-liams, and Barwick, all of whom are more reliable than Smythe where firearms are concerned, say something very different. As early as 1574, Rich claimed that a caliver could reach between 360 and 400 yards.[79] Barwick, writing twenty years later, asserted that harquebuses fired in volley would be effective 160, 200, even 240 yards from a target.[80] That Williams agreed can be seen from his remarks, quoted above, that bills and halberdiers should be armed with corselets that would withstand the shot of a caliver discharged 10 or 12 score yards away. Furthermore, whereas Smythe in a later passage recommended that harquebusiers, firing individually, should wait for the enemy to come within 8, 10, or 12 paces, Barwick stated that with a harquebuse he, at least, could hit a man standing 120 yards away.[81]

There was also some argument as to how many times a harquebusier might discharge his weapon in an hour. When this question was brought up among a group of Elizabethan captains, according to Barwick, one of them said ten, and "the rest of the captains did not reprove his answer, although that they did know he was far short of the matter." [82] The number, Barwick insists, should have been forty.

The equipment these men should carry into the field is listed in full by Barwick:

> The caliverman or harquebusier should have his mold to cast his bullets, his match well made and dry, his steel and flint to strike fire, his screws and worms to serve all for his scouring stick, and for every ten soldiers to have a casting pan. For flasks, it were better that the use of them were left, and in lieu thereof the Spanish use which is now had with us for our muskets [*i.e.,* the musketeers measured out their powder charges in advance, carrying them in little bottles attached to a bandolier]. This harquebusier must yet have a touch box, a purse for his bullets, . . . a priming iron for the clearing of the touch hole, . . . a good morion, with not too high a crest, a good short sword of a yard in blade, and a dagger of twelve inches in blade, with a good girdle and strong.[83] [See Figure 6.]

The main trouble with these weapons was that they would not always discharge (hence the phrase "flash in the pan");

they would often overheat, thus breaking (bringing "danger to the soldiers that do occupy them") or working "small effect" upon the enemy; [84] or, in the heat of battle, wads of paper or felt would not be employed, so that bullets would fall out, leaving only powder to be discharged.[85] When they broke, there would often be no artificer to repair them. Sir George Carew complained to Lord Burghley from Ireland in 1590 that among the firearms in his possession, "1,000 calivers are unserviceable; only 600 are worth the repairing; . . . timber to stock them, ready seasoned, is not to be had; neither sufficient workmen; for I know not but two in this realm that have knowledge how to stock a piece." [86]

The musket, which was "first devised to encounter heavily armed opponents, and for defense of towns and fortresses," [87] was a weapon liked by some, disliked by others. It weighed a good deal more than the harquebuse or caliver—about 20 pounds, therefore requiring a forked rest for firing—and, according to Smythe in 1590, was considered by many captains "too burdensome and heavy for soldiers to use in battles or great encounters." [88]

Sir Roger Williams, one of the greatest advocates of the use of the musket, does not hold with this opinion. He points out that "armed men [*i.e.,* pikemen, halberdiers, billmen and harquebusiers] are heavier laden than the musketeers," that the weight of cuirass, morion, and weapon was really greater than that of the musket and equipment. Furthermore, he adds, "no great troop marches ten miles without resting," and then "the musketeers are suffered to quit their weight," whereas "the armed men will not be suffered to disarm themselves in their march, let them stand never so often, if they be within five hours march of an enemy." [89]

Nevertheless, there were those who sided with Smythe

against Williams. Sir John Dowdall, a captain of English troops in Ireland in 1600, wrote to Sir Robert Cecil, Secretary of State, complaining that the "soldiers are compelled to carry muskets, which are very heavy . . . besides the charge of powder and lead, the weight of which, together with the musket, does clog and weary the bearer." [90] Whether Cecil discussed the matter with the Lord Deputy in Ireland or whether the Lord Deputy acted on his own initiative after receiving similar complaints from Sir John Dowdall and others, the fact remains that army ordinances published in Ireland in February of 1600 limited the number of muskets in a company to twelve. The reason given was that "the soldier, being weak and ill fed, will not be able to carry them in his long and continued marches." [91]

Humphrey Barwick would have considered this number too few. He recommends thirty muskets for every hundred men; [92] and although Sir Roger Williams does not commit himself, he notes that in the Spanish army under the Duke d'Alva, "25 of every hundred were commanded to be musketeers." [93] Moreover, he states, the Spaniards find "their service and terror such that I persuade myself shortly all or most of their small shot will be musketeers." [94]

Other reasons for preferring the caliver or harquebuse to the musket were that musketeers could not "skirmish so nimbly nor so often" with their weapons; [95] the musket was given to "churlish" or "sore" recoiling; [96] and it could not be fired as rapidly as other weapons. [97] Williams answers the first charge by stating that no one ever engages in light skirmishes with muskets anyhow, "unless it be raw men or lightheaded, that delight to hear the pieces crack." The service of musketeers, he emphasizes, "consists either to defend or assail passages, by water or by straits, or to assail towns, forts, for-

tresses, or whatsoever service you can invent." He adds that
against "great troops, the musketeers are the terriblest shot
and most profitable that ever was devised." [98]

To the second charge, that the musket had a tremendous
kick, both Barwick and Williams have their solutions, which
rest partly upon the manufacture of weapons and partly upon
the method of firing. Barwick would make sure that the
"vice" in the breech is long enough, "for when that is short,
whereby any of the powder does lie behind the touch hole,
then they recoil very much." [99] Williams would have the
muskets "straight stocked after the Spanish manner" rather
than "stocked crooked after the French manner." Furthermore he argues that they should not be fired from the breast
but from the shoulder "with the thumb betwixt the stock and
the face." Then, he insists, "there is neither danger nor hurt, if
the shooter have any discretion; especially not to overload
their pieces, and take heed that the bullets join close to the
powder." [100]

Musketeers needed approximately the same equipment as
the harquebusiers and caliver men, but they wore no breast
plates or other pieces of armor, and they sported broad-
brimmed, rakish hats instead of morions or burgonets. They
carried bandoliers, forked-rests, and swords. (See Figures 7
and 8).

The range and effectiveness of the musket was considerably
more than that of either the harquebuse or the caliver.
According to Williams, "the musket spoils horse or man
thirty score off, if the powder be anything good and the bearer
of any judgment. If armed men give the charge, few or any
carry arms of the proof of the musket, being delivered within
ten or twelve score." [101] And Barwick seconds him by stating
that the musket would "kill the armed of proof at ten score,

the common armors at twenty score, and the unarmed at thirty score, being well used in bullet and tried powder." [102] As for the fact that the caliver or the harquebuse would discharge two shots for every one of the musket, Williams points out that "one musket shot does more hurt than two calivers shot, far or near and better cheap." [103]

During this time there was as much argument about infantry tactics as there was about weapons. As we have seen in Chapters I and II, Elizabethan military tactics were based essentially upon classical tactics—especially Roman—modified by what could be learned from contemporary foreign theorists and first-hand experience in the field.

Roman military science, of course, varied from time to time and from general to general; but as understood in Elizabethan England, it was based on the Roman legion, a unit composed primarily of infantrymen armed with lances, swords, bows, and slings, but supported by certain elements of artillery (or, more correctly, engines of war) and cavalry. An arm of close combat, this legion had as its primary mission in the attack to close with the enemy and destroy or break him, and in order to succeed in its mission, it combined fire power, movement, and shock action. From the nature of its weapons, the legion was most successful when it came to grips with the enemy and assaulted him with swords, although the shot (*i.e.,* the bowmen and slingers), the artillery, and the cavalry could be effectively used to harass the enemy and prepare him for the shock action of the swordsmen.

The Roman army, which generally consisted of no more than two legions totaling approximately fourteen thousand men, fought on a narrow front with its elements disposed in depth to provide security and continuity of attack. The lightly armed men went before the formation to engage the enemy with bows and slings in an effort either to overwhelm and pursue him, or, if that were not possible, to provoke him to move to the attack and encounter the legion proper. The heavily armed men of the main body would then deliver the decisive blow, first hurling lances at the enemy and finally engaging him with swords.

The frontal assault was the operation most often used by the Romans in actual combat (although some generals were acquainted with the turning movement and the double envelopment, tactics which Vegetius describes in his *De re militari*), but such a relatively simple maneuver was arrived at only by a complicated recipe. The parts played by terrain, weather, and conditions of morale necessitated a commander of experience and ability; the shock of a frontal assault with its brutal, wearying sword play called for men of great stamina; and the method of renewing broken lines with elements of the reserves required the most careful training and drill.[104] So Roman military science was built upon cautious selection of officers and men, intense training and practice, and severe discipline.

In the main, except for a change in weapons and a refinement of maneuvering by the shot, Elizabethan infantry performed in the same manner. Generally speaking, when a regiment was involved and battle was imminent, the sergeant major had several different methods of placing his troops. He could establish "one common brute main battle" (which was sometimes used by the English but which Garrard and Digges describe as "barbarous"),[105] or form three battles in one front (equally "barbarous"),[106] or place his squadrons or battles in depth, with a forward, a main battle, and a rearward.[107] In each instance, the core of these squadrons would normally be made up of pikemen, billmen, and halberdiers, and the flanks of the shot. In other words, companies were divided up and reassembled according to the weapons they carried, pikemen being ranged with pikemen, harquebusiers with harquebusiers, and so on, so that during combat no captain had charge of all of his own men. (See Figure 9.)

Garrard is of the opinion that there was need of no "curious order . . . in placing the shot in any form of battle" except that these flanking shot should be divided into "sundry petty troops, of 25, 50, or 100 men apiece," each with a leader,[108] while Robert Barret states they should be composed of from 20 to 50 men.[109] In front of these battles skirmished the "forlorn hope," harquebusiers and calivermen who issued out of the flanks to take up positions much as the Roman lightly armed men had done, and for the same purpose: to overwhelm and pursue the enemy or provoke him to move to the assault.

There were many different tactics for the forlorn hope to use. On a narrow front, accompanied by "certain sleeves of pike" (as guards against charging horsemen) and backed by short weapons, such as swordsmen with targets or halberdiers (in case "they should come to the sword, or join pell mell with the enemy"),[110] successive troops of the forlorn hope could advance toward the enemy, fire, retire, reload, and advance again. Thus, according to Garrard, there would be a continuous "order of supply, succoring, seconding, shadowing and increasing the skirmish."[111]

On a broad front, the shot in the forlorn hope could unite (as German troops were wont to do) and, forming a ring, march round and round, firing when they faced the enemy, reloading as they turned away. Using such tactics, Garrard avows, the head of the forlorn hope "shall be sure always to have charged before the tail have discharged: and thus in a circular march the skirmish all day shall continue." [112]

On either a broad or a narrow front, these same shot could on occasion fight without keeping any order; that is, being lightly armed, they could engage the enemy by "running and traversing here and there, whether they pursue the enemies or be followed of them." In such instances, the accompanying pikemen would "do good service in backing and sustaining the harquebusiers, and may be able to make front to these that charge upon them, . . . and to make entrance and to thrust in among the enemies when they begin to stagger or sway." [113] Musketeers, being too weighed down with their weapons to skirmish nimbly, fought from stationary broad squares, [114] sometimes with the first rank kneeling and the second rank standing to fire by volley over their heads; [115] or they arranged themselves in semicircles or half-moons, providing cross-fire, or they fired from flanks, front, or rear of a squadron under the protection of couched pikes. [116] But such an account does not begin to describe the wild disorder that might occur were the shot to be overrun by horsemen, to find themselves holding over-heated weapons, or to run out of powder. Old soldier Bernardino de Mendoza, however, does mention the problem of powderless harquebusiers being forced during the heat of battle either "to beg more [ammunition from their companions] with great gabbling" or to retire to the rear to divide it out of the barrels. In the latter case, because of the haste the men were in, the casks could be set on fire, "and so the soldiers left clean without powder." He adds that, from his own experience in battle, the enemy hearing "the fire and the crack" of the barrels is quick to perceive the dire straits of the shot and "is the more animated to the close." [117] In August of 1598, the next year after Mendoza's work, translated into English as *Theorique and Practise of Warre,* was published in England, a graphic illustration of his comments was afforded by the actions of English and Irish soldiers pitted against one another at Armagh. During the engagement, two barrels of powder in one English regiment and two more in another were set afire, disranking and routing the men and "animating" the enemy, "as appeared by their cry." [118]

Eventually, the forlorn hope would cause the enemy to break and run—a situation which could occur only if the enemy were exceptionally weak—or, itself being broken, would be forced to retire to its own lines, leaving the way free for the opponents to join battle. Upon reaching its own lines, the shot could go to the rear, where the baggage was kept and where barrels of powder and shot could be tapped, or, if hotly pursued, could enter within the ranks of a squadron of pike for protection, issuing forth again when the pressure was off. This latter maneuver was so complicated—requiring, as it did, the pikemen to open and close lanes during the heat and confusion of battle—that in Garrard's view it could not be accomplished "without long abode in wars and 7 years service at the least of an army in sundry hazards of fights and battles." [119]

Just before the joining was to occur, Garrard recommends that the soldiers "flourish often their naked swords and halberds against the sun, for that the glistening of the weapons, and their shining points, through the brightness now of the one and now of the other against the resplendent beams of the sun, does show a certain horrible terror of war, the which will strike a dread and fear into the minds of the enemies." [120] Another psychological tactic was to advance "with rumors and shoutings, sometimes running with violence," all the while blowing trumpets, beating drums, and firing cannons, the noise of which "wonderfully troubles and fears the hearts of the adversaries." [121] But Garrard warns that as soon as contact between adversaries is made, "solemn silence" should ensue so that the men "may the better understand what commandments and directions proceed from their chieftain." [122]

Once opposing pikemen came clashing together, assault tactics necessarily varied with the particular training in hand-to-hand combat the men had had. According to Sir John Smythe, certain "principal" English military men believed that only the first rank of a squadron of pikemen should fight with their adversaries, the remaining ranks waiting until the first had "fought their bellies full, or until they can fight no longer." [123] When any man in the front ranks fell slain or wounded, the man next behind him, as Garrard remarks, was to "enter and step into his room and fill up the void place." [124] But this method of fighting, according to Smythe, could not be carried on in close formation, for it required that ranks and files be far enough apart so that "thrusts and foins" could be made, a method that he calls "a very scorn and mockery," since he felt it weakened a squadron. [125]

Instead of such tactics, Smythe would have the first four ranks, after closing up, "couch" their pikes, so that the men in the rear would present their weapons over the shoulders of the men in front, all pushing as a unit. The fifth and following ranks, the points of whose pikes would not reach far enough ahead to be of service, would hold their pikes upright, yet be "ready in an instant to let fall the points . . . and to succor the rank before them." [126] Following such a procedure, "all those four ranks marching or moving forward together pace with pace and step with step, carrying their pikes firmly with . . . points full in their enemies' faces," would "altogether give a puissant thrust . . ." [127] In a close formation, as Garrard describes it, it was possible for soldiers in the rear ranks to keep hard-pressed soldiers in the front rank from falling to the ground, these being held "straight up upon their feet" by the breasts of the men behind them.[128] Were the enemy pikemen fighting in more open formation, the kind of formation which Smythe scorned, they would not have "any leisure, any ways to pull back and recover the use of their pikes . . . , nor yet to close their ranks enlarged, . . ." They would, he remarks in colorful language, be overthrown, disordered, and broken "with as great a facility, as if they were but a flock of geese." [129] An attacking squadron such as Smythe envisioned would not be able to thrust and foin; that is, the foremost ranks of such a squadron, having with the points of the pikes "lighted upon the bare faces" of their opponents, would not be able to pull back their pikes to give a new thrust. They would therefore either drop their pikes or throw them as far as possible into the enemy ranks and then draw their swords and daggers for closer fighting. Since the rear ranks of pikemen would thus be rendered ineffective by the front ranks, Smythe advises that rear elements be armed, not with pikes, but with halberds which, "in the hands of lusty and well-armed [*i.e.,* armored] soldiers . . . work wonderful effects, and do carry all to the ground." [130] While other Elizabethan military authors may agree that the halberd had certain tactical uses, they generally feel that it should not be employed as Smythe suggests. Williams, as we have seen, would use it "to guard ensigns, . . . trenches or towns." [131] And Barret, exclaiming that he knows it "necessary for many pieces of service," limits those pieces to the execution of a broken or flying enemy, the backing of shot, the securing of convoys, the guarding of artillery, and the creeping along trenches and into mines.[132] No one but Smythe believes that halberdiers, however employed, should be mustered in large numbers. Barwick suggests that fifteen would be sufficient for a company of 100 men, while Barret is satisfied with but seven or eight.[133] Whether or not halberds were used in the rear ranks of a stand of pikes, Smythe argues that it must be apparent "to all such as are not obstinately ignorant, that battles and squadrons of pikemen in the field when they do encounter and charge one another, are not by any reason or experience military to stand all day thrusting, pushing, and foining one at another, as some do most vainly imagine, but ought according to all experience with one puissant charge and thrust to enter and disorder, wound, open, and break the one the other . . . ."[134] If this statement indicates that he is one of those who believe that "a battle is won or lost in the twinkling of an eye at the first joining,"[135] he is in total disagreement with Digges, who urges fighting in depth so that reserves may be committed to action when the vanguard or main battle cannot overcome the enemy.[136]

Smythe also envisions employment of a flanking attack in which several ranks of pikemen would be drawn from the rear of a squadron and used to assault the enemy's right or left flank, or both, while the main body engaged its front.[137] Mendoza would make these flankers number a fifth part of the squadron, although he adds that he has not known this maneuver "used in the fight of the infantry."[138] Smythe likewise describes the simple maneuver of making a flank a front and a front a flank,[139] a useful movement to change direction for an attack or to receive enemy troops who have themselves executed a flanking movement.

In defense against a charge by horsemen, the first four ranks of pikemen would kneel as described earlier in this chapter, unless it was deemed desirable to employ harquebusiers or musketeers in the formation. In the latter instance, according to Smythe, the pikemen would couch their weapons as if to engage another infantry squadron, and the shot would kneel beneath the pikes, loading their weapons with hailshot (if muskets) or full bullets (if harquebuses) and firing when the horse approached within 50 to 75 feet.[140] According to some others, the shot should commence firing when the horse were from 170 to 300 yards away, distances which would permit reloading and refiring but which, if one is to believe Smythe, would not be as effective as when the horse were closer.[141] Smythe quotes La Noue as saying that the shot could fight from within a squadron, firing over the heads of the pikemen; but again Smythe contends that this method is not only less effective than the one he proposes but also more dangerous.[142]

What one learns from all these theories concerning the arming and the tactical use of infantrymen, from all the agreements as well as disagreements, from all the bickering, outright quarrels, petulant statements, and dogmatic assertions, is that change and experimentation were in the air. The longbow, which had served its purpose nobly at Crécy and Poitiers and was a deeply respected weapon well into the reign of Henry VIII, was being replaced by caliver, harquebuse, and musket. Bills and halberds were giving way to the pike. If some weapons were becoming heavier, armor was becoming lighter—often because certain pieces were simply discarded by soldiers as being more cumbersome than protective. The one unchanging fact during the sixteenth century was that infantry, composed in large part of pikemen, dominated the battlefield. Fighting its enemy from positions formed in depth, infantry was the flower of Elizabeth's forces, usurping the place held so long in feudal times by heavily armored cavalry.

V

Cavalry

Cavalry had been the core of all medieval armies, but sometime in the fifteenth century the English army ceased to employ it to any great extent. In the sixteenth century, its importance continued to decrease and neither Henry VIII nor Elizabeth mustered large numbers of horses for their wars.[1] This neglect of cavalry was not due to a lack of faith in horsemen as military weapons, nor to a dearth of officers willing to muster and lead cavalrymen in battle. Sir Philip Sidney, Sir William Pelham, and the Earl of Essex are only three of a large number of high-ranking Englishmen to whom the command of horse companies seemed only right and proper. Furthermore, the authors of military texts, although they emphasized other matters, recognized the various uses to which cavalry could be put. There were two factors chiefly responsible for the decline of the cavalry: changing tactics and the high cost of breeding horses.

108

Bernardino de Mendoza stresses the shift from the medieval reliance on cavalry to the sixteenth century's dependence on infantry. In former days, he reminds his readers, "cavalry was of more estimation for their fury and readiness than the infantry." Now, "experience comes to discover the contrary, and to put the ground of a war in the squadrons of infantry, which serve with pikes, to which the first place is to be yielded in arms." [2] Matthew Sutcliffe elaborates upon the other reason that the army was not more liberally provided with cavalry. Disappointed at the lack of what he considered an essential arm of field forces, Sutcliffe complained in 1593 that "albeit we have hitherto had great want of horsemen in our expeditions in France, Flanders, and Portugal, yet there is no reason that this land should want hereafter, having such means. There only wants liberal minds and good order that some part of that is now spent in surfeit, silks, golden laces, and other vanities, may be employed in keeping horses for service." [3] Be that as it may, this particular arm of the service was certainly neglected during Elizabeth's reign. English forces in the Low Countries as early as 1585 and in Ireland as late as 1598 were especially weak in cavalry units. [4] The secondary role the cavalry had come to play on the battlefield is reflected in the military treatises, which, although they seldom fail to discuss cavalry, devote far less space to it than to infantry.

Most Elizabethan military writers felt that the English army should contain three types of horse units with varying degrees of mobility: men-at-arms, lancers, and shot-on-horseback. The missions of these units were manifold, for they included offensive action, exploitation and pursuit, seizing and holding terrain until the arrival of the main forces, reconnaissance, security for the front, flanks, and rear of other forces on the march, at the halt, and in battle, security for foragers, harassing action, and surprise action.[5]

The command of these units was vested in an officer who at various times was known by various titles. Barret, basing his description of sixteenth-century troops essentially on his knowledge of Spanish organization, calls him the captain general of the horse; [6] and it is this title which Lord Grey held for a time (along with that of high marshal) under Leicester in the Low Countries.[7] Official lists of lances and light horse under Leicester about the same time indicate that the Earl of Essex was in command of the cavalry and was known as the general of the horse.[8] Digges and Garrard prefer the title of lieutenant general of the horse, which they sometimes shorten to mere lieutenant.[9] It would seem, however, that the rank most frequently assigned the officer in command of the cavalry was general or lieutenant general of the horse.[10] According to Barret, whatever this officer might be called, he was commonly appointed by the prince—a practice that was certainly followed during Elizabeth's reign—and was supposed to be a titled person or some "very honorable gentleman" who had had considerable experience in war.[11]

Below him probably came the great variety of officers and noncommissioned officers found in the infantry, but except for the captains and color-bearers, none of the contemporary treatises on Elizabethan warfare mentions them.[12] By consulting John Cruso's *Militarie Instructions for the Cavallerie* (1632) and Robert Ward's *Anima'dversions of Warre* (1639), both of which were based on a knowledge of the organization of regiments in the Low Country as well as on a familiarity with foreign military texts, one discovers that by the time of the reign of Charles I, and probably during the reigns of Elizabeth and James as well, cavalry officers did not differ greatly in name or in duties from infantry officers—except that a quartermaster was added to the cavalry roster, the sergeant was omitted (his duties being taken over by the corporals and the color-bearer), and the ensign was given the title of cornet.[13]

The general or lieutenant general of the horse was, according to Digges and Garrard, comparable to the sergeant major general of the army because he, like the sergeant major, received his directions from the general or high marshal, and instructed his troops accordingly.[14] Later Garrard seems partly to contradict himself by stating that the lieutenant general of the horse was coadjutor to the lord marshal and sergeant major general.[15] Some explanation for this contradiction is given by Cruso, who points out that the general of the horse

was wont to supply the place of lieutenant general of the army, and in the lord general's absence to command the whole army. True it is that the lord marshal, forasmuch as he gives the orders, used to have some superiority of command, . . . whence it comes that the lord general, absenting himself from the army, used to take along with him either the general of the horse or the lord marshal to avoid the occasions of competition.[16]

In any event, the duties of this officer were to see that his captains had been suitably chosen and, if they had not, to advise the general of the army about it so that he could remove inexpert captains and replace them with experienced ones. He was also to keep a book and roll of all the bands of horse, check to see that they were kept at full strength, inspect the "furniture," reporting to the general or high marshal anything that was lacking, supervise their training, and assign them to their various missions.[17]

The captains ranking below the general of the horse were, according to military theorists, supposed to be of two sorts: the captain of the men-at-arms, who, according to Digges and Garrard, could be compared with a colonel of footmen, and the captains of the light horsemen and the shot-on-horseback, who were equal with captains of foot.[18] (There is some confusion of terms at this time because the arming of horsemen was undergoing a change. Both lancers and shot-on-horseback were often called "light horsemen," depending upon the armor worn by the men.) But since men-at-arms were never put into the field during Elizabeth's reign—at least by the English—the distinction between the two types of captains is meaningless. These captains of horse were ideally to be "vigilant, sober, continent, modest in apparel, curious to have good horses and arms, thereby to give example to soldiers, and to see them punctual in their service, and exactly observant of discipline."[19] They were also to see that their men were not "disfurnished of their horse and armor" and that they were properly trained.[20] In other words, they were to emulate their general.

The training of horsemen was of paramount interest to some military authors and, it may be presumed, to commanding officers of Elizabeth's troops in garrison and field, but the profusion of detail which is characteristic of discussions about training infantrymen is glaringly absent in accounts of the cavalry. Digges and Styward say nothing about training. Garrard states that cavalrymen should not be those individuals who know merely of "clean and gallant riding, or to run comely order with a lance upon the even gravel and sand," feats, he implies, that any man who knew but the rudiments of horsemanship could accomplish.[21] Barret wisely writes that cavalrymen ought to have some skill in recognizing diseases

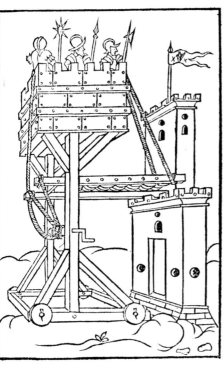

Figures 1 and 2. Engines of war. From J. Sadler's translation of Vegetius' *The Foure Bookes of Martiall Policye.* Reproduced by permission of The Huntington Library, San Marino, California.

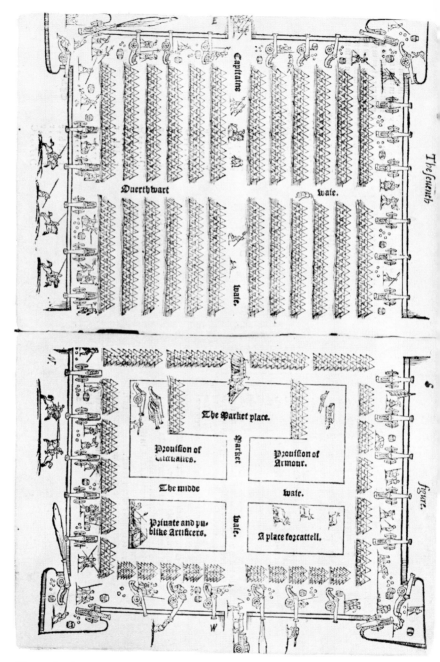

Figure 3. An encamped army. From Peter Whitehorne's translation of Machiavelli's *The Arte of Warre*. Reproduced by permission of The Huntington Library, San Marino, California.

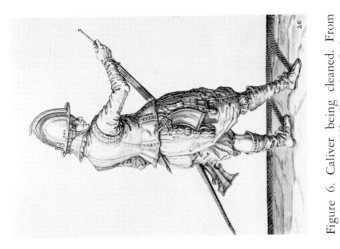

Figure 4. Pikeman at the push of pike. From Jacob de Gheyn's *The Exercise of Armes*. Reproduced by permission of The Huntington Library, San Marino, California.

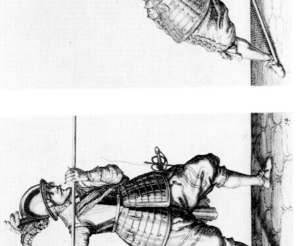

Figure 5. Pikeman ready to receive charge of horse. From Jacob de Gheyn's *The Exercise of Armes*. Reproduced by permission of The Huntington Library, San Marino, California.

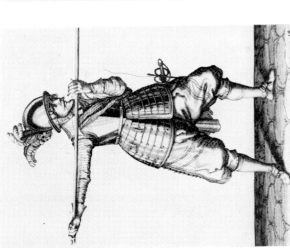

Figure 6. Caliver being cleaned. From Jacob de Gheyn's *The Exercise of Armes*. Reproduced by permission of The Huntington Library, San Marino, California.

Figure 7. Musketeer. From Jacob de Gheyn's *The Exercise of Armes*. Reproduced by permission of The Huntington Library, San Marino, California.

Figure 8. Musketeer firing from forked rest. From Jacob de Gheyn's *The Exercise of Armes*. Reproduced by permission of The Huntington Library, San Marino, California.

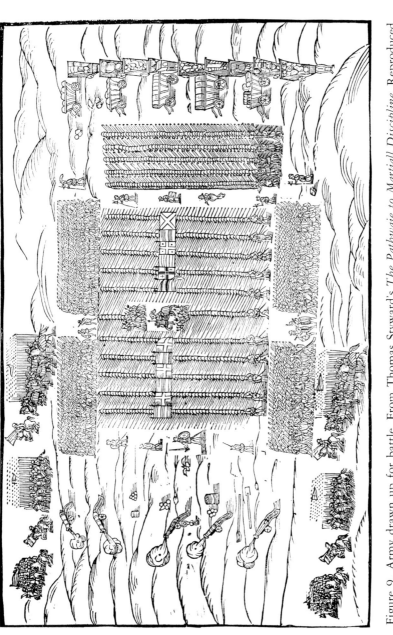

The Battell in Figure, shewing howv euerie Weapon should be placed to fight.

Figure 9. Army drawn up for battle. From Thomas Styward's *The Pathwaie to Martiall Discipline.* Reproduced by permission of The Huntington Library, San Marino, California.

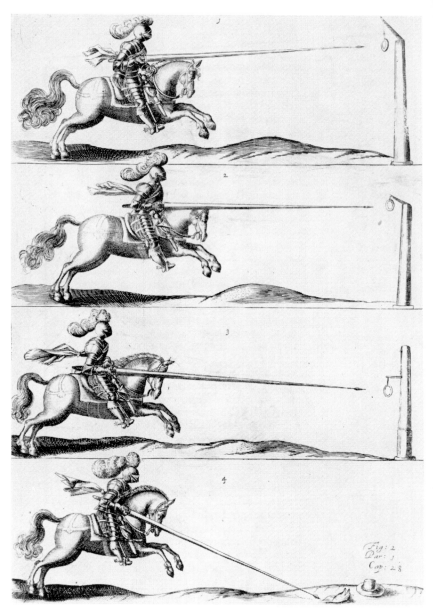

Figure 10. Lancers couching their weapons. From John Cruso's *Militarie Instructions for the Cavallerie*. Reproduced by permission of The Huntington Library, San Marino, California.

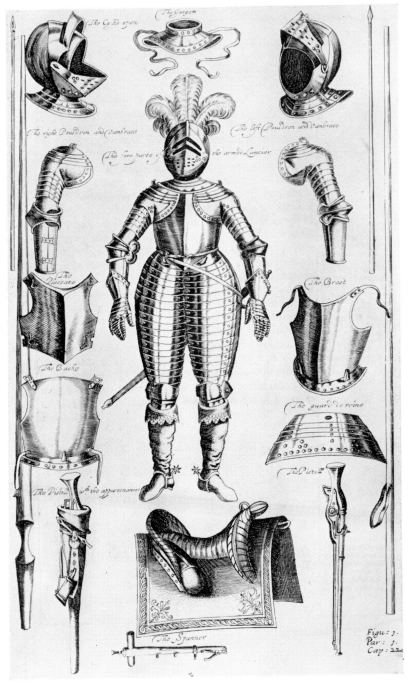

Figure 11. Armor for the lancer. The closed casque shown here was going out of favor. From John Cruso's *Militarie Instructions for the Cavallerie*. Reproduced by permission of The Huntington Library, San Marino, California.

Figure 12. Pistoleers charging in squadron formation. From John Cruso's *Militarie Instructions for the Cavallerie*. Reproduced by permission of The Huntington Library, San Marino, California.

Figure 13. Pistoleers forming a caracole. From John Cruso's *Militarie Instructions for the Cavallerie*. Reproduced by permission of The Huntington Library, San Marino, California.

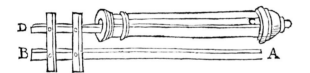

Figure 14 (*above*). Instrument to determine whether or not a cannon barrel was truly bored. From Cyprian Lucar's translation of Niccolò Tartaglia's *Three Bookes of Colloquies Concerning the Arte of Shooting*. Reproduced by permission of The Folger Shakespeare Library.

Figure 15 (*below*). Method of using the gunner's quadrant. From Cyprian Lucar's translation of Niccolò Tartaglia's *Three Bookes of Colloquies*. Reproduced by permission of The Folger Shakespeare Library.

Figure 16 (*at right*). Rear sight with sliding eye-piece and quadrant. From Cyprian Lucar's translation of Niccolò Tartaglia's *Three Bookes of Colloquies* (in the appendix by Lucar). Reproduced by permission of The Folger Shakespeare Library.

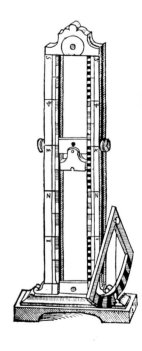

A peece mounted at 6. points or 72. minutes.

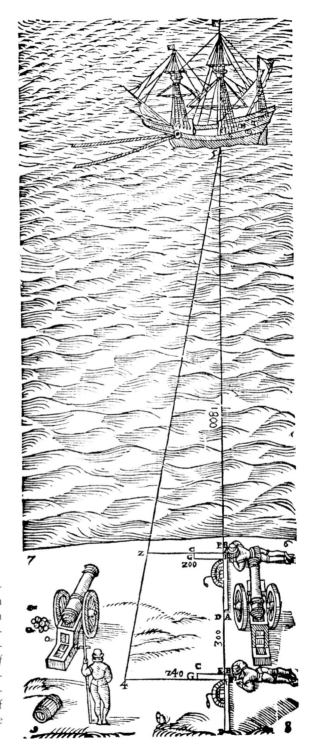

Figure 17. Method of determining range from cannon to target. From Cyprian Lucar's translation of Niccolò Tartaglia's *Three Bookes of Colloquies* (in the appendix by Lucar). Reproduced by permission of The Folger Shakespeare Library.

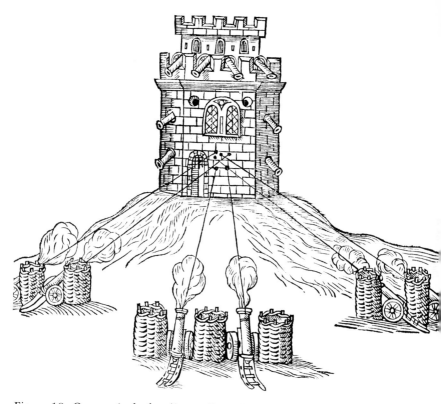

Figure 18. One method of wall-pounding. Illustrated in Thomas Smith's *The Arte of Gunnerie*. Reproduced by permission of The Huntington Library, San Marino, California.

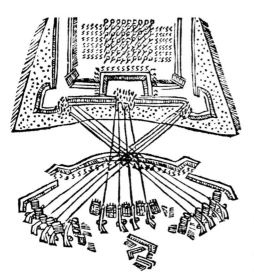

Figure 19. Batteries of cannon employing cross-fire to open several breaches in a fortification. From William Garrard's *The Arte of Warre*. Reproduced by permission of The Huntington Library, San Marino, California.

The type of a long Stater.

Figure 20. A "stater" used to weigh cannon in order to determine the amount of powder to use. From Cyprian Lucar's translation of Niccolò Taraglia's *Three Bookes of Colloquies* (in the appendix by Lucar). Reproduced by permission of The Folger Shakespeare Library.

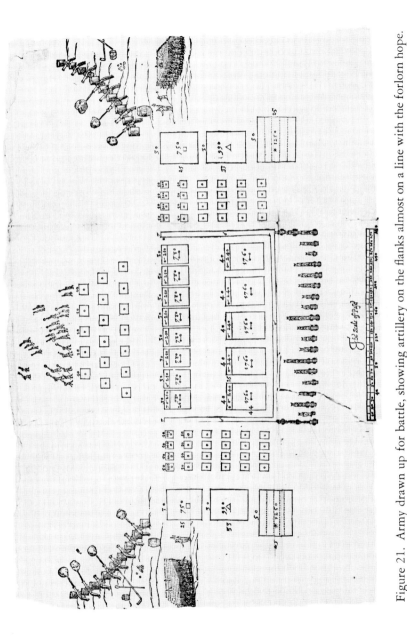

Figure 21. Army drawn up for battle, showing artillery on the flanks almost on a line with the forlorn hope. From Thomas Digges' *An Arithmeticall Militare Treatise, Named Stratioticos*. Reproduced by permission of The Huntington Library, San Marino, California.

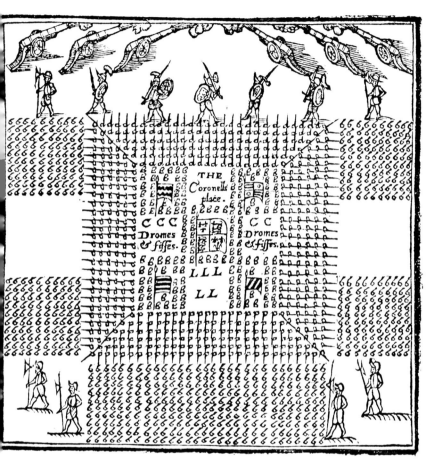

Figure 22. Army drawn up for battle, showing artillery on the front. From Thomas Styward's *The Pathwaie to Martiall Discipline*. Reproduced by permission of The Huntington Library, San Marino, California.

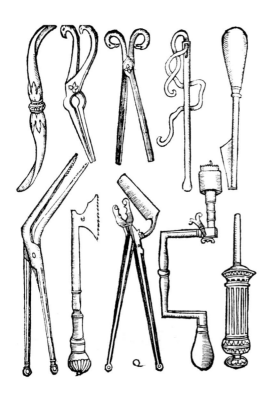

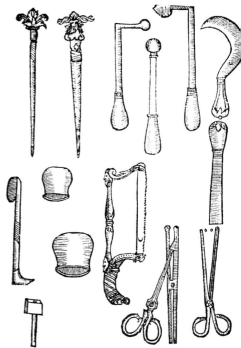

Figures 23 and 24. Surgical instruments. From William Clowes' *A Prooved Practise for All Young Chirurgians*. Reproduced by permission of The Huntington Library, San Marino, California.

of horses and knowing how to cure them, and should also be able, if necessary, to shoe a horse.[22] And Barwick points out that, although there might be many men who could ride and manage a horse well and many others who could shoot a pistol, there were few who could "rightly use both together," adding, "he that will be a pistoleer, must use [*i.e.,* accustom] his horse to know it, whereby he do not fear neither the crack nor the fire; and that done, he must learn to occupy his bridle hand, his pistol, and his spurs in due time and form, all at one instance." [23]

John Cruso, however, noting how little printer's ink had been expended on cavalry matters, devotes seven chapters to the exercising of cavalry "in general and particular," explaining that earlier works, although affording good directions, seem to have been written "as if none should read them but such as were already skillful in the art military." [24] Proper training involved teaching the horse at command by voice, leg, and hand to "pace, trot, gallop, or run in full career; also to advance, stop, retire, and turn readily to either hand, and all with alacrity and obedience." Especially the horse had to be taught to be unafraid of "the smell of gunpowder, the sight of fire and armor, and the hearing of shot, drums and trumpets." Cruso adds that this training should move slowly, "by degrees and with discretion." The soldier himself, of course, had to be trained to use his weapon—whether lance, pistol, or harquebuse—while charging the enemy.[25]

The unit to which the officers and noncommissioned officers were assigned might properly be termed a regiment, although much smaller than a regiment of foot, divided into companies (often called cornets) of various strengths—usually from 50 to 200 men. Each company employed one kind of weapon—lance, pistol, or harquebuse. In the Low

Countries in 1586, Leicester had two companies of lances, one of 200 and one of 150 men; the Earl of Essex, Sir John Norris, Sir Philip Sidney, Sir Robert Sidney, Sir Thomas Cecil, and Sir William Russell had 100 lances each; Sir Roger Williams (who at that time was lieutenant general of the whole force) had 50 lances, as did six other, lesser-known captains.[26] Shot-on-horseback are not indicated in this breakdown, but they soon appeared in the Netherlands and in Ireland in contingents of approximately the same size as the lancers. For instance, as early as September 1585, the musters of Elizabeth's forces in the Low Countries show an entry for Captain Peter Crispe, marshal of the army, of "30 footmen, to be changed next muster into hargeletiers on horseback." [27] Sir John Fortescue states that these shot—he calls them carbineers but Elizabethans called them also by such terms as petranells, hargulutiers, arquebusiers, harquebusiers, and pistoleers—replaced lancers in 1599.[28] But the "Ordinances to be Observed during the Wars in Ireland" (1600) indicate that, whatever may have been the situation in the Low Countries, only a third of the horse in Ireland were to be shot-on-horseback.[29] The probability is that in Ireland also the lancers were soon replaced by pistoleers or harquebusiers, for as Cruso explains, "lancers proved hard to be gotten." Their horses had to "be very good, and exceeding well exercised" and there was a "scarcity of such as were practiced and exercised to the use of the lance, it being a thing of much labor and industry to learn." [30]

The arms and equipment of Elizabethan cavalrymen depended upon whether they were lancers or shot-on-horseback, and, as in the case of infantrymen, on just what was available. The lancer carried a spear-like weapon made of ash, approximately 12 to 18 feet long. Thicker at the butt-end than the pike, the lance had a head similar to a pike head. Two feet from the butt-end it was bored through to take a thong of strong leather by which it could be fastened to the right arm.[31] Barwick states that some military men felt that the lancer should also carry a pistol "of a mean length," arguing that when the lance was broken the lancer could "yet therewith give a deadly blow."[32] Barret agrees with Barwick, adding that the lancer should carry his pistol at a saddle bow in a case of leather and should also be armed with a good curtilace (cutlass).[33]

Military books during Elizabethan days are unanimously silent as to the handling of the lance. Viscount Dillon refers to John Derricke's *Image of Ireland* (1581) for the information that English horsemen used the lance underhand, in contrast to the Irish, who used it overhand. This very slender fact is all we have, from the Elizabethan period, on the use of the lance.[34] However, Cruso's *Militarie Instructions for the Cavallerie,* which belongs to a somewhat later day, not only describes how the lance was handled but accompanies the description with some excellent pictures of lancers in action; and it is unlikely that the use of the lance had changed radically during the years between Elizabeth's death and 1632, when the book was published.

The lance was carried either "advanced" (that is, straight up in the air like a guidon with the butt-end in a socket affixed to the right stirrup) or couched. When couched, as Figure 10 illustrates, it could be held in three different positions, depending upon what the lancer wanted to hit: sloping upwards, for a blow to an enemy horseman's face; parallel to the ground, for a strike in his midriff to unhorse him; and sloping downward, for a blow to the horse's chest or to the chest and face of an infantryman. Occasionally a fourth position could be used: the lance might be borne across the neck of the horse so that it lay by his left ear.[35] Bernardino de Mendoza also gives us some notion of how the lancers sometimes employed the lance after it had been shivered. In his *Theorique and Practise of Warre* (1597), he states that even though the lance might be broken in the first encounter, "the great end of the staff" yet remaining could unhorse an opponent.[36]

Since it was well-nigh impossible to manipulate a lance and a burning match while engaging in a charge or melee, the pistol which the lancer carried was either a flintlock (*i.e.,* snaphance) or a wheel lock with the barrel 18 inches long and the bore of 20 bullets to the pound.[37] It was used only in emergencies, that is, when the lance was completely broken and utterly useless, or when it was dropped, or when the horsemen were too mixed up with the enemy to make their primary weapon serviceable. The sword was likewise considered a secondary weapon, to be employed after a charge when the lance was useless and the enemy thick about.

Ideally the lancer was to wear armor, of a sort, as Barret remarks, "as light as may be." [38] It consisted of a helmet with an open visor, a pair of cuirasses, "the fore part of pistol proof," pauldrons, vambraces, gauntlets, tasses, and cuishes.[39] These pieces were almost as many as men-at-arms had worn in the past, the only things missing being a closed helmet, a bevor, and a gorget.[40] Oddly enough, although he wrote later than Barret, Cruso stood by the closed casque and gorget.[41] But normally even Barret's list of armor was too long for the taste of most English cavalrymen, much to the disgust of that chronic complainer Sir John Smythe, who notes that horse-men thought themselves "very well armed with some kind of headpiece, a collar, a deformed high and long bellied breast, and a back at the proof; but as for pauldrons, vambraces, gauntlets, tasses, cuishes, and greves, they hold all for superfluous." [42] (Figure 11.)

The lancer was supposed to be provided with at least one strong horse "unbarded" (unarmored), fifteen hands high, and a saddle with two cuishes for the knees.[43]

The shot-on-horseback were of two sorts: pistoleers and harquebusiers. The pistoleer generally carried three pistols, "two in cases and one at his girdle, or at the hinder part of his saddle." [44] The argoletier carried a harquebuse with a snap-hance. Each carried a sword and a dagger for secondary defense.[45] Sometimes they both rode without armor, but Barwick writes that shot-on-horseback should be almost as well protected as the lancer, wearing "a good strong burgonet [headpiece], a collar with a pair of good cuirasses of the pistol proof, and a pair of well-arming pauldrons, one gauntlet for the bridle hand and no vambraces." He adds that one of the two reins to the bridle and the "head part" of the bridle should be of chain wire so that it could not be "cut in sunder with the blow of a sword." [46] Like his brother on foot, the shot-on-horseback also needed a "flask and touchbox for his piece, and a purse at his girdle with bullets." [47] According to Cruso, he was to "have a boy and a nag . . . to carry his spare arms and oat sack and to get him forage." [48]

Barret describes the horse that the shot should have as a "pretty light horse, such as be our northern nags," [49] and Cruso states that it should not be inferior in stature and strength to a lancer's horse.[50] But, as in the case of much other equipment for Elizabeth's army, what was needed for the cavalry and what was available were two different things. According to Sir Roger Williams, in the Low Countries some of the horses were "lame jades, sufficient with courtesy to pass the musters, being trimmed up with help of their witnesses how they were hurt in service." [51] Similarly in Ireland, as Captain Thomas Reade complained to Sir Robert Cecil in 1598, horses supplied the army were often weak and unserviceable; or if there were good horses, they became ill, as Captain Nicholas Dawtrey noted, because of lack of proper care and food. [52]

———

Cavalry tactics in Elizabethan times were about as complicated as infantry tactics although not so much was written about them. Horsemen were employed against enemy horse and foot, sometimes independent of their own infantrymen but generally in conjunction with them. When used with infantry, they operated from the flanks of the foot, never from the front; for as Digges and Garrard emphasize, horsemen charging from the front of a squadron of pike might be repulsed by the enemy and forced back on their own footmen. [53]

Barret warns horsemen, unless they have a definite advantage and are on favorable ground, to be wary of a standing band of footmen, remarking that "a resolute stand of pikes, with their convenient troops of shot, will give them sore stops and returns with dishonor." [54] The kind of unfavorable ground horsemen might encounter, according to Sutcliffe, would be that containing a trench, hedge, or wall; the kind of footmen they might successfully charge would be "men out of order in open field." In particular, Sutcliffe notes, any number of shot, however well-ordered, taken in open field without the protection of pikemen, could easily be overcome by a few horsemen, especially if lancers were employed.[55]

Generally speaking, lancers and shot-on-horseback used different tactics when attacking or repelling the enemy horse and foot. Lancers attacking enemy horse, if under the conduct of a captain who had learned his trade among the French, charged upon the enemy in a long single line, a method La Noue grants might be relied upon only if a small troop (twenty or thirty men) engaged in the charge.[56] La Noue's argument against the long single line of horse was based upon the stuff of which French cavalrymen were made, and might or might not apply to Englishmen. Many French horsemen, according to La Noue, had no stomach for a fight and would fall out of a charging line (on the specious ground of a broken stirrup, a bloody nose, or a lost horseshoe), leaving "glass windows" and "great breaches" in the file so that it could not break the enemy.[57] A better method, he feels, as does Sir John Smythe, was to fight as a compact squadron, with each rank containing as few as four, five, or six horsemen or as many as fifteen.[58] The first two or three ranks would be composed of the "choice men," assuming that there was a difference in the valor of the men and this difference was known; the remaining ranks would be composed of the fainthearted.[59] Although such a squadron would move as one body, only the first three ranks would level their lances, the remaining horse giving strength to the charge and supplying replacements for the killed or wounded in front.[60]

The purpose of such a charge was not only to kill and wound the enemy but also to break the squadron; that is, by speed, weight, and dexterity, to push completely through the enemy's formation so that it was disorganized. The ability to enter enemy ranks depended, of course, upon the strength of their horses as well as upon the sure use of their lances.[61] Once having pierced the enemy, the lancers could re-form and charge a second time.[62] If the enemy were completely broken by such a charge or a succession of charges, splintered lances, pistols, and swords could be put to work in the melee that followed.[63]

A third method of charging with lancers may have been that employed by *reiters* (German pistoleers) and recommended by Digges for English pistoleers. That is, successive ranks of lancers would charge one after the other, wheeling about after they had made contact with the enemy, and retiring to the tail of their own standing squadron.[64] At least, Cruso supports such a maneuver.[65] In spite of the danger involved, lancers could also be used as auxiliary troops against a well-ordered company or regiment of foot. Their very charge on his flanks or rear by file or squadron would bring the enemy to a halt.[66] In a desperate situation, they could advance on the enemy foot in squadron formation, the slain and wounded men and horses being replaced by men in the rear ranks, until eventually they rammed home upon the pikemen.[67] If the enemy foot were raw and untrained, such a maneuver might be successful in breaking their formation. Finally, if the lancers were well enough armed, upon reaching the infantry they could dismount and charge with their lances.[68] If their weapons were not as long as the pike, however, they would be at a great disadvantage, for pikemen also wore armor.

There were several ways lancers could defend themselves against enemy horse. One method, advocated by Smythe, was to straighten and close their ranks, couch their lances, and when the enemy had approached within fifteen or twenty paces, "with a terrible shout, . . . put spurs to their horses, . . . and so charge and shock with their enemies, to the disordering or breaking of them." [69] Cruso points out what might be a more prudent course: that when the lancers were attacked by superior cavalry, they could disband and scatter so that the enemy could not charge them all.[70] Another method of defense was to form a hollow square of two ranks, "standing back towards back, faced every way, to receive the charge wheresoever the enemy shall give on." [71]

Shot-on-horseback frequently operated as recommended by Digges above—in successive ranks of pistoleers or harquebusiers, wheeling about after giving fire and retiring to the rear of their standing squadron. After repeated charges of this type, the enemy might "sway or break," and then the successful rank of horsemen could enter the enemy squadron, backed up by other ranks or the whole troop if necessary.[72] Sometimes shot-on-horseback charged in full troop, like lancers, but upon coming within pistol or harquebuse range of the enemy, they would wheel about, every rank one after another, firing off volleys before galloping away again.[73] (Figure 12.) They could also serve with the forlorn hope, skirmishing "bravely upon the face of the enemy, discharging, and wheeling about, one troop seconding another." [74] Such action might be successful against lancers, especially if the latter were poorly trained, and it might also be successful against footmen.[75] Those shot-on-horseback carrying harquebuses could also dismount and fight as infantrymen and, as Williams remarks, "do no less duty than foot harquebusiers." [76]

Pistoleers and argoletiers could defend themselves against charging shot-on-horseback by making a caracole; that is, when the enemy in full career was all but upon them, they could divide by the half ranks, opening to the right and left to let the onrushing horsemen through, and then suddenly turn and charge them on the flanks. Such a maneuver could be performed by one company alone or by a unit composed of two companies. In the latter instance, one company could wheel to the left, one to the right, and both together could then face inwards and attack the enemy on the flanks or on his rear. Naturally, when using such tactics, pistoleers and argoletiers had to fire by ranks or, in some instances, by file.[77] (Figure 13.)

Because of its scarcity, cavalry was seldom used in great numbers at any one engagement. At the outset, Elizabeth's agreement to give formal aid to the Dutch States in 1585 included promise of an army of 5,000 footmen but only 1,000 horse. These horse trickled over the channel slowly and were husbanded with great care. When collected in numbers large enough to be put into the field, they were most frequently used in company strength. Thus, in September 1586 at the battle of Zutphen—according to Edward Grimestone, whose figures are not necessarily accurate—the English had 800 foot and only 150 horse; before Deventer, 1,200 foot and 200 horse; at Doesburgh, 800 foot and 200 horse.[78] Similarly, more than ten years later in Ireland, where the English poured in a greater number of troops than into the Netherlands, the Earl of Essex (then Lord Lieutenant), on his journey through Leinster and Munster to mop up the Irish rebels, assembled a force of 3,000 foot and only 300 horse.[79] Various entries in the *Calendar of State Papers, Foreign* and *Ireland,* from 1585 to 1600, show that these proportions of infantry to horse were normal for that period of Elizabeth's reign.

Even though, as Sir Roger Williams could persuade himself, a company of men-at-arms might be "the most honorable private charge that a man may have in the wars" [80] and even though the highest ranking Elizabethan officers nostalgically prided themselves upon being captains of horse (whatever other titles they might possess), so far as Elizabethan tacticians were concerned, cavalry had apparently seen its most glorious days.

VI

Field Artillery

Elizabethan field artillery, like its modern counterpart, was a unit of the army which contributed to the action of the field forces through fire support. Its command was vested in a general officer called the master of ordnance,[1] or, as was occasionally the case, the master of artillery, "one of the principal officers of the field." [2] His duties and responsibilities went far beyond the command of field pieces. He was in charge of all artillery, with mounts, carriages, ammunition, and the implements and material for making or repairing these. He also commanded a portion of the pioneers and, as a consequence, was sometimes responsible for preparing entrenchments, erecting fortifications, digging mines and counter-mines, and constructing bridges over rivers and streams. Besides supplying such powder and shot as would be needed for his own weapons, he had charge of munitions for the musketeers and harquebusiers. He was also a member of the commanding general's council of war.[3]

The organization of the ordnance master's command was in a state of flux during the Elizabethan period; but—theoretically, at least, if seldom in reality—he had under him a lieutenant with a staff of clerks, a master gunner,[4] a gunner and a gunner's mate for each cannon in the unit, and a great number of artificers, such as wheelwrights, carpenters, coopers, smiths, fletchers, masons, shipwrights, wagonwrights, and cable makers. Assigned to him by the high marshal on a more or less permanent basis was a band of pioneers under a captain,[5] and one or more companies of soldiers to protect the pioneers, to guard the artillery, and to see that the gunners did their duty.[6] Attached to him when the occasion warranted it were other bands of pioneers, such as those under the command of the trench master, mine master, or fire (*i.e.,* wildfire) master.[7]

The lieutenant of artillery was the commander's principal assistant; his duties combined those of a modern adjutant and an executive officer. He was to take charge of "inferior matters," such as those pertaining to supplies or the training of gunners; and, since it was "neither possible nor convenient that the master of ordnance should attend upon all the premises himself," the lieutenant was also to have delegated to him such other jobs as did not come under the rather vague heading of "great and most important."[8] Among these lesser jobs was that of disbursing munitions to infantry companies.[9]

The master gunner was to take charge of the gunners, principally looking to their maintenance and conduct. He was also "to have in readiness, bullets, powder, ladles, and sponges, . . . to peruse the carriages and wheels that they be strong, and the pieces themselves that they have no honeycombs or flaws in them."[10] Upon occasion he was likewise to demonstrate his pieces and ammunition "in the presence of the master of the ordnance." [11]

The gunners themselves were something of a problem. Thomas Smith, author of *The Arte of Gunnerie* (1600), warned officers assigning men to artillery units not to "suffer every tag and rag to be a gunner, as is too much used in these days," but to choose only those soldiers who had been "truly instructed in the principles" of gunnery.[12] Once properly trained, they were not only to service their pieces but also to make "trunks, balls, arrows, and all other sorts of wildfire and fire work." [13]

The pioneers, like the gunners, posed a problem to their commanding officers, although presumably not for the same reason. According to William Garrard, they were "not men of estimation and honor, such as men of war be"; and he pointed out that they had a tendency to leave units "without license at their own pleasure" and without "respect of incurring danger of punishment." [14] For this reason, he recommended that they should be paid their wages every night (the anticipation of additional wages the following night would keep them in camp) and be watched by infantry guards assigned to the artillery.[15] Their duties were to "accommodate and make easy every foul way, strait passage and encumbrance, . . . to clear the ways before the great ordnance," [16] and "to plant artillery, and to entrench the place in the camp . . . assigned for munition." [17]

The unit to which these officers and men were assigned was a field army, roughly comparable in organization, though not in numbers, to a modern division. That is, it was the largest administrative and tactical force placed in the field during the period, and it was composed of a varying number of infantry, cavalry, and pioneer companies grouped together as regiments. Unless placed in a fortress, units smaller than a field army apparently never had artillery regularly assigned to them, but frequently regiments and even companies had artillery attached to them to carry out small-scale operations.

The size of the artillery unit assigned to a field army depended upon the mission to be accomplished and the availability of cannon and cannoneers, neither of which were really plentiful in Elizabeth's reign. When the mission was to lay siege to a fortified city, as many cannon as possible were assembled; when, however, the mission was to engage the enemy in the field, very few cannon were required, since field tactics for artillery was in a most rudimentary stage during this period. Thus, to quote extremes, at one point in the siege of Ostend (1601), the Spanish, with approximately five or six regiments, managed to bring thirty-five pieces of ordnance to bear upon the city; [18] while at the battle of Nieuport in 1600—a field engagement pitting 13,800 English and Dutch and their allies against 12,000 Spanish—only twelve or fourteen cannon were brought into the field by both parties together.[19]

Something of the anomalous position of the general of artillery and his command can be seen in the organization of the English expeditionary force sent by Elizabeth to aid the Dutch in 1585. The "head officers of the field," appointed in late July of that year, included a master of ordnance. An examination of the financial accounts of this force, however, reveals no mention of artillery or gunners; but it does reveal that the master of ordnance had nominal command of an infantry company and that he and his company were transferred on August 23 from the field forces to the garrison of Ostend, where he assumed the governorship.[20] If the field forces, which consisted of approximately 8,000 men, had field artillery, it was not significant enough to be placed under separate command and listed in army financial accounts.

By 1590, these accounts begin to show evidence of expenditures on artillery, but the amounts are so slight as to be rather startling. Thus, of £442,059 paid out by Elizabeth between February 1587 and October 1590 for all purposes—wages and supplies—£1,558 were disbursed to artillery officers (ranks not designated) and £394 for ordnance.[21] Of these small sums, what share went to fortified towns and what to the field forces is not stated. These figures, of course, do not give a true picture of the forces in field and garrison, for the Dutch were also supplying men, munition, victuals, and cannon to the combined armies. Nevertheless, it is obvious that, in spite of some significant advances in the development of ordnance in the sixteenth century,[22] field artillery was one of the less important components of the Elizabethan army.

———

For every piece of field artillery a good deal of supplementary equipment had to be provided. It was absolutely necessary, of course, to have horses or oxen to draw the cannon, and wagons to carry munitions. But how many horses, oxen, and wagons? Robert Barret, who had, as we have seen, spent a good portion of his life "in the profession of arms . . . among foreign nations, as the French, the Dutch, the Italian, and Spaniard,"[23] felt that the greatest cannon should be pulled by twenty-four animals, the demi-cannon by eighteen, the culverin by twenty-four, the saker by twelve, and the falcon by eight—with greater numbers in foul weather;[24] whereas Thomas Smith, likewise an experienced soldier,[25] cut down the number of animals considerably and made a distinction between the drawing power of oxen and horses. According to Smith, three yoke of oxen could draw as much as three horses; seventeen yoke of oxen could pull a cannon of 8,000 pounds, while three yoke could pull a 1,400–pound saker or a 900–pound falcon.[26] Barret estimated that a good cart or wagon drawn by six or eight horses could carry sixty cannon shot.[27] Since a double cannon could fire about thirty times in every twenty-four hours and a falcon one hundred and twenty times,[28] some idea of the size of Elizabethan ammunition trains can be gained from this figure. Some cannon balls were of stone; others were of iron or lead (called "whole iron shot" and "small base shot"). There were also chain shot, clive shot, and dice shot;[29] and gunners devised special shells, using "certain little vessels full of nails and bullets chained together" and "little sacks full of musket bullets."[30]

Wagons also carried a wealth of powder, chemicals, and tools. Barret's list of equipment includes

axletrees, wheels, ladles, rammers, iron crows, levers, shovels, mattocks, gabions [cylindrical wicker baskets to be filled with earth or stone, used as a defense in fortification], ropes, chains, quoins . . . , powder both serpentine and corn powder, cotton match, lintstocks, priming irons, their rules or instruments to take the level, taladros, that is, engines to mount and dismount the ordnance; shot of all sorts and sizes; cartridges of all sizes, trunks, arrows, and balls of wildfire and stuff to make the same . . .[31]

The "stuff" to make fireworks, as listed by Digges in his *Stratioticos* (1590), was "sulphur, saltpeter, rosin, calx vive [quick lime], linseed oil and common lamp oil, pitch, tar, camphor, wax, tutia [possibly tutin or britannia metal, an alloy of tin and regulus of antimony], arsenic, quicksilver, and aqua vitae."[32]

Since the master of ordnance had charge of conveying all troops over rivers, the field artillery was equipped with "boats made . . . with flat covers of square planks, which chained together may make suddenly a bridge to pass an army over any water." [33]

Finally, there was the artillery itself. When cannon were first employed on the battlefield, any size and weight would serve for any purpose. But toward the end of the Elizabethan period, careful distinctions in the use of pieces began to be made. Cyprian Lucar recognized eight different types: double-cannon, demi-cannon, quarter-cannon, culverin, saker, minion, falcon, and falconette; and the first four types were cast in several different sizes, which bore individual names. [34] The largest of these—the double cannon (or cannon royal) and the demi-cannon—varying in weight from 8,000 pounds to 5,000 pounds, were used as siege guns to batter down walls; quarter-cannons and most culverins, weighing from approximately 5,000 pounds to 4,000 pounds, were mounted on fortified walls to repel the besieging enemy; and some culverins and all sakers, falcons, and falconettes—weapons which weighed between 2,000 pounds and 360 pounds—were employed as field pieces. [35] The double-cannon had a caliber of 8½ inches, was 12 feet long, and shot a ball of 66 pounds; while the falconette had a caliber of only 2 inches, was 5 or 6 feet long, and shot a ball of 2 pounds. [36] These weapons were supplemented by mortars—instruments, as Thomas Smith pointed out, "invented only to annoy the enemy, when other ordnance cannot be used against them, as being charged with stone shot to beat down the houses of the enemy or to fall among men being assembled together, or charged with balls of wildfire to burn the enemy's ships, houses, or corn." [37] Some of these mortars were of tremendous size. At the siege of Grave, for instance, Maurice of Nassau had one—called a "great murderer" by a man who saw and described it—which shot "pieces of blue square stone and other great stones out of it, of such bigness, that a man (with all his power and strength) is but able to lift one of them." [38] But most of the mortars, it would seem, were of the same proportions as normal cannon, except for the shortness of the barrels.

———

The science of gunnery during the early years of Queen Elizabeth's reign was in its rudimentary stages. Artillerymen, both on land and at sea, knew how to make powder after the Continental method, being aware of the theory that the ingredients should be pure, and that different proportions of saltpeter, charcoal, and sulphur should be used for different sizes of artillery; and they adhered to the customary—and often dangerous—mode of charging their pieces with powder that weighed two-thirds of the weight of the ball. [39] When lading their pieces, they also followed the custom of using wads (generally wisps of straw or pieces of wool cloth) to keep powder and shot solidly in place. [40] Besides the solid projectiles they ordinarily used, they experimented with fragmentary shot and incendiary shells.

But when it came to aiming their weapons, they simply sighted along the barrels of their pieces, from the breech to the muzzle, until the target was covered; [41] consequently —assuming that their pieces were truly bored—they could be expected to do fairly well only at point-blank range, a range, with most artillery, too close to the enemy to be comfortable.

The effective range of Elizabethan artillery varied widely with the size of the cannon, the excellence of its construction, and the type of powder employed. William Bourne, author of

Inventions or Devises. Very Necessary for All Generalles and Captaines (1578) and *The Arte of Shooting in Great Ordnaunce* (1587), mentions point-blank ranges of 26, 40, and 80 yards, and a maximum range of almost a mile.[42] Thomas Smith notes a range of 700 yards, but he reports the maximum range for wall-pounding to be 240 paces.[43] Cyprian Lucar, translator of Tartaglia and omnivorous reader of contemporary Continental treatises on gunnery, suggests that the ideal distance for wall-pounding was 80 paces, adding that cannon should be no farther from the wall than 150 paces.[44] John Sheriffe, who about 1590 prepared a chart of "the secret of the art of great ordnance," indicates that the greatest point-blank range of the farthest shooting cannon was 400 paces. At the same time, he notes that such cannon were most effective when they were within 80 paces of their mark.[45]

Whatever the effective range of various Elizabethan cannon may have been, targets beyond point-blank range could be hit only by chance; for without the aid of fixed front sights and adjustable rear sights and with no mechanism for determining the proper muzzle elevation necessary to deliver a shot a certain distance, Elizabethan cannoneers had to guess themselves onto a target. They observed their shots carefully, however, and, by altering the elevation of their pieces with "quoins" or wedges beneath the tails, approached their targets by creeping or bracketing fire. Since their guns recoiled six to eight feet,[46] and so had to be completely remounted after each firing—without the use of gauges or sights—it is not surprising that the effects were sometimes discouraging.

By the late 1570's decided improvements had been made in Elizabethan gunnery methods. Front sights came into general use, although, since cannon were not equipped with them in the gun foundries, gunners had to manufacture their own.

The process of preparing such sights was quite simple. Elizabethan ordnance was generally tapered down from breech to muzzle, so that the bore of the piece was not level when the top of the barrel was level. Therefore, a front sight had to be devised in such a way as to take this tapering into consideration. Gunners figured the diameter of the breech (for instance, by using calipers when they were available or by placing a string around the breech and figuring seven twenty-seconds of the result) and the diameter of the muzzle, subtracted one from the other, and took half the result. This figure represented the correct height of the front sight. It was an easy matter to cut a length of straw the right number of inches and affix it to the muzzle with wax.[47] This procedure was termed "disparting" the piece, and the front sight was therefore called "the dispart." [48]

Of course, such a method would not work unless the gun was "truly bored," so a means was devised for determining whether or not the bore was centered in the barrel. As William Bourne described it: "Take two straight staves and make them fast at the one end, that they be not wider asunder at one end than . . . at the other, and then put one of the staves into the mouth of the piece near unto the touch hole, and then try the piece round about on every side with an inch rule. . . ." [49] (See Figure 14.) Were the bore not true, the "dispart" could be lengthened or shortened, put to the left or right, to allow for its inaccuracy, although such a gun, Bourne declared, would never shoot accurately. [50]

The rear sight at this time was merely another piece of straw affixed to the breech. An immobile rear sight, as is generally known, is useful only when the target is within point-blank range. Beyond that range, the sight must be elevated, little by little, according to the distance of the piece from the target. Instead of manipulating their rear sights, however, Elizabethan gunners did what amounts to the same thing: they placed a quadrant in the muzzle of their cannon (see Figure 15) and adjusted the muzzle elevation to the degree required to project a ball the desired distance.

Two things were requisite before this practice could produce good results. In the first place, the cannoneers had to know how far their weapons would fire with every degree of muzzle elevation; and, in addition, they had to be able to judge ranges. In general, the first time that gunners had a chance to fire their cannon was in battle, for not until the late seventeenth century was regular artillery practice instituted in England.[51] If they kept their heads, they might work out a rough table of ranges with two shots—assuming, of course, that they had level fields of fire. For they could determine the point-blank range of their pieces with one shot, the range of one degree of elevation with a second shot, and, by noting the distance between these two marks, could have an approximation of how much farther their pieces would throw a cannon ball "at the mount of every degree" up to twenty degrees.[52] Since the ranges involved never exceeded the range of a modern rifle, most gunners probably estimated distances by eye, a method that experience can make very accurate. As a matter of fact, since, according to Bourne, many gunners did not use quadrants in making their muzzle elevations, they frequently had to make "a guess what advantage will reach the mark. . . ."[53] They may also have paced off distances to fortified walls if they could do it without jeopardizing their lives; indeed, as late as 1587 Bourne could write that few gunners knew any other method.[54]

Had Elizabethan gunners studied available military literature, they could have improved their accuracy and speed of fire, but they would have had to have the cooperation of the government to do it. One of their greatest deficiencies—inability to place shots on given targets at various ranges—was due in part to the fact that they were unfamiliar with their weapons. Although Bourne stated that "ordnance has been had into the field [for range practice] both in Master Bromefield's time when that he was Lieutenant of the Ordnance, and at divers times since," [55] he found that the methods of testing weapons were inadequate. And Thomas Smith, writing in 1600, complained that he had "never heard nor read of any that has as yet fully put the same [*i.e.,* range firing] in practice." [56]

There were several methods suggested for zeroing in cannon on artillery ranges. After leveling their piece with the quadrant and shooting across horizontal ground until they found the point-blank range of their weapon, the gunners could elevate their piece from minute to minute and from degree to degree, firing after each change in elevation. Then, by marking down the distance the shot was conveyed at every elevation, they could construct a table of ranges or "randoms." [57] In time of battle, gunners would merely have to estimate a target's distance from the piece, consult the table, elevate the piece to the proper degree, and, with a plumb line or a piece of straw as a rear sight, lay on the target and fire.

Another method was to construct a rear sight out of a rule and a sliding eyepiece and, by practicing on a target range, translate degrees of muzzle elevation into inches of breech depression. [58] (See Figure 16.) Gunners could then either mark yardages off on the rear sight or consult a table of randoms.

Having once prepared a table of randoms or a graduated rear sight, gunners could also hit targets on hills without wasting innumerable shots to discover the proper number of degrees to elevate their weapons. Assuming that they knew the distance to the target and the point-blank range of their piece, gunners could, in four movements, lay on the target—and the method prescribed for them was precisely the method used by gunners today. They could (1) raise their piece the number of degrees it would take to reach the target on level ground, (2) determine with their quadrant the number of degrees the target on the hill stood above the piece, (3) raise their piece this additional number of degrees, and (4) align target, dispart, and rear sight.[59] In other words, they could do what modern gunners do when they add the angle of elevation to the angle of site. If their powder was good, their measurement of it accurate, their balls of the proper size, their dispart of the correct length, and their weapon truly bored, they could hit the mark—or close to it—when they fired.

A special, if obvious, skill before gunners could possibly hit targets was that of estimating the range. As has already been pointed out, most gunners probably judged distances by eye or, when the terrain was favorable, paced off distances between gun emplacements and walls. But Elizabethans had another way of resolving distances which, though slow and therefore only useful against stationary objects, was nevertheless safe and accurate. As described by Cyprian Lucar (see Figure 17), it was not greatly different from the method used by modern gunners. One of the gunners first placed his quadrant on a level spot, *1*, and sighted the target, *5*. Second, without moving his quadrant, he sighted back along it several hundred paces to another point, *3*, which he marked. Third, he turned his quadrant 90 degrees, and sighted a point, *2*, several hundred paces from point *1*, which he also marked. Fourth, he took his quadrant to point *3* and, after aligning it with points *1* and *5*, turned it 90 degrees and marked a point, *4*, which was in alignment with points *2* and *5*. By measuring the distances between points *1* and *2*, and *1* and *3*, and *3* and *4*, he had enough information to calculate the range to his target. The formula was as follows:

$$\frac{(\text{distance from } 1 \text{ to } 3) \times (\text{distance from } 3 \text{ to } 4)}{(\text{distance from } 3 \text{ to } 4) - (\text{distance from } 1 \text{ to } 2)}.$$

For instance, suppose (as Cyprian Lucar does—see Figure 17) that the gunner found the distance from *1* to *3* to be 300 paces, the distance from *3* to *4* to be 240 paces, and the distance from *1* to *2* to be 200 paces. He would then find that the distance to his target was 1,800 paces, as follows:

$$\frac{300 \times 240}{240 - 200} = \frac{72,000}{40} = 1,800 \text{ paces.}$$

By planting his piece at point *1*, raising the muzzle the necessary number of degrees to convey a ball 1,800 paces, and aligning his sights on the target, the gunner (theoretically, at least) would hit his mark.

Early in Elizabeth's reign, the theory for wall-pounding was anything but scientific. The master of ordnance would mount his cannon as close to the walls as possible and let his gunners fire at will. This indiscriminate sort of bombardment was, later on, not approved by those who theorized about or experimented with cannon. Two other methods of opening breaches were advocated instead. Faced with a curtain or cullion point that was successful in repelling besiegers, the master of ordnance could plant his cannon in three positions, each approximately the same distance from the target, and have his gunners aim in such a manner that "the 2 side mounts would quoin or cut out that which the ordnance from the middle mount does batter or pierce." [60] Or, he could set up two batteries of three guns each and have the Number 1 guns in both batteries shoot at the bottom of the mark, the Number 2's one foot higher, and the Number 3's one foot still higher—all at once.[61] These methods were obviously better than blasting away at will at a stubborn fortification. (See Figures 18 and 19.)

Even guns with good sights manned by gunners who could estimate ranges correctly would not fire properly without good powder; and in spite of the fact that in Elizabethan times "the making of the powder and also the making of the saltpeter" had "become . . . a common thing," [62] gunners could never be sure that the powder they received in barrels was good or that its explosive force would be consistent from keg to keg. As a result, if they wanted to know where their shots would fall, they had to be prepared to test the powder. This they did in two ways. First, upon opening a keg, they noticed whether or not the powder was dry, as it should be; they tasted it, to see that it was "sharp" enough; examined its color ("bluish" was considered to be the best); felt it to note whether it was as "fine as sand, and as soft as flour"; and finally, lit a portion of it to determine whether or not it would fire in "the twinkling of an eye" and burn with a white smoke.[63] Second, by making for themselves a small can with a hinged lid, a notched metal arc above the lid to catch it, and a touch hole, they were able to fire a portion of the powder and note how high it forced up the lid.[64] From these procedures they were able to judge what quantities to use out of different barrels.

During this period, gunners were also presented with a new theory concerning the amount of powder which should be used to convey cannon balls the maximum distance with the minimum damage to their weapons. Instead of charging their pieces with powder weighing two-thirds of the weight of the ball, as was customary at the time, they were directed to divide the weight of their shot into the weight of their cannon and apply the following rule for computing the weight of the powder required for the shot used by artillery pieces of various sizes:

Artillery piece: *pounds of metal per pound of shot*	*Weight of powder in proportion to weight of shot*
100–150	⅔
150	⅞
150–200	⅘
200	equal
300	1⅑

For instance, according to this rule, a double cannon weighing 8,000 pounds and being serviced with a ball of 70 pounds, would need 46 pounds of powder to cast its projectile; while a little saker weighing 1,800 pounds and being serviced with a ball of 9 pounds, would need 9 pounds of powder to cast its projectile.[65] (See Figure 20.)

These powder and shot weights were figured out so as to obtain the greatest force at the maximum range without bursting the cannon. To make sure that the cannon did not become overheated and were not subjected unduly to the strain of constant firing, gunners also were instructed to limit the firing of their weapons to a predetermined number of shots a day. Thus, one table of firings indicates that the ordinary double cannon could be fired thirty times within twenty-four hours, the culverin sixty times, and the falcon one hundred twenty times.[66]

Projectiles for sixteenth-century cannon were normally

loaded into pieces with ladles and rammers, a slow and cumbersome method which, in the heat of battle, would result in unequal charges and spilled powder. Consequently, Elizabethans were introduced to a manner of charging cannon which, though hardly new, had not been practiced very often, even on the Continent. Instead of lading powder directly from a keg into the bore, the gunners prepared cartridges of paper or canvas before the battle, making sure that all the cartridges contained the same amount of powder. In an engagement, gunners provided with such cartridges were able to fire with greater rapidity and accuracy than those who had to charge with a ladle.[67]

As might be expected from a people whose ancestors had perfected the use of the long bow, Elizabethan gunners were well aware of the method of hitting targets that were in rapid motion across their front. Instead of firing directly at a galloping troop of horsemen or a sailing ship, they took what the modern soldier calls "leads." That is, they noted a spot which the horsemen or the ship would cross, aimed their cannon at it, and just before the target reached the spot, fired.[68] Sailors naturally had greater difficulty in getting good results, for they used cloud formations rather than landmarks for aiming.[69]

In general, the practice of naval gunners was, as I have suggested above, the same as the practice of artillerymen on land, except that naval gunners had more complications to worry about. In addition to the common problems of correct boring, good powder, and accurate sights, they had to deal with heaving seas, wet powder and barrels, constantly moving targets, and unsteady emplacements. But in spite of Elizabethan success at sea, we cannot say that they were any more scientific than were their brothers on land. They were counted good gunners, William Bourne points out, because they were "hardy or without fear about their ordnance," not because of their knowledge; [70] and when it comes down to sheer effectiveness against fortifications, it would seem that army gunners were sometimes worthy of the applause usually reserved for Elizabethan seamen.[71]

It is quite possible that some, if not all, of the methods described in this chapter for increasing the accuracy of cannon were put into practice by Elizabethan cannoneers at one time or another. But one suspects that their use was not widespread; for, in spite of the fact that gunners were notably successful at sea and against Irish fortifications, there is plenty of evidence in contemporary histories and military newsbooks to the effect that on the Continent, either because the gunners and gun founders were poor, or because the fortifications were superior, cannon were not especially effective. The contempt in which artillery men were sometimes held is amusingly illustrated by the tale of the defenders of Steenwijk in the early nineties, who came to their ramparts after a cannonading "with brooms to sweep the walls in mockage." [72] And it seems particularly significant that the Dutch and English troops, assembled in great numbers to undertake the momentous Flanders campaign of 1600, had only six pieces of artillery with them. A. R. Hall, in *Ballistics in the Seventeenth Century,* explains this situation by pointing out that there is always a "lag of artillery training behind the science of each age." [73] Toward the end of the Elizabethan period, however, the lag was not as obvious as it had been at the beginning. Englishmen, after all, trained in the Low Countries under Maurice of Nassau, who, as Oman relates, was a master of siege craft. With artillery he caused the surrender of Zutphen, Deventer, Hulst, Nijmegen (in 1591) and Steenwijk, Coevorden, and Gertruidenberg (in 1592), and he did it with amazing tactical perspicacity, concentrating more on the employment of weapons than on the clash of men.[74] It was only a question of time before tacticians and scientists got together and these gunnery theories, proved by practice on the range and in the field, became the common property of cannoneers.

———

The field tactics of Elizabethan field artillery were extremely elementary, a fact due partly to the limitations of sixteenth-century weapons and partly to the lack of imagination of sixteenth-century tacticians. Elizabethan artillery, unlike modern artillery, gave no depth to combat and was incapable of rapidly shifting its fire without changing its position. Its immobility is suggested by the general directions given by Thomas Digges in his *Stratioticos* for the emplacement of cannon: "In the field, whensoever any day of service is, it is the office of the master of the ordnance to select a convenient place to plant his ordnance, as well to annoy the enemy, as also to be in such sort guarded and fortified that it be not surprised of the enemy." [75]

The normal position of artillery in the field was on one or both of the flanks almost on a line with or even in advance of the leading infantry and cavalry elements.[76] (See Figure 21.) This position was sometimes varied by placing it directly in the front and center.[77] (See Figure 22.) It could not fire over the heads of troops from the rear because of range limitations and the unpredictability of weapons and powder: one's own troops were always placed in jeopardy by cannon firing from behind. When on the flank it could maneuver, clumsily, forward and backward or to the left or right, and of course it could traverse in any direction. When directly in front, it could move only to the right or left. But these maneuverings were obviously so slow (particularly if oxen were used to draw the cannon or if the target were beyond point-blank range) that after the initial stages of combat, artillery was not especially effective in the field as a supporting weapon in the offense. Machiavelli's interesting description of the role of artillery in the field, although written in 1516 and, therefore, somewhat out of date in the Elizabethan period, is nevertheless an accurate description of the tactics often employed in the late sixteenth century.

Do you not hear the artillery? Ours have already shot, but little hurt the enemy; and the extraordinary Veliti, issuing out of their places together with the light horsemen, most speedily and with most marvelous fury and greatest cry that may be, they assault the enemy, whose artillery has discharged once and has passed over the heads of our footmen, without doing them any hurt; and because it cannot shoot the second time, the Veliti and our horsemen have now gotten it, and the enemies for to defend it are come forward so that neither our ordnance nor the enemies' can any more do their office . . . the army . . . with the men of arms on the sides, . . . marches in good order to give the charge on the adversary. See our artillery, which to give them place and to leave them the space free, is retired to the same space from whence the Veliti issued. . . .[78]

Noteworthy in this account is the fact that the artillery is described as being of little use for two reasons: not only is it inaccurate—the cannon balls pass over the troops "without doing them any hurt"—it is also extremely vulnerable to attacks by the light infantrymen and light horsemen, being overrun before it can "shoot the second time."

In defense in the field, when elaborate, semi-permanent fortifications were thrown up, the artillery was naturally more useful. Planted in protected positions and bolstered by gabions, it served to cover routes of approach and could fire, as if from a fort, as long as sorties did not mask enemy troops, or as long as it managed to withstand assaults by opposing cavalry.

———

Elizabethan gunnery practice reflected three chief influences. First of all, during the reign of Henry VIII, artillerymen learned the barest elements of gunnery from experience in the field with the Dutch and the Flemish.[79] Secondly, from 1560 onward, Englishmen were confronted with an increasing number of books—some of them foreign works, some of them translations of foreign works, and some of them the product of native Englishmen—on gunnery and ballistics; [80] and from these works they slowly developed improved methods of employing cannon. Finally, from 1572 until well into the seventeenth century, Englishmen volunteered or were pressed into the army to go to France and the Low Countries, there learning from the French, the Dutch, and the Spanish still further methods of improving their science of gunnery.

But in spite of books and experience, improvement was not rapid. For more than twenty-five years after Elizabeth ascended the throne, a good number of soldiers and sailors were still employing the elements of gunnery learned during the reign of Henry VIII.[81] One of the reasons for the slow development of English artillery was, as we have seen before in connection with other aspects of the art of war, that Elizabethan military science had its roots in the classics; and for this reason, for the first two decades of Elizabeth's reign, English military writings emphasized Roman tactics based upon the legion, an infantry unit supported in a very minor way by cavalry and artillery.

Now while a return to Roman military science was a definite improvement over medieval methods of warfare, with its emphasis on heavy cavalry and its minimization of infantry, a close adherence to Roman methods and, particularly, to the theories of its most articulate admirer, Machiavelli, inhibited the development of gunnery. In field engagements, the Romans eschewed artillery (or, more correctly, engines of war) because they found such engines relatively ineffective except when used against fortified walls. There are instances in ancient history, of course, in which the employment of weapons like the ballista and the catapult materially affected the tide of battle; but on the whole their value was essentially that of harassment. Machiavelli likewise dismissed artillery as "unprofitable," except against fortifications, because, as we have pointed out above, his observations taught him that on the battlefield it generally had a chance to fire but once before it was masked by advancing friendly troops or neutralized by enemy cavalry.[82] Thus discouraged, Englishmen but slowly produced anything like a science of gunnery.

Another reason for the slow development of English gunnery was undoubtedly the fact that the first half of Elizabeth's reign was relatively peaceful, and there was no pressing need for the development of either artillery or an art of war.[83] But once Elizabeth was forced to desert diplomacy for warfare, mathematicians and physicists, in cooperation with experienced gunners, devised scientific methods of increasing the effectiveness of artillery, publishing their findings in short, readable, and often well-illustrated textbooks.

The cooperation of the scientists and the gunners was probably not very "scientific" in the modern sense of the word. Thomas Digges, one of the more learned mathematicians of the age, says that he was aided in his studies by the "conferences" of his father with "the rarest soldiers of his time." [84] And Humphrey Barwick, author of *A Breefe Discourse, Concerning the Force of All Manuall Weapons of Fire* (*ca.* 1594), also speaks of "conferences with persons of sundry callings." [85] Most thinkers seem to have drawn upon the extant work of scientists. Cyprian Lucar, for instance, lists twenty-five scientists from whose works he borrowed, including such well-known authorities as Niccolò Tartaglia, Vanoccio Biringuccio and Girolamo Cardano of Italy, Diego de Alaba y Viamont and Luya Collado of Spain, Daniel Santbech of Austria, and Leonard and Thomas Digges and the soldier-scholar Whitehorne. Foremost among these men was Niccolò Tartaglia (1506–1557), a mathematician who published two important works on ballistics: *La nova scientia* (Venice, 1537) and *Quesiti et inventioni diverse* (Venice, 1546). [86] The latter text was presented to Henry VIII of England in manuscript form (Tartaglia's dedication to King Henry was later used to preface the first English edition) and either from copies made therefrom or from copies of the Italian printing, Tartaglia's theories circulated among Englishmen. As Hall has pointed out, they translated him (Cyprian Lucar brought out his *Quesiti* as *Three Bookes of Colloquies* in 1588), imitated him, and plagiarized his statements. [87] Indeed, as Hall says, "there were few further contributions to the theory of gunnery before the middle of the seventeenth century," [88] although, as he shows, a few useful footnotes were contributed by the Englishmen Thomas Digges and William Bourne, and by the Continental writers

Diego de Alaba y Viamont, Luya Collado, Vanoccio Biringuccio, Girolamo Cardano, and Daniel Santbech. Portions of Continental theories and experiments were presented to English readers from time to time by Smith, Barwick, and Lucar. Eventually they were compiled and made available in one volume by Robert Norton in *The Gunner* (London, 1628).

There is no proof, of course, that the works of these men were immediately accessible to interested Englishmen during the period of our study. Indeed, it is well-nigh impossible to state to what extent the science of gunnery percolated down to the rank and file of Elizabethan gunners. Hall feels that these works really influenced the science of gunnery in the field very little, contending that the "emphasis of the experts and of the artillery schools was on a sound education in straight forward field gunnery in which scientific ballistics played a very small part." [89] Bourne, writing in the late seventies, supplies evidence for Hall's contention, in his remarks that among gunners of his acquaintance there were "divers that will have instruments, and yet be utterly void of the use of them." He assumed, moreover, that many gunners, who "would not have their ignorance known," might be displeased with his attempt to explain the details of gunnery.[90]

On the other hand, we have a good deal of circumstantial evidence that, during Elizabeth's reign, all sorts of military books were being read by different classes of Englishmen; [91] and it seems quite probable that masters of ordnance, if not the rough gunners themselves, read artillery manuals and insisted that their men conform to some of the textbook rules of gunnery.

VII

Military Medicine
and Surgery

There was a revival of the art of surgery during the reign of Elizabeth,[1] but at the same time there was a great dearth of works on military medicine and military surgery, probably because in Elizabethan England the army or navy doctor, unlike his modern counterpart, who has prestige, rank, and relatively adequate pay, was not an important man.[2] During most of the Queen's long sovereignty, every band or company of men and every warship had attached to it, or was supposed to have, a physician or "chirurgeon," who was generally obtained in one of three ways. By order of the Privy Council, he was sent to the army or navy by the Company of Barbers and Surgeons; or he was impressed by the aldermen, sheriffs, and justices of the peace in England; or he was taken up by the particular captain needing his services.[3] In any case, he possessed neither rank nor distinction, and his wages, during a good portion of Elizabeth's reign, amounted to only twelve pence a day, a sum equivalent to that received by the company trumpeter.[4] By the late eighties, this sum was increased to twenty pence, still considerably less than the wages of a lieutenant or a captain, who received two and four shillings respectively.[5]

On special occasions, when the need was great and when men of considerable rank were involved, physicians of exceptional background or reputation might have something to say about their remuneration. Thus in 1588 (the year of the Spanish Armada), when "disease and sickness began to increase in Her Majesty's Navy," the Privy Council called upon the president of the College of the Doctors of Physick in London to send two renowned doctors down to the ships. These two were to be selected from four men, already known to their lordships for their "sufficiency" and "learning" and for being "very fit persons to be employed in the said Navy to have care of the health of the noblemen, gentlemen and others in that service." They were ordered to have with them, when they reported for duty, "a convenient quantity of all such drugs as should be fit for medicine and cure," and, strangely enough, after conferring with the Lord Admiral, they were to be given such payments "as should be to their contentment." [6]

But special occasions of this sort were rare. During most of Elizabeth's reign the military surgeon remained something of a nonentity, being consistently classed with drummers, trumpeters, and smiths. Hardly a letter from the Privy Council called attention to a surgeon without mentioning in the same breath, as it were, a musician or artificer of some sort. Typical of many such letters was one sent in 1589 to the "Lord Mayor of the City of London and to all other mayors, sheriffs, justices of peace, etc." In it, the addressees were ordered to aid and assist "in the impressing and taking up of trumpeters, drummers, fifers, surgeons, and armorers," the authors of the letter apparently seeing no incongruity in placing menders of breastplates and menders of bones in the same category.[7]

From time to time, surgeons were assigned to elements larger than companies or warships and, as a result, received greater compensation for their services. In Ireland, for instance, army surgeons were "maintained by certain stipends given them by the Lord Deputy and Councillors, and by the chief officers, captains, and commanders of the army, out of their private purses, according to the rates agreed upon of their voluntary liberalities."[8] One William Kelly, who was sent over in the nineties with the new and imposing title of Surgeon General, received two shillings a day—a lieutenant's pay—getting two pence from one captain, one pence from another, and so on, until the full sum was collected. In time of war, when this allowance would be too little for Kelly's maintenance, it was understood that the officers whom he was to attend would increase their contributions. In 1595 the surgeon received an allowance of one man's pay out of every company then in Ireland. Since a foot soldier's pay was eight pence per day and since there were approximately eighteen companies in Ireland during this period, the surgeon got twelve shillings a day, or three times as much as a captain.[9] In 1599, this amount was raised to thirteen shillings, four-pence.[10]

In the Netherlands at this time, each regiment of ten companies had assigned to it two surgeons, each receiving a salary of five shillings a day, part of which was used to remunerate their assistants.[11]

Although the Irish pay may seem fairly good, it must be remembered that there were seldom more than two surgeons assigned to the entire army stationed in Ireland—and Ireland, like the Low Countries, even when actual combat was not in progress, was death on Englishmen. Besides suffering from wounds, the soldiers had to put up with the unfamiliar "raw and waterish climate" and the "disease of Ireland," which seized them two or three months after shipping overseas.[12] Sir George Carey, Treasurer at War and Lord Justice of Ireland in the late nineties, was aghast at the devastation nature wreaked on his army. "The soldiers fall sick and die fast," he wrote to Sir Robert Cecil. "I have freighted two or three barks, and have sent into England, out of this town [Dublin], almost 300 sick, hurt, and unserviceable men . . . ; and yet there remains here six or seven score sick."[13] Their illnesses were aggravated by "the unseasonableness of a great portion of their victuals sent out of England," which had been spoiled by "evil carriage at sea, and by long and close keeping . . . in the several magazines."[14] Sir John Smythe, one of the army's most voluble critics, had summed up the problem in the Low Countries several years earlier: poor soldiers suffered because of "the naughtiness or scarcity of their victual or by their evil lodging, or by the pestering, or lying of two or three hundred of them together in some one church, and so in divers churches, upon the bare pavements . . ."[15] The result was an army of pitiful ghosts and shadows of men who were well aware, as Sir Ralph Lane remarked in December 1600, that "sickness and mortality [*i.e.,* death by contagious disease] does consume more than the sword."[16] Consequently, the burden of the surgeons' work must have been almost insupportable. If they obtained assistants, they paid for them out of their own pockets, and what medicines and instruments they had were supplied, not by the Queen, but by themselves. For instance, two surgeons sent to Ireland in 1599 were given twenty pounds to "furnish themselves with divers necessaries,

for the better performance of their charge and service." But
the sum was later deducted "out of their several entertain-
ments." [17]

William Clowes (1540?–1604), a "master in surgery"
with extensive military experience, had something to say
about poorly equipped physicians, and his particular background and success give weight to his words. In 1563 he was
a surgeon in the army commanded by Ambrose, Earl of
Warwick, in France, and in 1585 he served in the same
capacity under the Earl of Leicester in the Low Countries. He
also served several years in the navy, being with the fleet
which defeated the Spanish Armada in 1588. When not with
the armed forces, he practiced in London as a member of the
Barber-Surgeons' Company and as a member of the surgical
staff of St. Bartholomew's Hospital.[18] According to Clowes,
surgeons "in Her Majesty's service, with General Norris and
Sir Francis Drake" were "very poor men, and so poor indeed,
that some of them went out very slenderly furnished: some
with a little surgery stuff in a scholar's satchel . . ." [19]

To add to the frustration of those military physicians sent
to the Irish wars, there was but one army hospital in all of
Ireland, and that one was not constructed until the turn of the
century. This hospital was described in a letter written to
Lord Burghley by Sir Henry Docwra in September of 1600 as
"within the walls of an old church . . . made fit and com-
modious to contain twenty-eight beds, with a kitchen and
other rooms. . . . The charge of governing the house was
committed to an overseer and other officers, a contribution of
4d. a month allowed from every man's pay to maintain it"
(on the basis of eighteen companies, this would be approximately six pounds).[20] Docwra's administration of the hospital
was defended in December of that year in these terms: "But if

any man will say that all the sick men were not relieved in it, I must acknowledge that, for I do know the best hospital in London cannot contain all the sick men in that army, nor was it held fit . . . that such infectious men should be brought in there; for the hurt men (of whom there is greater hope) should not only be in danger of death by his wounds received in service, but by the infectious disease of others (of whom the tenth man does not recover)." [21]

It can readily be understood that men were not anxious to serve their Queen under such circumstances. Good surgeons, loath to leave profitable civilian practices for the pittance offered them by the army, were obtained only with difficulty. Sometimes they tried to slip out of their obligations. On such occasions, the authorities took severe measures to retain the services of the men selected. A letter from the Privy Council to the Master and Wardens of Chirurgeons Hall in London colorfully sets forth the problem:

Whereas we gave direction unto you by our former letters to impress two surgeons for Her Majesty's service to be employed at Lough Foyle in Ireland, and choice being made of Peter Peine and John Raunger, we do understand by Sir Henry Docwra, Raunger being sick, one Foster did offer himself to the service, and at the instant when they were now to set forth, they do find fault [with] that is appointed to be given them, though the same be very large, and the entertainment greater than has heretofore been given unto any of their sort. Because Her Majesty's service might receive no hindrance, and they are to be at the Port of Chester by the last day of this month, this shall be in Her Majesty's name to command you that considering they already did undertake the service, that you compel them without delay to set forward or else that you commit them to prison. [22]

Serve or be imprisoned, ordered the Queen; but still some surgeons tried to wriggle out of appointments to the army or navy. Clowes scornfully condemned his unpatriotic colleagues who used subterfuge to remain free, even to the extent of denying their profession:

And what shall be said to some which not long since have been commanded to prepare themselves and with all speed to serve Her Majesty in the wars, then presently with many solemn circumstances did desire to be excused, protesting that they had no knowledge in surgery . . . But . . . let the services be once furnished with sufficient surgeons, which oftentimes is very hard to do, then they begin to shake their chains and keep a stir that they can cure that which all the best surgeons in London or elsewhere do forsake . . .[23]

Once impressed, surgeons occasionally deserted. In 1587, English forces in the Netherlands, according to a report sent to the muster-master general, had "not one surgeon among them" notwithstanding there were "no such defects" in the muster books.[24] William Jones, Commissary for Munster in 1600, complained to the Privy Council that there had been a defection of a surgeon out of every company in his sector—a fact which greatly aggrieved the captains, who resented paying "for the entertainment of one they never see, nor know so much as his name." [25] Moreover, Jones pointed out reasonably, these same captains were less valiant in combat, "knowing there is no surgeon in their company to look to them when they are wounded." [26]

Unfortunately, even when the army had its full complement of surgeons, soldiers were not always well cared for. Shirkers, such as those Clowes condemns above, made it possible for dangerously ignorant quacks to fill medical posts. Thomas Gale, while practicing surgery at the battle of Montreuil in 1544, complained that "there was a great rabblement there that took upon them to be surgeons. Some were sow-gelders, some were horse-gelders, with tinkers and cobblers . . . [The] surgery stuff they had to cure men withal [was] such trumpery as they did use to grease horses' heels withal and laid upon scabbed horses' backs, with nerval [*i.e.,* ointment for the sinews] and such like. And others that were cobblers and tinkers, they used shoemaker's wax with the rust of old pans and made therewithal a noble salve. . . ." [27] An anonymous "Student in Physick and Chirurgerie," writing a commendatory letter to Clowes' *A Prooved Practise for All Young Chirurgians* (1588), complained that the lack of proper medical and surgical knowledge among army practitioners "cost many poor soldiers full dear":

For when they have been anyway maimed or endangered with loss of life or limb, then comes the bare, single-soled surgeon, as he rightly terms them, and what to do by art knows not, yet something he must attempt, treading in his old cow path as though he were healing a broken head or plastering of kibed heel [*i.e.,* a heel bothered by chilblains], having one or two boxes of green salves with a plaster of diachylon [made of lead oxide, olive oil, and water] and a green grass melilot [for making poultices], with their moth-eaten mucilage, and these are good forsooth for all sores, and so commits the health of the patient to the main chance, a miserable thing that warlike men should first fall into the hands of men and afterward to be as it were massacred by such ignorant beasts.[28]

Clowes also condemned these "stragglers which did thrust themselves into captains' bands for principal surgeons": "I am persuaded there be more killed by such wicked practicers than there are many times slain by the sword of the enemy . . . many of them . . . do practice their malignant, corrosive, biting or gnawing medicines to the utter subversion and overthrow of their patients." [29]

Undoubtedly it was also a great temptation for surgeons,

whether honest men or "stragglers," to slight the treatment of sick or wounded soldiers in order to save the cost of medicines. Among the French at least (whatever may have been the situation with the English), it apparently was customary to doctor patients according to their station in life. Thus, Joseph Du Chesne, known as Josephus Quercetanus, in his *Sclopotarie of J. Quercetanus, or His Booke Containing the Cure of Woundes Received by Shot of Gunne* (translated into English by John Hester, "practitioner in spagirical art" [*i.e.*, alchemy] and published in 1590 and 1596), classifies his concoctions as remedies either for "common soldiers" or for "the rich." [30]

In the midst of this chaos on land and on sea, three London physicians published several manuals dealing with military medicine and surgery. They were George Baker (1540–1609),[31] Thomas Gale (1507–1587), and William Clowes, who has already been mentioned. Clowes' work, entitled *A Prooved Practise for All Young Chirurgians, concerning Burnings with Gunpowder, and Woundes made with Gunshot, Sword, Halbard, Pyke, Launce, or such other* (1588, 1591, 1596), is the only one written during Elizabeth's reign specifically "for young practicers of surgery . . . which follows the wars either by sea or land." But the others—Gale's *Certaine Workes of Chirurgerie* (1563, 1586) and Baker's *The Composition or Making of the Moste Excellent and Pretious Oil Called Oleum Magistrale* (1574)—although not written especially for military doctors, contain material which would have been useful to them.

Thomas Gale, who was a member of the Barber-Surgeons' Company, had seen action at Montreuil (1544) and, under

Philip II of Spain, at the siege of St. Quentin (1557).[32] He was therefore as well qualified as any Englishman to write of military surgery. Dedicated to Robert, Lord Dudley, his *Certaine Workes of Chirurgerie* is divided into four parts: an "institution" of surgery; an "enchiridion" (*i.e.* handbook or manual) treating the cure of wounds, fractures, and dislocations; a treatise on gunshot wounds; and an "antidotary" describing various medicines used in surgery. Of these four parts, only the second and third are of particular interest to our study, the first being merely a discussion of "the sure grounds and principles of surgery," and the fourth a sixteenth-century version of our modern pharmacopoeia.

In the "enchiridion" and in the gunshot treatise, Gale endeavors to discuss the treatment of every kind of wound with which he was familiar, drawing upon his own knowledge as well as upon such authorities as Galen and Avicenna, Hippocrates and Abulcasis. He presents cures for "great and deep wounds," wounds in veins, arteries, nerves, sinews, "wounds in which are fixed thorns, splints of wood, arrowheads, gunshot, or such like," wounds in the bones, head, face, stomach, intestines, and so on. He also discusses the different approaches necessary when dealing with "contused, bruised, or crushed wounds," as well as "the cure of those that are burnt with gunpowder" and the amputation of legs and arms.

One of his most interesting chapters deals with determining the location of "deep and hidden wounds, which cannot be well perceived." He writes: ". . . you shall know in deep wounds what part is hurt by these signs following. As the brain being wounded, he shall void scum and foam at the mouth. If the heart be wounded, there issues out blood black in color. Also, if the lungs be wounded, the blood is like a scum. But if the stomach be pierced, the meat undigested comes out. In like manner, the intestines being wounded, the odor issues . . . the urine flows out in wounds of the bladder." [33] The last-named wound, that of the bladder, he notes as being fatal.

Gale's explanation of the proper method of healing a wound made with gunshot is illuminating; in some respects it is far more modern than might be expected of the period. The wound, he says, should be cleaned "not only [of] shot, iron, splints, or shivers of wood, cloth, dust, oil, or such like, but also the clods of blood, matter, bruised flesh." If necessary, an incision should be made with a pair of scissors to enlarge the opening, and the foreign matter should be drawn out with "tongs or nippers." [34] Then a mixture of "precipitate mercury" and "simple oil, or oil of roses, or with butter, or fresh barrow's grease" should be applied. [35]

But the most fascinating chapter by far—and perhaps to the Elizabethan surgeon the most valuable—is the one on amputations. Gale exhorts the surgeon to hold consultations with others before removing an arm or leg, to make sure that such an operation is absolutely necessary. Once removal is decided upon, the surgeon should determine whether the cut should be made above or below the knee (or in the case of an arm, the elbow). If the cut is to be below the knee, Gale notes that it should be made "one good handbreadth beneath the knee. So shall the party have a resting place of a stilt to go upon." Even if no more were to be amputated than a foot, a cut lower down would have no advantage and only be a nuisance to the patient. Moreover, "the pain will be all one and the danger is least in that place." When amputating above the knee, the surgeon should make the cut "three fingers high." [36] A quarter of a century after this description was penned, William Clowes gave Gale's procedure his blessing by stating that a gangrenous arm or leg should be amputated "as Master Gale very skillfully has appointed in the whole and sound parts . . ." [37]

Gale realized that with an operation so painful and so shocking, the patient needed a certain amount of psychological preparation, and therefore he urges, ". . . before you make any incision, put the party in very good comfort, declaring unto him that the fear is much more than the pain." He also recommends that the patient's eyes be covered. [38]

One method of stopping the flow of blood after an amputation was to apply a hot iron to the stump. Gale, however, recommends a powder composed, among other ingredients, of alum, lime, and clay. And he had another invention. Instead of using a saw to take off fingers or toes, he had devised pincers to "nip the bone asunder." [39]

As might be imagined, Gale was much concerned that young surgeons, particularly military surgeons, be well prepared "in the time of necessity to serve princes and other noble persons . . .":

Remember what great charge is committed unto you in the time of wars. You have not only the charge of men's limbs, but also of their lives, which if they should perish through your default, either in neglecting of anything that were necessary for their health, which you ought to be furnished withal, either else through lack of knowledge which you ought to have in your art—I say, if these defaults be in you and the people perish in your hands, you cannot excuse yourselves of your brother's death. [40]

George Baker, who published his *Composition or Making of the Moste Excellent and Pretious Oil Called Oleum Magistrale* eleven years after Gale's first edition of the *Certaine*

Workes of Chirurgerie, did not have the military experience of his predecessor. But, besides being a member of the Barber-Surgeons' Company, he was Sergeant Surgeon to Queen Elizabeth and had a considerable practice in London.[41] Altogether, he saw through the press at least six volumes dealing with some aspect of medicine. Several of these were translations of works written earlier in the century: Conrad Gesner's *The Newe Jewell of Health* (1576) and a revision of this work entitled *The Practise of the New and Old Phisicke* (1599); Vidius Guido's *Questions* (1579);[42] Joannes de Vigo's *Chirurgical Works* (1586);[43] and the *Antidotarie of Select Medicine* (1579).[44] Only his first work, on *oleum magistrale,* considers the treatment of wounds which soldiers were most likely to suffer. This volume also contains "Galen's Third Book of the Composition of Medicines" and "A Brief Gathering Together of Certain Errors Which the Common Surgeons Use."

The origin of this "precious oil," or *oleum magistrale,* Baker relates, was in Spain among the "Moriscus" (*i.e.,* the Moors), a people well versed in "the properties of herbs and generally in the art of curing."[45] Their famous oil was composed of ten ingredients: white wine, olive oil, hypericum, carduus benedictus, valerian, sage, Venice turpentine, olibanum, myrrh, and sanguis draconis; and an unguent made from it was composed of equal parts of the oil, Venice turpentine, and new wax.[46] The method of its use was simple if startling. After a wound had first been cleaned with a mixture of hot white wine and "incense," this concoction was to be applied "as hot as ever it can be possible."[47] Understandably, there were certain variations in the application, depending upon whether the wound was old or new, or whether it was in "the head, arms or legs, . . . [or] other places"; [48] but in any case, according to Baker, *oleum magistrale* had almost magical powers. Not only was it efficacious in the treatment of injuries made with the "harquebuse and thrusts with swords, pikes, and such other like," [49] it would cure such diverse things as "cankers, pain of the reins [kidneys], apostumes [abscesses], hemorrhoids, old ulcers, pain of the joints and gout, and indifferently all manner of diseases." [50]

Although the brevity of the work keeps detail to a minimum, Baker manages to advise his readers to do more than just add *oleum magistrale* to cuts and gashes. They should watch the patient's diet and method of rest and see to it that he abstains "from the company of women." When a wound went completely through an arm or leg, Baker advises using "tents" (rolls of linen to keep wounds open) on both sides of it in order to "purge the wound of contusion or bruised blood." Such a wound, he notes, should be washed and dressed twice a day. If the wound happened to be through the body, the attending surgeon was warned to "tie the tent with a thread lest it should slip into the body and so annoy the patient." [51]

In spite of the title of the book, *oleum magistrale* is not the only oil or unguent which Baker feels can be used successfully with wounds. Going back to Galen, "the father and light of physic," [52] Baker marshals up a number of salves which would do the trick, arranging some of them in three categories: "Medicines for strong and boisterous people . . . for delicate and tender complexions . . . [and] for mean complexions." [53] Foremost among these were euphorbium (a vesicant) combined with various proportions of oil, wax, and/or turpentine; certain gum resins, such as propolis (*i.e.,* bee glue), labdanum, galbanum, sagapenum, etc.; and certain herbs or roots which "have a bitterish taste without . . . immoderate sharpness." [54]

Besides remedies for "ordinary" wounds, Baker was interested in methods to cure wounds of the nerves and to stop pain in them. His discussion of them is illuminating, and one wonders how many soldiers fighting in the Low Countries, in France, and in Ireland submitted to these treatments. Into a wound which involved a nerve, Baker states, the surgeon should put one of the following concoctions: oil of turpentine and alcohol; euphorbium and sulphur, "applied very warm"; or sulphuric acid and alcohol. And "round about the place," he should put a "catoplasma" or poultice composed of vinegar, farina, and camomile: "If by this order the pain does not cease," Baker writes, "you shall apply speedily hot seething oil with lint being dipped in it, as well at the bottom as the edges of the wound; which must be done two or three times at one dressing, for by this kind of cauterization, you shall cease the pain, by reason of the burning of the oil, the nerves or tendons do lose their sensible feeling." [55]

He also discusses the treatment of skull fractures, shoulder, arm, and leg wounds, and large wounds in the "interior parts and under the arm holes, the bend of the arm, in the wrists or in the hams or groins"—wounds which should be stitched up "leaving an orifice in the lower part thereof for to give issue to the matter." [56]

We can only speculate whether or not Baker's surgical methods were successful and his ointments and salves efficacious. Perhaps the modern physician and surgeon can bring his knowledge to bear here. But Baker was respected by Clowes (although they got into at least one argument),[57] for Clowes mentions him favorably in his own book.[58]

William Clowes, whose military and civilian experiences as physician and surgeon have been briefly outlined above, published two other works besides his *A Prooved Practise for All Young Chirurgians*. These were *De morbo Gallico* (1579), which is a dissertation upon the cause and cure of the French pox, or venereal diseases, and *A Right Frutefull and Approved Treatise for the Artificiall Cure of the Struma* (1602).

A Prooved Practise was written "for the benefit of all young practicers of surgery," but it was of especial value to military surgeons in that it was replete with remedies for "wounds made with gunshot, sword, dagger, halberd, pike, or lance." [59] In this respect, it is similar to the works of Gale and Baker, but it is unlike their works in that much of the material which it presents is based directly and specifically upon cures which Clowes himself had effected. Chapter IV, for instance, deals with "The cure of one Master Andrew Fones, a merchant of London, who being in a ship at sea, was set upon by the Flushingers, in which fight he was very dangerously wounded with gunshot." [60] Often, names of patients are given; sometimes the victim is designated merely as "a certain soldier." Only rarely is a remedy suggested which had not been successfully tested on a patient.

Besides cures for wounds, the work contains a section on the diet which should be prescribed for a wounded man; another on the "manner of the purging of your patients being at the sea"; a very valuable and informative list of the "necessary medicines and instruments, good for young practicers of surgery to be furnished with, which follow the wars either by sea or land"; and an "Apostematibus" or catalogue of "most imperfections, which daily assaults man's body." In short, it was a work which any young military physician during Elizabeth's reign might have considered extremely useful—a fact which accounts for the three editions between 1588 and 1596.

The cures which Clowes effected both in the army and at home were sufficiently various so that, although he does not present his readers with a thorough exposition of his subject or even with a compendium, he offers them a working basis for the treatment of most kinds of wounds encountered in the wars. Thus, since he was writing in an age of unpredictable propellants and defective guns, he sagely begins with the treatment of persons "grievously burned with gunpowder" and later devotes a chapter to cures of men hurt by exploding weapons, burns and explosions being kinds of injuries frequently suffered by Elizabethan soldiers and sailors on the battlefield and on ships of war.

Except for the application of unguents, there was, then as now, little one could do for burns. Clowes' unguents were essentially mixtures of oil, wax, and lard, with infusions of such homely herbs as navelwort, St.-John's-wort, houseleek, violets, and so on, with variations demanding egg white and human milk, depending on whether medication was to be applied to blistered flesh, flesh "burned off and the parts made raw and painful," eyelids, or the eyes themselves.[61] Whatever one might think today of Clowes' remedies, he himself seemed satisfied with them, remarking that he had, since 1577, successfully used them "infinite times." [62]

Wounds caused by exploding weapons, however, demanded other and more complicated treatment, since flesh would frequently be torn and bone would be shattered. Precisely what the "young practicers of surgery" should do is described in fascinating detail, from the preliminary stitching and the application of restrictives to "restrain the bleeding" to the final dressing. For instance, Clowes devotes four pages to the treatment of a man whose bursting gun "made a great wound upon his chin, . . . carried away a good part of the mandible and teeth . . . [and] rent his hand in three parts very greatly." Incredible though it may seem, the patient, Clowes insists, recovered "without maim or deformity," and he gives the man's name and place of occupation as proof of a successful operation.[63]

Gunshot wounds were of two kinds: those in which bullets went entirely through the body and those in which bullets lodged within the wound. Clowes discusses each type, taking care to include information on the handling of such complications as might be caused by fractured bone and putrefying flesh. The procedures for handling both types of wounds are essentially the same. After consulting with a "Doctor of Physic" concerning the patient's "diet, purging, and bleeding," the surgeon should apply a cataplasm or poultice to appease the pain and stop the inflammation, add a "defensive" to stop the advance of gangrene and a "mundificative" to cleanse and purge the area involved, cut away (if necessary) all the spongy flesh and remove the loose bones, and finally dry up "superfluous moisture." [64] When the bullet lodged within the wound, the surgeon would naturally have to make an incision to remove it, and if the wound was deep, he would have to add "digestives" to promote suppuration, or the forming of pus, using tents to keep the wound open. Sometimes he might find it necessary to inject a mundifying or purifying lotion into the wound.[65] Clowes gives the formulas for all the cataplasms, defensives, mundificatives, and digestives employed in these treatments.

In one of his most engrossing accounts of a complicated wound—and such wounds were probably far from uncommon during Elizabeth's reign—Clowes describes the cure of a soldier who still retained a shot which had been fired at him three years before. According to Clowes, the man "was shot in at the bottom of his belly on the left side, and the bullet passed through and rested in the right buttock near unto anum, where . . . it became a fistula" difficult to heal. Clowes conceded that the task of removing the bullet would be difficult because its position could be determined "neither by probing nor conjecture." First of all he tried to "destroy and remove the callous hardness which was environed about the circuits or compass of the hollowness of the fistula" by the application of two specially prepared powders. He was partly successful in this endeavor, but the fistula had so many "creeks or turnings" that the bullet still could not be located. In order to reach the bottom of the fistula, he decided to use a liquid instead of a powder, stopping up the orifice for twenty-four hours once the liquid was induced. This treatment caused pain and swelling "upon the buttock near unto anum." Here he made an incision and recovered the bullet.[66]

Clowes' description of the method for amputating "mortified and corrupt" legs and arms is an expansion of Gale's account, to which he generously refers. Realizing that such operations were fraught with danger, he suggests that the patient be given "some good exhortation by the minister or preacher" to fortify him spiritually for the ordeal, and that he be provided with some broth two hours before the amputation to fortify him physically.

During the operation itself, he advises, the surgeon should be assisted by three strong men, one to hold the patient's arms, one his leg above the incision point, and one his leg below the incision point. The second man's hands, Clowes warns, should be large, with "a good grip," so as to be able to stop the flow of blood. The actual cutting should be done "boldly with a steady and quick hand." Once the leg was removed, a restrictive powder (of a composition entirely different from Gale's powder described above) mixed with finely cut rabbit's hair and egg white should be applied to the stump to curtail the bleeding, the large veins being stopped up by "bolsters or buttons" of tow.[67]

Clowes wisely includes in *A Prooved Practise* a list of things "very needful and necessary for all young practicers of surgery to be furnished with which follow and serve in the wars." An army surgeon's chest should contain suppuratives to induce the forming of pus, "mundifying or cleansing medicines," "incarnatives or regeneratives" to promote the growth of flesh, "desiccatives," "unguents for burning with gunpowders," syrups, waters, electuaries, poultices, lotions for sore mouths, cataplasms, and eggs. Since, throughout the book, formulas for making these various concoctions abound, the young army surgeon might prepare his medicines before departing for the wars or carry a miniature apothecary shop along with him in a surgeon's chest. The chest (a picture of it accompanies Clowes' text [68]) should be supplied with splints, tape, cupping or boxing glasses, a chafing dish, a mortar and pestle, blood porringers, wax candles, a sharp saw, a catlin (which was a knife used in amputations to divide tissues between close-lying bones), an incision knife, needles, buttons of tow, cauterizing irons, a trepan or instrument for boring holes in the skull, a head saw, an elevator to raise bones, certain birds' bills (to be used as tweezers, etc.), a syringe, and stitching quills.[69]

"There are also many other instruments, I know, which are in use," concludes Clowes, "but these may suffice for young practicers of the art." Yet he, or perhaps his publisher (*A*

Prooved Practise for All Young Chirurgians was printed by Thomas Orwyn for Thomas Cadman), augments the list by furnishing pictures of several tools not mentioned in the text. (Figures 23 and 24.)

With such instruments and medicines packed in his surgeon's chest and with the works of Gale, Baker, and Clowes tucked under his arm, the youthful and perhaps inexperienced physician was ready to march off to the wars as part of Elizabeth's forces on land and on the sea.

VIII

The Books
and the Practice

Authors of Elizabethan military books covered every conceivable aspect of the sixteenth-century art of war. Many of these men wrote complete textbooks, as useful to a commanding general as to a noncommissioned officer, as valuable to a muster-master as to a company clerk. Some of them dealt with more limited matters, such as how to feed a garrison of 1,000 soldiers or how to form infantrymen into fighting battalions or how to manipulate pike, caliver, and musket. From the earliest days of Elizabeth's reign to the latest, a number concentrated upon what Shakespeare's Fluellen reverently called the "disciplines of the pristine wars of the Romans." That is to say, with the armies of classical antiquity in mind, they gave their readers advice on the type of soldiers to procure, the arms they should bear, the training they should undergo, the tactics they should employ, the encampments they should make, the fortifications they should throw up, and the ordinances they should obey. Others, while acknowledging that there was much to be admired in Roman discipline, altered tactics to make use of weapons never dreamed of by Agrippa or Caesar. Still others, ignoring methods of warfare which seemed completely outmoded, focused their attention upon the most devastating of late sixteenth-century instruments of war—artillery. Even when these military thinkers got mired down in the more trivial intricacies of drill regulations or were led astray by a patriotic devotion to the longbow, all had something valuable to say on a subject of great interest to their fellow countrymen.

There is hardly any doubt that these works on the art of war were widely read. Their very number—almost two hundred if one includes reprints, enlarged editions, and military newsbooks—argues for their popularity. Of course one can only guess at what sort of people read them. They would be most apt to appeal to military leaders and those who aspired to military leadership. Sir John Smythe, for instance, was convinced that quite a number of soldiers had read his first book—and that they were partly responsible for having it censored. Whitehorne and Rich had read Machiavelli; Hitchcock had read Garrard; Garrard had consulted Fourquevaux, Digges, and Styward; Styward had borrowed from Digges and Fourquevaux; Williams and Barwick had argued with Smythe. The list could be prolonged so that one wonders just how many soldiers were cast in the image of the classical-minded Fluellen and how many were, like Cassio, arithmeticians fond of "bookish theoric."

And in that age which valued the well-rounded man, scholars and gentlemen, even those who were not themselves involved in military affairs, might have been expected to thumb through some of these books. Such an introduction might have encouraged them to read more. And the average literate citizen could hardly have ignored them. The time was ripe for him to peruse such literature. Soldiers were everywhere, particularly after 1585, when men were levied to serve against the Spanish in the Low Countries. Even before that date, troops had been raised to fight the Scots, to aid the Huguenots, and to support the Dutch. Conscripts and volunteers were constantly in the public eye, going to and from the fields where they trained, or marching down to wharves where they boarded ships for destinations overseas. They were seen coming back home, too, sometimes proud and eager to tell of glowing exploits, but often as not, diseased and maimed, pitiful ghosts and shadows of men whom the wars had broken.

There is ample evidence that people were aware of these returned veterans, particularly when they became rogues, vagabonds, thieves, and beggars, for, throughout the sixteenth century, they crop up in plays and essays. As early as 1535 Robert Copland wrote, in *The Hye Way to the Spyttell Hous,* a passage that was echoed in one form or another in literature and proclamation for the next eighty years:

> Come here any of those masterless men,
>   That everywhere do go and run,
> That have served the king beyond the sea,
>   And now that they out of wages be
> They must beg, or else go bribe and steal?
>   Methink it is a great soul-heal
> To help them, till they were purveyed
>   Into some service; for, if they were arrayed,
> Some of them were proper men and tall,
>   And able to go whither they shall.[1]

John Awdeley, explaining the tricks of various rogues in *The Fraternitie of Vacabondes* (1565, 1575), describes a "courtesy-man" as one who pretends to be begging for ex-soldiers "which have come lately from the wars, and as God knoweth, have nothing to take to, being both masterless and money-less . . ." [2] Thomas Harman, author of *A Caveat or Warening for Commen Cursetors* (1567, 1573, 1592), commented that discharged soldiers, "if they be without relief of their friends, . . . will surely desperately rob and steal, and either shortly be hanged or miserably die in prison." [3] Henry Porter in his prologue to *The Pleasant History of the Two Angry Women of Abington* (1599) managed to show his scorn for "this new world's new-found beggars, mistermed soldiers" by ridiculing their method of obtaining favors.[4] The tone of this prologue is similar to Ben Jonson's description of Brainworm, the cunning servant in *Every Man in his Humour* (1601). Although it is well known to every student of Renaissance drama, the passage is well worth quoting here, so superb is it in its satirical effect. Disguised as a maimed lance-knight, Brainworm accosts Edward Kno'well and endeavors to sell him his sword, saying that he has been wounded and beggared in the service of his country. Kno'well, later discovering Brainworm's disguise, says of him:

> He had so writhen himself into the habit of one of your poor infantry, your decayed, ruinous, worm-eaten gentlemen of the round; such as have vowed to sit on the skirts of the city, let your provost and his half-dozen halberdiers do what they can; and have translated begging, out of the old hackney pace to a fine easy amble, and made it run as smooth off the tongue as a shovegrost shilling. Into the likeness of one of these reformados had he moulded himself so perfectly, observing every trick of their action, as, varying the accent, swearing with an emphasis, indeed, all with so special and exquisite grace, that, hadst thou seen him, thou wouldst have sworn he might have been sergeant-major, if not lieutenant-colonel to the regiment.[5]

This passage gives the impression that vagabond-soldiers were rather successful in their attempts at begging. Perhaps many of them were. But the words of Stumpe, the lame lieutenant in *A Larum for London* (1602), reflect a different opinion. Speaking bitterly to an Antwerp citizen concerning the lot of a soldier, Stumpe remarks:

> But let a soldier that hath spent his blood,
> Is lame'd, diseas'd, or any way distressed,
> Appeal for succour, then you look askance
> As if you knew him not; respecting more
> An hosteler, or some drudge that rakes your kennels,
> Than one that fighteth for the commonwealth.
>
> (ll. 612–17)

Looking askance was not the only method used to make begging veterans disappear. In 1591 a proclamation was issued to the effect that "the Treasurer of War is to make payment, in every port where any shall arrive with lawful passports, of sums to conduct them to the places from which they were levied." [6] The sum with which the treasurer was to provide the soldiers amounted to five shillings, a few pence more than the average weekly pay received by a private. The proclamation, however, did not have its desired effect, which was, of course, to get honest soldiers back to their homes as soon as possible so that the dishonest ones might be rounded up and punished. Justices of the peace, no doubt horrified by the sudden appearance of pitiful scarecrows in their counties, did all in their power to make the rehabilitation impossible. They had a habit of sending discharged men "from the place where they were impressed to the place where they were born, and vice versa, and refused to sign their certificates." [7] The necessity of obtaining a certificate from a justice of the peace is ridiculed in *The Life of Sir John Oldcastle* (1600):

> *Old man.* If a poor man come to a door to ask for God's sake, they ask him for a license, or a certificate from a Justice.
>
> (ll. 337–38)

The government expended more effort to bring rascals to justice than to ameliorate the pitiful condition of the honest men. The very proclamation which had been issued in 1591 to help disbanded soldiers return to their homes devoted more space to the arrest and punishment of rogues than to the care and transportation of upright men-of-arms. And more proclamations were issued. The effect was not always very great. In 1596 a Somersetshire justice wrote to the Privy Council complaining that "of wandering soldiers there are more abroad than ever were, notwithstanding Her Majesty's most gracious proclamation lately set forth for the suppressing of them." [8] By 1600, however, the situation was such that the author of *Sir John Oldcastle* could have a character remark:

> There be more stocks to set poor soldiers in,
> Than there be houses to relieve them at.
> (ll. 327–28)

Whether or not these vagabond-soldiers were successful as thieves or beggars, they were around, were observed, often made nuisances of themselves, caused the government to stir itself both in their behalf and against them, and got into literature and upon the stage. Conceivably, these men and their actions created the sort of interest in military affairs that would carry over into an interest in books more directly concerned with military problems.

Not only were these men seen and heard, or read, about. They—along with friends and relatives, merchants, seamen, and displaced Dutchmen—spread rumors. George Gascoigne wrote *The Spoyle of Antwerpe* (1576), he tells us, out of a desire to correct "the manifold light tales which have been engendered by fearful or affectionate rehearsals" and "doubtful reports." [9] Similarly, the author of *The True Reporte of the Skirmish betwene the States of Flaunders and Don Joan* (1578) complains that "many tales go, and men are desirous to know the truth." [10] The next year, Thomas Churchyard remarked in his *A Generall Rehearsall of Warres* that he wished to write of the battle at Guines, "not because I had some charge there, but for that sundry reports have been raised thereof by those that never thoroughly knew or understood the matter." [11] Thomas Digges had two pamphlets published to defend Leicester, because, he said, he felt that calumnies on Leicester were circulating and the man was "not alive to answer for himself." [12] Again, the anonymous author of *A Particuler of the Yeelding Uppe of the Towne of Zutphen* (1591) manages to convey the impression that all London was buzzing with the deeds of Vere, whose exploits had "eternized his renown and rung the fame of his name." [13] Some civilians must have turned to military literature in an effort to satisfy the curiosity and concern aroused by the sight of returned soldiers and by the tales they told.

It is almost impossible to determine the precise effect of Elizabethan military texts upon the selection of personnel, training, organization, arming, and tactics of the English army. First of all, it must be remembered that they present diverse, sometimes violently conflicting points of view. Secondly, they were published over a long period of time, during which Englishmen came into contact with the armies of the Spanish, Dutch, French, Germans, and Irish, and were strongly influenced by their ways of doing things.

But one thing at least is clear. They reflected the dramatic change which the Elizabethan army was undergoing and they no doubt helped to convince Englishmen that this change was not only inevitable, but good. For instance, Machiavelli's *The*

Arte of Warre, which dismissed the usefulness of artillery in the most cavalier fashion, was bound in the same volume with Whitehorne's discussion of the employment and value of ordnance; and this book, in turn, was succeeded by very sophisticated treatises on the science of gunnery by such eminent authors as Digges, Bourne, Barret, Smith, and others. Again, reflecting the growing preference for infantry over cavalry, these books emphasized the role of footmen on the battlefield, re-examining Roman theories and practices of warfare which in the past had been so successful. Such studies of the use of infantry were of particular value at a time when there was a dearth of horses and trained horsemen. Moreover, some of these books carefully spelled out the recommendation that shot should be substituted for the longbow, however much Smythe might protest, thereby helping to retire a weapon which, having seen its years of glory, needed to be replaced by one more modern. They also, along with letters from commanders in garrisons and in the field, made Crown and public alike aware of the need for carefully selected troops strenuously trained, adequately paid, decently lodged, and properly fed and clothed. Finally, they proved repositories of technical information which commissioned and noncommissioned officers, no matter how experienced, could not readily carry in their heads; and for the unexperienced who cared to use them, they provided a thorough education in every aspect of the art of war. One is therefore tempted to conclude that, over the years, Elizabethan military books were in part—perhaps in large part—responsible for a remarkable improvement in Elizabeth's fighting force.

Reference
Matter

Notes

CHAPTER I: THE CLASSICAL BACKGROUND

1   See especially Henry Burrows Lathrop, *Translations from the Classics into English from Caxton to Chapman* (*University of Wisconsin Studies,* No. 35; Madison, 1933).

2   Alexander Barclay, tr., Caius Sallustius Crispus, *Here Begynneth the Famous Cronycle of the Warre, Which the Romayns Had agaynst Jugurth,* Preface to the 1557 edition, sig. aiv ᵛ.

3   Thomas Proctor, *Of the Knowledge and Conducte of Warres* (1578), sig. ¶ iv ᵛ.

4   Richard Morison, tr., Sextus Julius Frontinus, *The Strategemes, Sleyghtes and Policies of Warre* (1539), "The Epistle to the Kynges Hyghnes," sig. Aiiii ᵛ.

5   Fifty years earlier Caxton had translated and published a military book which, though interesting, was not influential in the way these four books were—*The Book of Fayttes of Armes and Chyvalrye* (1489).

6   See *Onosandro Platonico dell' ottimo Capitano generale, e del suo ufficio,* tr. Fabio Cotta (Venice, 1546).

7   Peter Whitehorne, tr., Onosander's *Of the Generall Captaine, and of His Office* (1563), sig. Aii ᵛ.

8   *Dictionary of National Biography,* "Tiptoft, John."

9   So inscribed on the title page.

10 See the dedication and appendix of Arthur Golding, tr., *The Eyght Bookes of Caius Julius Caesar Conteyning His Martiall Exploytes in Gallia* (1565).

11 *Ibid.,* sigs. *4 ᵛ–*5 ʳ.

12 Sir Roger Williams, *A Briefe Discourse of Warre* (1590), p. 37 and sig. A3 ʳ.

13 Louis le Roy, *Of the Interchangeable Course of Things in the Whole World,* tr. R. Ashley (1594), pp. 73–74.

14 Matthew Sutcliffe, *The Practice, Proceedings and Lawes of Armes* (1593), pp. 44–45.

15 Sir Clement Edmondes, *Observations, upon the Five First Bookes of Caesars Commentaries, Setting Fourth the Practise of the Art Military, in the Time of the Roman Empire* (1600), Dedication.

16 Besides the first edition, printed in 1600, there were two in 1604, one in 1609, and another bearing no date.

17 Unless we are to include Roger Ascham's *Toxophilus, the Schole of Shootinge* (1545, 1571, 1589), which is a treatise on archery, the most frequently printed military works during this period were those by Edmondes, Whitehorne, and Styward.

18 Edmondes, *Observations,* p. 1.

19 *Ibid.,* p. 3.

20 Fluellen, though placed by Shakespeare in the age of Henry V, was by speech and actions characteristically Elizabethan. Undoubtedly Shakespeare had seen him and his fellows about London, possibly at the musters making caustic remarks about recruits and drill masters.

21 Edmondes, *Observations,* pp. 1–3, 26, 30, 189.

22 *Ibid.,* pp. 14, 16, 19, 23, 56–57, 69, 81–83, 107, 126–27, 149 ff., 183.

23 *Ibid.,* pp. 43, 44, 84, 119, 188, 198.

24 *Ibid.,* pp. 23, 63, 67–68.

25 *Ibid.,* p. 67.

26 John Sadler, tr., Flavius Vegetius Renatus, *The Foure Bookes of Martiall Policye* (1572), sig. C*i ᵛ.

27 Plutarch, *The Lives of the Noble Grecians & Romans,* tr. Thomas North (1579) (London: The Nonesuch Press, 1929), III, 333. Thomas Digges, of whom much will be said later, attempting in his military treatise *Stratioticos,* first published

in 1579, to prove that all military leaders should be learned men, used Alexander as one of his examples: "Was not Alexander the great trained up in philosophy under Aristotle? and had the Iliads of Homer in such veneration, that he never traveled or rested without them."—Leonard and Thomas Digges, *An Arithmeticall Militare Treatise, Named Stratioticos* (1590), p. 307.

28 From *Achilles Shield* as quoted by Lathrop, *Translations from the Classics*, p. 283.

29 Peter Betham, translator of Jacopo di Porcia's *The Preceptes of Warre* (1544), has this interesting comment to make in his dedication to the Lord Chancellor: ". . . if we call to remembrance the Greeks and Trojans, and search which of them deserved greatest praise in that long battle (among whom the feats of chivalry were most used) we shall soon see that wisdom had ever the highest praise. For Ulysseys both of Homer and other writers, was much more praised than either was Achilles or Ajax, which both in strength passed all other. For how many things were conveyed by Ulysseys' wisdom, which the puissance of Achilles, the strength of Ajax, the fierceness of Diomede could never bring to pass, nor once equal" (sig. Aiiij ᵛ).

30 Peter Whitehorne, tr., Niccolò Machiavelli, *The Arte of Warre* (1560), Dedication to Queen Elizabeth, sigs. aii ʳ and aiv ʳ.

31 *Ibid.,* fol. xj ʳ.

32 At the conclusion of the book, there is the statement, "Thus ends the book of James the Earl of Purlilie, dedicated to King Ferdinandus, in the year of our Lord. MD.xxvii."

33 Porcia, *Preceptes of Warre*, sigs. A5 ᵛ–A6 ʳ.

34 *Ibid.*

35 See Paul Ive, *The Practise of Fortification* (1589, 1597).

36 Raimond de Beccarie de Pavie, Sieur de Fourquevaux, *Instructions for the Warres,* tr. Paul Ive (1589), sigs. b ʳ⁻ᵛ.

37 *Ibid.*

38 Sir Edward Hoby, in his translation of Bernardino de Mendoza's *Theorique and Practise of Warre* (1597), sig. A4 ʳ.

39 Whitehorne's dedication to Queen Elizabeth in his translation of Machiavelli's *The Arte of Warre*, sig. aij ᵛ.

40 Thomas Styward, *The Pathwaie to Martiall Discipline* (1581), sig. Aiv ʳ.

CHAPTER II: ENGLISH MILITARY WRITERS

1 Leonard and Thomas Digges, *An Arithmeticall Militare Treatise, Named Stratioticos* (1579), "The Preface to the Reader," sig. Aiij ʳ. (Much of the material for the discussion of Thomas Digges in this chapter was originally published in my article "The Mathematical and Military Works of Thomas Digges," *Modern Language Quarterly,* VI [1945], 389–400.) *Stratioticos* was published by Thomas Digges from a manuscript written by his father, Leonard, which he had reworked and to which he had added.

2 *Ibid.,* sig. Aiij ᵛ.

3 Leonard and Thomas Digges, *A Geometrical Practise, Named Pantometria* (1591), "The Preface to the Reader," sig. [A1] ᵛ. Like *Stratioticos, Pantometria* had been begun by Leonard Digges but was reworked and completed by his son Thomas.

4 *Ibid.,* sigs. [A1] ᵛ–[A2] ʳ.

5 Digges, *Stratioticos,* Dedication, sig. Aij ʳ.

6 *Ibid.,* sigs. Aij ʳ⁻ᵛ.

7 *Ibid.*

8 *Ibid.,* "The Preface to the Reader," sig. Aij ʳ.

9 *Ibid.,* pp. 55–57.

10 *Ibid.,* p. 258.

11 *Ibid.,* pp. 62–63.

12 Digges may have had elementary training in the militia, for he speaks of "having partly by experience myself seen what extreme disorders grow and dishonors are received for want of military discipline" (*ibid.,* sig. a ʳ). It is clear, however, from the nature of the Preface, that had Digges experienced actual combat service, he would have mentioned it. The *Calendar of State Papers* does not place him with the army until 1585.

13 Digges, *Stratioticos,* "The Preface to the Reader," sig. Aiv ʳ.

14 Robert Barret, *The Theorike and Practike of Moderne Warres* (1598), p. 5.

15 Digges, *Stratioticos,* "The Preface to the Reader," sig. Aiv ᵛ.

16 Eleanor Rosenberg in her interesting *Leicester, Patron of Letters* (New York: Columbia University Press, 1955) goes so far as to state that *Stratioticos* was "a work designed to revolutionize the science of warfare" (p. 283).

17 Thomas Digges, "A brief discourse," ed. T. W. Wrighte, *Archaeologia: Miscellaneous Tracts Relating to Antiquity* (Society of Antiquaries of London, 1794), XI, 214.

18 *Ibid.,* p. 211.

19 *Ibid.,* pp. 214–22.

20 Great Britain, Public Record Office, *Calendar of State Papers, Foreign* (September 1585—May 1586), p. 213.

21 For Digges' authorship of this work, see my article, "Two Additions to the Military Bibliography of Thomas Digges," *MLQ,* XII (1951), 131–33.

22 Thomas and Dudley Digges, *Foure Paradoxes* (1604), p. 40.

23 *Ibid.,* pp. 42–43.

24 *Ibid.,* pp. 61–63.

25 *CSP, Foreign* (June 1586—March 1587), p. 172.

26 For Digges' authorship of this work, see my article, "Two Additions to the Military Bibliography of Thomas Digges," pp. 131–33.

27 Digges, *Stratioticos,* p. 66.

28 *Ibid.,* pp. 62–63.

29 John Stow, *A Survey of the Cities of London and Westminster,* ed. John Strype (1720), I, 71, 72. For a discussion of Digges' contributions to science, see Francis R. Johnson and Sanford V. Larkey, "Thomas Digges, the Copernican System, and the Idea of the Infinity of the Universe in 1576," *Huntington Library Bulletin,* V (1934), 69–117; and F. R. Johnson, *Astronomical Thought in Renaissance England* (Baltimore: Johns Hopkins Press, 1937), *passim.*

30 For an account of Rich's life, see Thomas M. Cranfill and Dorothy Hart Bruce, *Barnaby Rich, A Short Biography* (Austin: University of Texas Press, 1953).

31 See, for instance, the following non-military works: Thomas Nashe, *Pierce Pennilesse, His Supplication to the Divell* (New York: E. P. Dutton, 1934), p. 70, and *The Unfortunate Traveller* (London: Charles Wittingham, 1892), pp. 30–31; Thomas Dekker, *The Guls Horn-Book* (London: J. M. Dent & Sons, 1908), pp. 239–40; *The Overburian Characters,* ed. W. J. Paylor (Oxford: Basil Blackwell, 1936), pp. 49–50.

32 *Dictionary of National Biography,* "Rich, Barnabe." Rich's *A Right Exelent and Pleasaunt Dialogue, betwene Mercury and an English Souldier* (1574) carries a dedication to Warwick.

33   Barnabe Rich, *The Irish Hubbub or, The English Hue and Cry* (1617), sig. B2 ʳ.

34   Rich's appreciation of the value of reading is amply illustrated by the following passage from his *Allarme to England* (1578): ". . . considering that there is nothing which may be either pleasant, profitable, or necessary for man but is written in books wherein are reported the manners, conditions, governments, counsels, and affairs of every country; the deeds, acts, behavior, and manner of living of every people; the forms of sundry commonwealths, with their augmentations, and decays, and good persuasions comprehended in quick sentences; to conclude, in books and histories are actually expressed the beauty of virtue and the loathesomeness of vice . . ." (sigs. Ei ʳ⁻ᵛ).

35   Whether Rich read these authors in their original tongue, in Continental translations, or in English epitomes, it is impossible to say. He could have consulted some of them in English: William Blandy, *The Five Bookes of Hieronimo Osorius, Containing a Discussion of Civile and Christian Nobilitie* (1576); Robert Whittington, *The Thre Bookes of Tullyes Offyces* (1534, 1540), or Nicolas Grimald, *M. Tullius Ciceroe's Thre Boks of Dueties* (1553), and other works of Cicero's; Thomas Wilson, *The Three Orations of Demosthenes* (1570); John Alday (?), *A Summarie of the Antiquities Abstracted out of Plinie* (1566); Alexander Barclay, *Here Begynneth the Famous Cronycle of the Warre . . . agaynst Jugurth* (1520).

36   The following passages, the first from the *Dialogue* and the second from Whitehorne's translation of *Dell' arte della guerra,* illustrate how closely Rich imitated Machiavelli:

   "The Romans punished with death him that lacked in the watch, he that forsook the place that was given him to fight, he that carried any thing out of the camp, if any man should say he had done some worthy thing in fight and had not donȩ it, if any for fear, had cast away his weapon . . ." — Rich, *Dialogue,* sig. Fii ᵛ.

   "The Romans punished with death him that lacked in the watch, he that forsook the place that was given him to fight in, he that carried any thing, hid out of the camp, if any man should say that he had done some worthy thing in the fight and had not done it, . . . if any for fear, cast away his weapons

. . ."—Niccolò Machiavelli, *The Arte of Warre*, tr. Peter Whitehorne (1560), fol. lxxxv ᵛ.

37 Rich, *Dialogue*, sig. Diii ᵛ.
38 See Paul A. Jorgensen, "Theoretical Views of War in Elizabethan England," *Journal of the History of Ideas,* XIII (1952), 469–81.
39 Rich, *Allarme,* sig. Ai ʳ.
40 *Ibid.*
41 *Ibid.,* sig. Bii ᵛ. Rich's point of view is very similar to that expressed by early writers on the law of war. See the works of Franciscus de Victoria, Pierino Belli, Balthazar Ayala, Alberico Gentili.
42 *Ibid.,* sig. Biii ᵛ.
43 *Ibid.,* sig. Biiii ʳ.
44 *Ibid.,* sig. Biiii ᵛ.
45 *Ibid.*
46 *Ibid.,* sigs. Bv ʳ⁻ᵛ.
47 Barnabe Rich, *A Path-way to Military Practise* (1587), sig. A2 ʳ.
48 Compare the passage from *Stratioticos* on p. 20 with: "And as by the knowledge of war and exercise of arms, empires have been purchased, kingdoms enlarged, princes preserved, justice maintained, good laws protected, and the commonwealth defended, so in neglecting martial exercises and laying aside of their weapons, how many kingdoms have been brought to calamity, how many flourishing cities, sacked, beaten flat to the ground, covered over with mould, and almost worn out of memory." —Rich, *Path-way,* sig. A3 ʳ.
49 Digges, *Stratioticos,* "The Preface to the Reader," sig. Aij ʳ.
50 Rich, *Path-way,* sigs. k2 ʳ⁻ᵛ.
51 Barnabe Rich, *The Fruites of Long Experience* (1604), p. 68.
52 *Ibid.,* Dedication to Prince Henry, sig. A3 ʳ.
53 *Ibid.,* p. 17.
54 *Ibid.,* p. 18.
55 *Ibid.*
56 *Ibid.,* p. 31.
57 Rich, *Dialogue,* p. 27; see also his *Faultes Faults, and Nothing Else but Faultes* (1606), pp. 48–51.
58 Rich, *Allarme,* sig. Fi ʳ.
59 *Ibid.,* sigs. Fi ᵛ–Fiij ʳ.
60 *Ibid.,* sig. Giij ᵛ.

61 Rich, *Path-way*, sig. B ᵛ; see also *Allarme*, sig. Giiij ʳ.
62 Rich, *Fruites*, p. 6.
63 Rich, *Dialogue*, p. 98; see also *Faultes*, p. 51.
64 Rich, *Allarme*, sig. Kiij ʳ; see also *Fruites*, pp. 6–7, 33.
65 Rich, *Dialogue*, p. 113.
66 Rich, *Path-way*, sig. G4 ʳ.
67 Rich, *Dialogue*, p. 113.
68 *Ibid.*, pp. 113–15.
69 *Ibid.*, p. 47; see also *Allarme*, sig. Gi ʳ; and *Fruites*, Dedication, sig. A3 ᵛ.
70 Rich, *Dialogue*, p. 50.
71 *Ibid.*, p. 42.
72 Rich, *Allarme*, sig. Kiij ʳ; *Path-way*, sigs. D4 ʳ–E2 ᵛ; *Fruites*, pp. 29–31.
73 Rich, *Dialogue*, p. 51; *Faultes*, p. 51. See also Digges, *Foure Paradoxes* (which, as we have seen, Rich held in small esteem), pp. 2–5, 39.
74 Rich, *Faultes*, pp. 70–71.
75 Rich, *Dialogue*, p. 28; *Allarme*, sigs. Eiiij ʳ⁻ᵛ; *Path-way*, sigs. C3 ʳ⁻ᵛ. Erasmus had a deep-rooted conviction that there was "no course of life in the world more wicked or more wretched" than that of a soldier: see *The Colloquies of Desiderius Erasmus* (London: Gibbings & Co., 1900), I, 68, 69, 282, 283.
76 Rich, *Dialogue*, p. 30.
77 *Ibid.*, pp. 32–33.
78 Rich, *Path-way*, sig. B2 ᵛ.
79 *Ibid.*, sigs. B3 ᵛ–B4 ʳ.
80 *Ibid.*, sig. G4 ʳ.
81 *Ibid.*, sigs. G4 ᵛ–H ʳ; *Dialogue*, p. 84; *Allarme*, sigs. Kiij ᵛ–Kiiij ʳ.
82 Rich, *Allarme*, sig. Giiij ʳ.
83 Rich, *Fruites*, p. 13.
84 *DNB*, "Smith or Smythe, Sir John," and Anthony Wood, *Athenae Oxonienses* (2d ed.; London, 1721), I, 285. Smythe's mother, Dorothy, was the youngest daughter of Sir John Seymour and sister of the Duke of Somerset and Jane Seymour, Henry VIII's queen.
85 John Strype, ed., *Annals of the Reformation and Establishment of Religion* (1824 ed.), IV, 413.
86 Letter from Smythe to Burghley, May 20, 1590, *Original*

Letters of Eminent Literary Men, Camden Society Publications, Old Series, No. 23 (London, 1843), p. 61.

87 Maurice J. D. Cockle, *A Bibliography of Military Books up to 1642* (London: The Holland Press, 1900; reprinted 1957), p. 42.

88 Sir John Smythe, *Certain Discourses Concerning the Formes and Effects of Divers Sorts of Weapons* (1590), sig. (a) 2 ʳ.

89 *Ibid.,* sigs. *4 ʳ⁻ᵛ.

90 *Ibid.,* sigs. **3 ᵛ–***3 ʳ.

91 He was wrong—or partly wrong—on one point. The Earl of Leicester had, in the Netherlands, established, or at least published, a set of "laws and ordinances" for his troops. These were printed in England by C. Barker in 1586, four years before Smythe wrote his *Certain Discourses.*

92 Smythe, *Certain Discourses,* sigs. A2 ᵛ–A3 ʳ.

93 In the dedication to his *Instructions, Observations and Orders Mylitarie* (1595), Smythe states that there are "some other books that I have in times past composed, and do intend (God willing) hereafter to print, in case I shall see that these discourses of mine shall be accepted and allowed of according to my good intention and meaning" (sig. ¶¶¶ 4 ᵛ). One of these works "by me composed 1585, and not yet printed" was entitled *Certen Military Discourses, Arithmeticall Tables, Formes and Demonstrations to Reduce Both Horsemen and Footmen into Many Formes of Squadrons, &c.* (p. 171).

94 The dedication is dated 1594. Smythe admits culling material from his earlier work (*ibid.,* p. 101).

95 *Ibid.,* sig. ¶¶¶ 4 ᵛ.

96 *Ibid.,* sig. ¶ 2 ʳ.

97 *Ibid.,* p. 90.

98 *Ibid.,* p. 103.

99 *Ibid.,* p. 220.

100 According to accounts given by various witnesses, Smythe asked the soldiers willing to follow him to hold up their hands. He said that Thomas Seymour (who had accompanied him to the field) should be their captain; that the country was being consumed in foreign wars; that those who followed him and Seymour would not have to go outside the realm although there was a press out for 1,000 men; that 9,000 men had been foolishly confined, with the result that the

land was weakened; that 5,000 to 6,000 men had been slain near Greenwich and lay in bloody heaps; that there were traitors about the Court; that the Lord Treasurer Burghley was a traitor of traitors; and that the common people had been oppressed for a long time and would have redress and see a reformation if they would go with him.—*CSP, Domestic* (1595–1597), p. 235 *et passim*.

101   Thomas Styward, *The Pathwaie to Martiall Discipline* (1581), sigs. Aii ʳ⁻ᵛ. William Garrard states that Styward borrowed "the greatest part of his Pathway to Militarie Discipline" from Captain Francesco Ferretti, *Osservanta Militare*. See Garrard's *The Arte of Warre* (1591), p. 194.

102   Styward, *Pathwaie to Martiall Discipline*, sig. Aiv ʳ.

103   *Ibid.*

104   *Ibid.*, p. 107.

105   *Ibid.*, p. 135.

106   *Ibid.*, p. 157. Digges, of course, put the infantry first also. But he had great admiration for cavalry and thought that a captain of men-at-arms should be equal to an infantry colonel.

107   *Ibid.*, p. 27.

108   Smythe, *Certain Discourses,* sig. *2 ʳ.

109   Digges, *Stratioticos* (1590), sig. Bii ʳ. Francisco de Valdes in *The Sergeant Major*, tr. J. Thorius (1590), thinks that such arguments are sheer rationalization. He states: "For as much as the greater part of soldiers lose their time in games, love idleness, and have not from their youth either will or power to apply themselves to any virtuous exercise, wanting the due grounds of speculation, they despair that ever they shall be able to study any such art, and so to cover their exceeding fault, they scoff at the art of war, which men attain unto by study" (fol. 3 ʳ).

110   An epithet George Pettie applies to them in the preface to his translation of *The Civile Conversation of M. Steeven Guazzo* (1581), (New York: A. A. Knopf, 1925), p. 7.

111   Richard Morison, tr., Sextus Julius Frontinus, *The Strategemes, Sleyghtes and Policies of Warre* (1539), sig. Av ʳ.

112   Garrard, *Arte of Warre*, p. 64.

113   Sir Roger Williams, *A Briefe Discourse of Warre* (1590), p. 37.

114   See Digges, *Foure Paradoxes*, pp. 41 ff.

115   From the Hulton MS as quoted by L. W. Henry in "The

Earl of Essex as Strategist and Military Organizer, 1596–7," *English Historical Review,* LXVIII (1953), 370.

116 Matthew Sutcliffe, *The Practice, Proceedings, and Lawes of Armes* (1593), sig. B3 ʳ.

117 Digges, *Foure Paradoxes,* pp. 52–53.

118 Garrard, *Arte of Warre,* sig. A4 ʳ.

119 *Ibid.,* p. 1.

120 *Ibid.,* pp. 333 ff.

121 *Ibid.,* p. 169.

122 Like most writers, he confuses Fourquevaux with Du Bellay.

123 Garrard, *Arte of Warre,* p. 32.

124 *Ibid.,* p. 206.

125 *Ibid.,* p. 169.

126 Humphrey Barwick, *A Breefe Discourse Concerning the Force and Effect of All Manuall Weapons of Fire* (1594?), sig. B1 ʳ.

127 *Ibid.,* sig. B1 ᵛ.

128 *Ibid.,* sigs. B1 ᵛ–B2 ʳ.

129 *Ibid.,* sig. A4 ʳ.

130 *Ibid.,* fol. 30 ᵛ.

131 *Ibid.,* fol. 11 ʳ.

CHAPTER III: MILITARY PERSONNEL

1 Onosander, *Of the Generall Captaine, and of His Office,* tr. Peter Whitehorne (1563), p. 8.

2 Flavius Vegetius Renatus, *The Foure Bookes of Martiall Policye,* tr. John Sadler (1572), fol. 3 ʳ.

3 *Ibid.*

4 Count Jacopo di Porcia, *The Preceptes of Warre,* tr. Peter Betham (1544), sig. A6 ʳ.

5 Raimond de Beccarie de Pavie, Sieur de Fourquevaux, *Instructions for the Warres,* tr. Paul Ive (1589), p. 260.

6 Niccolò Machiavelli, *The Arte of Warre,* tr. Peter Whitehorne (1560), fols. xij ᵛ–xv ᵛ.

7 *Ibid.,* fol. xvi ᵛ.

8 Fourquevaux, *Instructions,* pp. 13, 20–21.

9 Onosander, *Of the Generall Captaine,* p. 16.

10 Leonard and Thomas Digges, *An Arithmeticall Militare Treatise, Named Stratioticos* (1590), pp. 305–6.

11 Sir John Smythe, *Certain Discourses Concerning the Formes*

and *Effects* of *Divers* *Sorts* of *Weapons* (1590), sigs. **3 ᵛ–*** ᵛ.

12 William Garrard, *The Arte of Warre* (1591), title page.
13 His military career is briefly summarized in my article, "Dr. Matthew Sutcliffe," *Philological Quarterly*, XXIII (1944), 85–86.
14 Garrard, *Arte of Warre*, pp. 335, 337–38.
15 Matthew Sutcliffe, *The Practice, Proceedings, and Lawes of Armes* (1593), pp. 38–40.
16 *Ibid.,* p. 40.
17 Garrard, *Arte of Warre*, p. 337.
18 Sutcliffe, *Lawes of Armes*, pp. 35–36.
19 Robert Barret, *The Theorike and Practike of Moderne Warres* (1598), p. 9.
20 Giles Clayton, *The Approoved Order of Martiall Discipline* (1591), p. 11.
21 Garrard, *Arte of Warre*, p. 139.
22 Barret, *Theorike,* p. 23. Cf. Digges, *Stratioticos* (1590), p. 95, and Sir Roger Williams, *A Briefe Discourse of Warre* (1590), p. 11.
23 Barret, *Theorike,* p. 23. Cf. Sutcliffe, *Lawes of Armes,* p. 61.
24 See Thomas Fenne, *Fennes Frutes* (1590), fol. 65 ᵛ.
25 Thomas Styward, *The Pathwaie to Martiall Discipline* (1581), pp. 34–35.
26 Digges, *Stratioticos* (1590), pp. 96–97.
27 *Ibid.,* p. 98.
28 *Ibid.,* pp. 79–81.
29 Sutcliffe, *Lawes of Armes,* pp. 63–64.
30 *Ibid.,* p. 66.
31 Barret, *Theorike,* pp. 8–9.
32 Garrard, *Arte of Warre,* pp. 30–31. These points, without elaboration, are also found in Styward, *Pathwaie to Martiall Discipline,* pp. 46–47.
33 Garrard, *Arte of Warre,* p. 1.
34 *Ibid.,* pp. 11–14.
35 Thomas Smith, *The Arte of Gunnerie* (1600), sigs. Aii ʳ⁻ᵛ.
36 John Hester's dedication to Essex in his translation of Joseph Du Chesne (Josephus Quercetanus), *The Sclopotarie of J. Quercetanus, or His Booke Containing the Cure of Woundes Received by Shot of Gunne,* sig. A2 ᵛ.
37 Garrard, *Arte of Warre,* sig. A2 ᵛ.

38 Sutcliffe, *Lawes of Armes,* sig. B2 ʳ.

39 *Extremeties Urging the Lord General Veare to Offer the Late Anti-parle with the Arch-duke Albertus* (1602), p. 16.

40 *Newes from Ostend* (1601), sig. A4 ᵛ.

41 Sir Robert Naunton, *Fragmenta regalia,* p. 41, as quoted in *The Commentaries of Sir Francis Vere* (1657), sig. A6 ʳ.

42 Emanuel van Meteren, *A True Discourse Historicall of the Succeeding Governours in the Netherlands* (1602), pp. 27–28, 32.

43 However, Digges may not have been a very circumspect crusader. Edward Burnham, writing to Walsingham on April 2, 1587, said: "The muster-master and the auditor . . . run a violent course; I think no more than their instructions do guide them, but it might be done with more moderation. It is a great authority to the muster-master that the treasure cannot be disbursed without his warrant. He was pontifical enough before; this makes him more so."—Great Britain, Public Record Office, *Calendar of State Papers, Foreign* (April–December, 1587), p. 3.

44 Edward Grimestone, *A Generall Historie of the Netherlands* (1609), p. 955.

45 *Ibid.,* p. 934.

46 See *A Breife and True Report of the Proceedings of the Earle of Leycester for the Reliefe of Sluce* (1590), *passim.*

47 Digges vouches for his courage in *A Briefe Report of the Militarie Services Done in the Low Countries by the Erle of Leicester* (1587), *passim.* And Leicester's own letters to Walsingham and Burghley indicate a definite interest in the condition of his men. See *Correspondence of Robert Dudley, Earl of Leycester, during his government of the Low Countries, 1585 and 1586,* Camden Society Publications, Old Series, No. 27 (London, 1844), *passim.*

48 Roger Ascham, *The Scholemaster,* ed. Edward Arber (Westminster: A Constable & Co., 1903), p. 54.

49 See Paul A. Jorgensen, *Shakespeare's Military World* (Berkeley and Los Angeles: University of California Press, 1956), *passim,* and G. Geoffrey Langsam, *Martial Books and Tudor Verse* (New York: King's Crown Press, 1951), *passim.*

50 The best contemporary account of these abuses may be found in Smythe, *Certain Discourses,* sigs. *** ᵛ–***2 ʳ. They are also impassionedly repeated in a letter from Smythe to

Lord Burghley, dated May 20, 1590—see *Original Letters of Eminent Literary Men,* Camden Society Publications, Old Series, No. 23 (London, 1843), pp. 56–62. See also Sir Henry Knyvett, *The Defence of the Realme* (1596) (Oxford: Clarendon Press, 1906), pp. 56–57; and Thomas and Dudley Digges, *Foure Paradoxes* (1604), p. 20. *The Calendar of State Papers (Foreign, Domestic,* and *Ireland)* for the age of Elizabeth and *The Salisbury Manuscripts* are full of letters despairing of the abuses concurrent with the pocketing of "dead pays."

51 Note especially an interesting letter from William Saxey, Chief Justice of Munster, to the Earl of Essex, dated October 9, 1599, *CSP, Ireland* (April 1599—February 1600), p. 182.

52 *Acts of the Privy Council,* New Series, XIV (1586–1587), 374.

53 *CSP, Ireland* (1601–1603), p. 178.

54 Letter from Anthony Reynolds to Sir Robert Cecil, November 22, 1601, *CSP, Ireland* (1601–1603), pp. 176–78.

55 *Ibid.* (April 1599—February 1600), p. 248 and *passim.*

56 *Ibid.,* pp. 192–93.

57 *Ibid.,* p. 212.

58 Smythe to Burghley, *Letters of Eminent Literary Men,* p. 50.

59 Smythe, *Certain Discourses,* sig. ***2 ͬ.

60 Knyvett, *Defence of the Realme,* pp. 30–31.

61 Digges, *Foure Paradoxes,* p. 53.

62 *Ibid.,* p. 81.

63 He places captains among others who "do wholly bestow themselves upon pleasure, and that pleasure they divide . . . either into gaming, following of harlots, drinking, or seeing a play." See *Pierce Penilesse His Supplication to the Divell,* in *The Works of Thomas Nashe,* ed. Ronald B. McKerrow (Oxford: Basil Blackwell, 1958), I, 212.

64 Thomas Dekker, *The Devils Answer to Pierce Pennylesse,* in *The Complete Works of Thomas Dekker,* ed. Alexander B. Grosart (The Huth Library: London, 1885), II, 96.

65 Barnabe Rich, *Allarme to England* (1578), sig. **1 ͬ.

66 Williams, *Briefe Discourse,* p. 7.

67 Barret, *Theorike,* p. 7.

68 *Ibid.*

69 *CSP, Ireland* (April 1599—February 1600), p. 351.

70 *Ibid.*

71 Geoffrey Gates, *The Defence of Militarie Profession* (1579), p. 43.
72 *Ibid.*
73 Rich, *Allarme,* sigs. Ai ʳ⁻ᵛ.
74 Sutcliffe, *Lawes of Armes,* pp. 62–63.
75 Barret, *Theorike,* p. 7, and Barnabe Rich, *A Right Exelent and Pleasaunt Dialogue, betwene Mercury and an English Souldier* (1574), sigs. G6 ʳ–G7 ʳ.
76 Sutcliffe, *Lawes of Armes,* p. 63.
77 Gates, *Defence,* pp. 45–46.
78 *CSP, Domestic* (1547–1580), pp. 224, 226.
79 *I Henry IV,* IV, ii.
80 Historical Manuscripts Commission, *Calendar of the Manuscripts of the Marquis of Salisbury,* IV, 4–5. Smythe makes a similar statement in his *Certain Discourses,* sigs. *** ᵛ–A ʳ, adding, however, that rogues "were levied in the city of London by commission, and . . . in one year . . . in other shires."
81 *Salisbury Manuscripts,* IV, 15–18.
82 *CSP, Foreign* (September 1585—May 1586), p. 437.
83 *Leycester Correspondence,* pp. 166–67.
84 *Ibid.,* p. 285.
85 *Ibid.,* pp. 338–39.
86 *CSP, Foreign* (June 1586—March 1587), p. 385.
87 Smythe to Burghley, *Letters of Eminent Literary Men,* p. 51.
88 *Ibid.*
89 *CSP, Ireland* (April 1599—February 1600), pp. 483–84.

CHAPTER IV: INFANTRY

1 Leonard and Thomas Digges, *An Arithmeticall Militare Treatise, Named Stratioticos* (1590), p. 258; Giles Clayton, *The Approoved Order of Martiall Discipline* (1591), pp. 3–4. Sir John Norris' commission as leader of Elizabeth's expeditionary force to the Low Countries in 1585 was that of colonel general. Because of special circumstances—mainly, it would appear, because the Earl of Leicester had not yet arrived to assume his duties as Lord Lieutenant General—Norris for a time also commanded the artillery and briefly had under him as well the treasurer-at-war, the provost marshal, the muster-master, and sundry other "head officers of the field."

See Historical Manuscripts Commission, *Manuscripts of Lord de L'Isle and Dudley*, III, xxxii. Later, Norris was given a temporary commission "to conduct and command the troops, horse and foot," a commission that caused bickering among a number of high-ranking officers in the field. See Great Britain, Public Record Office, *Calendar of State Papers, Foreign* (June 1586—March 1587), p. 127 and *passim*. The colonel general could have cavalry attached to his command. In Ireland in 1598 Sir Urian Leigh was chief commander of the horse company under the colonel general (*CSP, Ireland* [January 1598—March 1599], p. 322).

2 Each captain could choose his own colors. According to Robert Barret, "if the service be for the field, he makes it somewhat less, the lighter and easier to be handled; but in garrisons it is made somewhat larger, because it is most often camped upon the wall."—*The Theorike and Practike of Moderne Warres* (1598), p. 20.

3 Barret, *Theorike,* and Digges, *Stratioticos* (1590), *passim*. See also *Mss. of Lord de L'Isle and Dudley*, III, xxxii, and *CSP, Foreign* (June 1586—March 1587), *passim*.

4 Digges, *Stratioticos* (1590), p. 261. That this was a theory not always held to in practice can be illustrated by a letter from Dr. Thomas Doyley to Burghley, dated Utrecht, June 24, 1586. The writer complains that, although Sir John Norris "incessantly urges" that the army be sent into the field "to make head against the enemy," his advice is ignored and "contrary advice by those which know no wars" is heeded (*CSP, Foreign* [June 1586—March 1587], p. 49). This is confirmed by Sir Edward Norris (*ibid.*, p. 173). Whether or not Elizabeth and her Privy Councilors harkened to these specific complaints, it is interesting to note that in the Queen's "Articles of Instructions to be put in execution by the Lord Willoughby," dated December [24?], 1587, is the statement that since "it has always been the custom with princes to appoint some persons of judgment and experience as Counsellors of war to assist the General," she is nominating four officers to give Willoughby "counsel and advice." These men were Sir William Russell (at various times Governor of Flushing and captain of both horsebands and footbands), Sir William Reade (lieutenant colonel general and sergeant major general), Captain Nicholas Errington

(sometime master of ordnance and commander of a footband),
and Thomas Wilford (likewise a sergeant major). See *CSP,
Foreign* (April–December 1587), p. 463.

5 Barret, *Theorike*, p. 93.
6 Digges, *Stratioticos* (1590), p. 229; William Garrard, *The
Arte of Warre* (1591), p. 171.
7 Digges, *Stratioticos* (1590), p. 228.
8 *Ibid.,* pp. 225–26.
9 *Ibid.,* p. 120.
10 Barret, *Theorike*, p. 93.
11 Digges, *Stratioticos* (1590), p. 228. Clayton states (*Martiall
Discipline,* p. 10) that the corporals of the field were "either
to be captains of experience, which are discharged of their
companies, or to prefer such lieutenants as be of good
government and knowledge, well experienced in these
exercises of martiality, for that they are to discharge the head
governors of the field of many travails and pains." Elizabeth's
expeditionary force to the Low Countries in 1585 contained
two corporals of the field. See *Mss. of Lord de L'Isle and
Dudley,* III, xxxii.
12 Thomas Styward, *The Pathwaie to Martiall Discipline* (1581),
p. 30.
13 Digges, *Stratioticos* (1579), p. 106; *Stratioticos* (1590),
p. 229.
14 Sir Roger Williams, *A Briefe Discourse of Warre* (1590), p. 8.
15 Matthew Sutcliffe, *The Practice, Proceedings, and Lawes of
Armes* (1593), p. 60.
16 Digges, *Stratioticos* (1590), pp. 100–101. The Commission to
the Earl of Cumberland in October 1597 reads: ". . . we have
made choice of you, and do by these presents give you
authority to make choice and constitute such principal officers,
as well by sea as land, and also to appoint such meet captains
and other persons whom you shall depute thereunto by
writing under your hand, to take up, levy, assemble, arm, and
furnish with all manner of victuals and warlike provision
whatsoever, within any part of this realm, such and so many
of our loving subjects as are fit and apt for the war to serve
by sea and land, as shall be willing thereto. . . ."—*The Eger-
ton Papers,* Camden Society Publications, Old Series, No. 12
(London, 1840), pp. 263–64. Apparently the Queen was
sometimes jealous of her prerogative or the prerogative of

members of her Privy Council to appoint all officers, regardless of rank, for we find Sir John Norris, colonel general in the Low Countries, writing to Walsingham in 1587 requesting that the latter procure a company for one of his veteran captains whose band had been discharged (*CSP, Foreign* [April–December 1587], p. 15). Lord Willoughby, Lord General of the Queen's forces in the Low Countries, agreed with Elizabeth's feelings on this matter. On July 4, 1588, he wrote to Burghley "that every man according to his worth for his deserts should be recommended from the general and Council of wars where he serves and the honor of the gift and disposing of the place left to Her Majesty only."— *CSP, Foreign* (July–December 1588), p. 9. These statements are at variance with Oman's that "the Lord-Lieutenant designated the subordinate officers from captain downward." See Sir Charles Oman, *A History of the Art of War in the Sixteenth Century* (New York: E. P. Dutton, 1937), p. 374. I suspect that the Lord Lieutenant did a certain amount of appointing when war was not imminent and great numbers of men were not needed.

17 Digges, *Stratioticos* (1590), pp. 100–101.

18 *Ibid.,* and Garrard, *Arte of Warre,* pp. 73–78.

19 Garrard, *Arte of Warre,* p. 152.

20 *Ibid.* Garrard's interest in the special treatment of the lieutenants extraordinary may readily be explained by the fact, as he recounts on page 154, that he had held such a post "under my colonel, the Baron of Sheverau, in service of Don John of Austria, and the Prince of Parma."

21 Digges, *Stratioticos* (1590), p. 102.

22 *CSP, Ireland* (January 1598—March 1599), p. 279.

23 Digges, *Stratioticos* (1590), p. 95.

24 Sutcliffe, *Lawes of Armes,* p. 61. In the Orders for the Musters, March 15, 1589/90, captains were instructed "to have an especial care to make choice of able and meet men to serve under them as soldiers, which they shall sort to their armor and weapon according to the stature of their bodies."— Historical Manuscripts Commission, *Calendar of the Manuscripts of the Marquis of Salisbury,* IV, 15–18.

25 Digges, *Stratioticos* (1590), pp. 95, 101.

26 *Ibid.,* p. 95.

27 *Ibid.,* p. 98. The notion of shooting for wagers with harque-

buse—or target practice—was an admirable one, for one cannot learn without trial, and will grow rusty without practice; but in actuality the soldier often had to pay for such activity. Thomas, Lord Buckhurst, for instance, urged in 1600 that "the expense of powder by the soldier, except in days of service, be at the soldier's charge," adding that such was the rule until the Earl of Essex became Lord Lieutenant in Ireland. However, Lord Mountjoy, in the same month and year, requested that "the Lord Deputy have power to give allowance of powder, lead, and match unto the soldier for his signal and training days of service." Buckhurst was Lord High Treasurer of England and Mountjoy was Lord Deputy of Ireland. See *CSP, Ireland* (April 1599—February 1600), pp. 380 and 488.

28 Digges, *Stratioticos* (1590), p. 97.

29 *Ibid.,* p. 96. Clayton describes the reason thus: ". . . for the practice of the enemy is to set suddenly upon such men so laden with baggages, a great hindrance to the soldier and an encouragement to the enemy."—*Martiall Discipline,* p. 29.

30 Digges, *Stratioticos* (1590), p. 96.

31 *Ibid.,* pp. 93–94. Digges saw no great use for this officer. Not only was the rank unknown to the Romans but the Spanish did not employ it. According to Digges, "if the ensign and other officers sufficiently knew their duty," the lieutenant could readily be done away with. See *Stratioticos* (1590), pp. 94–95.

32 *Ibid.,* pp. 93–95.

33 *Ibid.,* pp. 91–93.

34 *Ibid.,* and p. 108.

35 *Ibid.,* pp. 83–85.

36 According to Sir Roger Williams, some English bands in the Low Countries numbered 200 (*Briefe Discourse,* p. 59). Clayton favors this number of men (*Martiall Discipline,* p. 12). The expeditionary force which Elizabeth sent to the Low Countries in 1585 had foot companies composed of 150 men each, except for one under Colonel Thomas Morgan, which mustered at 200 men (*Mss. of Lord de L'Isle and Dudley,* III, xxxii). In 1595 in Ireland, footmen were divided into companies of 50, 60, 100, and 120 men. See "A note of all the Footmen in Ireland and of their several places of Garrison," *Calendar of the Carew Manuscripts* (1589–1600),

p. 128. Garrard states that the colonel should make up companies of "300 for a band, which number is most convenient quantity; for by reducing companies to a less number, as in our times is used, specially among the Spaniards and Italians, and well followed by the French and our English, they may rather carry the name of lieutenants and centurions, than bear the title of captains."—*Arte of Warre,* p. 73. Sir John Smythe in *Instructions, Observations and Orders Mylitarie* (1595) goes Garrard one better and raises the number in a company to 500 (p. 100). The larger companies were not put into the field in Elizabeth's time, but at least Humphrey Barwick, author of *A Breefe Discourse, Concerning the Force and Effect of All Manuall Weapons of Fire* (1594?), would not appear to understand this. He writes that footbands should be of "divers numbers," depending on the ability of the captains and the service to be done (fol. 6 ᵛ).

37 Oman, *History of the Art of War,* p. 379. These proportions differ from Spanish proportions which, according to Luis Gutierrez de la Vega in *A Compendious Treatise, Entitled De Re Militari* (1582), were one-third shot to two-thirds pike (fol. 6 ʳ).

38 Oman, *History of the Art of War,* p. 381.

39 Emanuel van Meteren, *A True Discourse Historicall of the Succeeding Governours in the Netherlands* (1602), p. 47.

40 *Mss. of Lord de L'Isle and Dudley,* III, xxx–xxxvi.

41 *Ibid.,* pp. xxxii–xxxiii.

42 Sir John Smythe, *Certain Discourses Concerning the Formes and Effects of Divers Sorts of Weapons* (1590), fols. 6 ʳ, 9 ʳ. Humphrey Barwick would vary the number of men per regiment from 3,000 to 1,000, depending upon the ability of the colonel in command (*Manuall Weapons,* fol. 7 ᵛ).

43 *CSP, Ireland* (April 1599—February 1600), p. 113.

44 Niccolò Machiavelli, *The Arte of Warre,* tr. Peter Whitehorne (1560), fol. xxij ʳ; Sutcliffe, *Lawes of Armes,* p. 187.

45 Garrard, *Arte of Warre,* p. 214.

46 Barwick, *Manuall Weapons,* fol. 23 ʳ. George Silver, thinking in terms of hand-to-hand combat, calls for a short pike only eight or nine feet long, feeling that such short weapons can, by crossing and uncrossing, "safely pass home to the place where he may strike or thrust him that has the long

weapon, in the head, face, or body at his pleasure."— *Paradoxes of Defence* (1599) p. 29.

47 Smythe, *Certain Discourses*, fols. 4 ᵛ–5 ʳ.

48 *Ibid.*, fol. 5 ʳ. Sutcliffe states: "The pike I would have, if it might be, of Spanish ash, . . ."—*Lawes of Armes*, p. 187.

49 Jacob de Gheyn, *The Exercise of Armes* (The Hague, 1607), sigs. a ʳ ff.

50 *Ibid.* See also Garrard, *Arte of Warre*, p. 229.

51 Garrard, *Arte of Warre*, p. 229.

52 *Ibid.*, p. 54; Williams, *Briefe Discourse*, p. 43; Barret, *Theorike*, p. 33. Barret, quoting from the Spanish, calls the pike "the queen and mistress of weapons."

53 Sutcliffe, *Lawes of Armes*, pp. 185–86.

54 Smythe, *Certain Discourses*, fols. 3 ᵛ–4 ʳ.

55 Silver, *Paradoxes of Defence*, sigs. A5 ʳ⁻ᵛ. Silver waxes eloquent in his defense of the short sword, pointing out that "our forefathers were wise, though our age account them foolish, valiant though we repute them cowards. They found out the true defense for their bodies in short weapons by their wisdom. They defended themselves and subdued their enemies with those weapons with their valor." He then wisely informs his readers that in battles, there is no room to draw long weapons, and even if drawn, what could be done with them? "Can they pierce [the enemy's] corselet with the point? Can they unlace his helmet, unbuckle his armor, hew asunder their pikes . . . ?" (sigs. A4 ʳ–A5 ᵛ). Apparently captains liked the rapier; at least they carried rapiers in Ireland at the turn of the century. Barwick feels that the blade should be a yard long (*Manuall Weapons*, fol. 23 ʳ). Sir John Dowdall noted that English soldiers in Ireland preferred "a scalde [*i.e.*, scurvy] rapier before a good sword." —*Carew Mss.* (1589–1600), p. 354.

56 Smythe, *Certain Discourses*, fols. 4 ʳ f. Barwick perfers a dagger with a ten- to twelve-inch blade, and gives the pikeman a pistol besides (*Manuall Weapons*, fol. 23 ʳ).

57 Raimond de Beccarie de Pavie, Sieur de Fourquevaux, *Instructions for the Warres*, tr. Paul Ive (1589), p. 27.

58 Williams, *Briefe Discourse*, p. 45. Garrard thinks that "if every shot had . . . at his back a light leather or Venetian target . . . , they would do great good service" (*Arte of Warre*, p. 171); and Robert Barret feels that every band of one

hundred men should contain two or three targets (*Theorike,* p. 27).

59 Letter from Dawtry to Cecil, February 9, 1601, *CSP, Ireland* (November 1600—July 1601), p. 183.

60 Fourquevaux, *Instructions,* pp. 24–27.

61 Smythe, *Certain Discourses,* fol. 3 ˢ.

62 Gheyn, *Exercise of Armes, passim.*

63 See *CSP, Ireland* (November 1600—July 1601), pp. 113, 183.

64 Digges, *Stratioticos* (1590), p. 81. Barwick would have halberdiers and billmen armed alike, with "burgonets, cuirasses with tasses and pouldrons, and no vambrases."—*Manuall Weapons,* fol. 23 ˢ.

65 Williams, *Briefe Discourse,* p. 45. In Elizabethan times, a score was 20 paces or yards.

66 H. C. B. Rogers, *Weapons of the British Soldier* (London: Seeley Service & Co., 1960), p. 19.

67 *Carew Mss.* (1589–1600), p. 40.

68 Williams, *Briefe Discourse,* p. 44.

69 *Ibid.,* pp. 44–45.

70 Machiavelli, *Arte of Warre,* fol. xxij ˢ. Barwick remarks: "I wish no halberds into the hands of any that has no skill to use the same, for it is a weapon that can abide no blows, as the bill will do, but yet in the hands of officers, and such as have skill how to use the same, it is a very good weapon, . . ."—*Manuall Weapons,* fol. 23 ˢ.

71 Williams, *Briefe Discourse,* p. 45.

72 Gheyn, *Exercise of Armes, passim.*

73 *Ibid.*

74 Smythe, *Certain Discourses,* fol. 16 ˢ. Barwick points up this confusion by stating: "It is supposed by many that the weapon called commonly a caliver is another thing than a harquebuse, whereas in truth it is not, but only a harqubuse, saving that it is of a greater circuit or bullet than the other is of . . ."—*Manuall Weapons,* fol. 8 ˢ.

75 Smythe, *Certaine Discourses,* fol. 5 ˢ.

76 *Ibid.,* fols. 5 ˢ and 16 ˢ.

77 *Ibid.,* fol. 6 ˢ.

78 *Ibid.*

79 Barnabe Rich, *A Right Exelent and Pleasaunt Dialogue,*

betwene Mercury and an English Souldier (1574), sig. Hiiii ʳ.

80 Barwick, *Manuall Weapons,* fol. 17 ᵛ.

81 Smythe, *Certain Discourses,* fol. 15 ᵛ; Barwick, *Manuall Weapons,* fols. 16 ᵛ–17 ʳ.

82 Barwick, *Manuall Weapons,* fol. 4 ᵛ.

83 *Ibid.,* fols. 8 ʳ⁻ᵛ.

84 Smythe, *Certain Discourses,* fols. 18 ʳ–19 ʳ.

85 *Ibid.,* fol. 18 ʳ.

86 *Carew Mss.* (1589–1600), p. 20.

87 Letter, January 2, 1600, from Sir John Dowdall to Sir Robert Cecil, *ibid.,* p. 354. Sir John Smythe notes that the musket "was first used in Italy above 60 years past [*i.e.,* about 1530] . . . and at that time they were employed for defense of places fortified, as also out of trenches against places fortified being besieged."—*Certain Discourses,* fol. 13 ᵛ.

88 Smythe, *Certain Discourses,* fol. 14 ʳ.

89 Williams, *Briefe Discourse,* p. 41.

90 Letter, January 2, 1600, from Sir John Dowdall to Sir Robert Cecil, *Carew Mss.* (1589–1600), p. 354.

91 "Ordinances to be Observed during the Wars in Ireland," *Carew Mss.* (1589–1600), p. 366.

92 Barwick, *Manuall Weapons,* fol. 7 ᵛ.

93 Williams, *Briefe Discourse,* p. 19. Barret, much impressed by the Spanish method of organization, specifically states that there should be 25 muskets for every 100 men (*Theorike,* p. 27).

94 Williams, *Briefe Discourse,* pp. 42–43.

95 *Ibid.,* p. 41.

96 Barwick, *Manuall Weapons,* fol. 23 ᵛ; Williams, *Briefe Discourse,* p. 41.

97 Williams, *Briefe Discourse,* p. 41.

98 *Ibid.,* pp. 42–43.

99 Barwick, *Manuall Weapons,* fol. 23 ᵛ.

100 Williams, *Briefe Discourse,* p. 42. Barret agrees (*Theorike,* p. 33).

101 Williams, *Briefe Discourse,* pp. 40–41.

102 Barwick, *Manuall Weapons,* fol. 10 ᵛ.

103 Williams, *Briefe Discourse,* p. 41.

104 For a clear and detailed description of the movements re-

quired by elements of the Roman legion, see F. E. Adcock, *The Roman Art of War under the Republic* (Cambridge, Mass.: Harvard University Press, 1940), pp. 8–11.

105 Garrard, *Arte of Warre*, p. 197; Digges, *Stratioticos* (1590), p. 320.

106 Garrard, *Arte of Warre*, pp. 192, 197; Digges, *Stratioticos* (1579), p. 177. Bernardino de Mendoza agrees that the fight should not be begun by engaging all the squadrons, in the *Theorique and Practise of Warre*, tr. Sir Edward Hoby (1597), p. 109. This gradual engagement of troops was the Order of the Day at Armagh, August 14, 1598. See *CSP, Ireland* (January 1598—March 1599), p. 253.

107 Garrard, *Arte of Warre*, pp. 192 ff.

108 *Ibid.,* p. 170.

109 Barret, *Theorike*, p. 43.

110 Garrard, *Arte of Warre*, p. 171.

111 *Ibid.,* p. 170.

112 *Ibid.,* p. 171.

113 *Ibid.,* p. 209.

114 Mendoza, *Theorique and Practise of Warre*, p. 108.

115 *Ibid.,* p. 169.

116 Smythe, *Instructions*, p. 156.

117 Mendoza, *Theorique and Practise of Warre*, p. 108.

118 The account of this unfortunate occurrence is given in a declaration to Lord Justices Loftus and Gardner, the Earl of Ormonde, and the rest of the Council by Captains Ferdinando and George Kingsmill, August 23, 1598. See *CSP, Ireland* (January 1598—March 1599), p. 242. See also Cyril Falls, *Elizabeth's Irish Wars* (London: Methuen & Co., 1950), p. 217.

119 Garrard, *Arte of Warre*, p. 169.

120 *Ibid.,* p. 191.

121 *Ibid.*

122 *Ibid.,* p. 212.

123 Smythe, *Instructions*, pp. 24–25.

124 Garrard, *Arte of Warre*, p. 210.

125 Smythe, *Instructions*, p. 25.

126 *Ibid.,* p. 23.

127 *Ibid.,* p. 25.

128 Garrard, *Arte of Warre*, p. 219.

129 Smythe, *Instructions*, p. 26.

130 *Ibid.,* pp. 26–27. According to Smythe, a squadron consisting only of pikes, which the Italians and Spanish "have . . . altogether used of late years," was far inferior to a squadron of pikes with battleaxes or halberdiers in the middle—a Swiss formation which he had seen in France (*ibid.,* pp. 62–63). He knew full well, of course, that certain military men—those that "do regard the new fashions and fancies of the disordered and corrupted militia that of late years in divers civil wars have crept into Christendom"—would not approve of his theory. But he dismisses them by saying that he is "not carried with new fashions and fancies, but with the observations of that which I have read, has been in use and observed by divers brave nations in many ages, as also by mine own hearing the opinions of divers great captains, colonels and sergeants majors of divers warlike nations, some of late years dead, and some yet alive; and therewithall by that which I have seen and observed myself, . . ." (*ibid.,* p. 90).

131 Williams, *Briefe Discourse,* p. 45.

132 Barret, *Theorique,* p. 4.

133 Barwick, *Manuall Weapons,* fol. 7 ᵛ; Barret, *Theorike,* p. 4.

134 Smythe, *Instructions,* p. 27.

135 Thomas and Dudley Digges, *Foure Paradoxes* (1604), pp. 52–53.

136 *Ibid.*

137 Smythe, *Instructions,* p. 44.

138 Mendoza, *Theorique and Practise of Warre,* pp. 50–51.

139 Smythe, *Instructions,* pp. 44–45.

140 *Ibid.,* p. 29.

141 *Ibid.,* p. 30.

142 *Ibid.,* pp. 31–34.

CHAPTER V: CAVALRY

1 Sir Charles Oman very briefly discusses this dearth of cavalry in *A History of the Art of War in the Sixteenth Century* (New York: E. P. Dutton, 1937), pp. 289 and 333.

2 Bernardino de Mendoza, *Theorique and Practise of Warre,* tr. Sir Edward Hoby (1597), p. 54.

3 Matthew Sutcliffe, *The Practice, Proceedings, and Lawes of Armes* (1593), p. 185.

4 Great Britain, Public Record Office, *Calendar of State Papers,*

Foreign (September 1585—May 1586), pp. 5, 31, 112; *Calendar of State Papers, Ireland* (January 1598—March 1599), pp. 399 and 403.

5   Robert Barret, *The Theorike and Practike of Moderne Warres* (1598), p. 141; Leonard and Thomas Digges, *An Arithmeticall Militare Treatise, Named Stratioticos* (1590), pp. 262 ff.; William Garrard, *The Arte of Warre* (1591), pp. 225 ff.; Mendoza, *Theorique, passim.*

6   Barret, *Theorike,* p. 139.

7   *CSP, Foreign* (June 1586—March 1587), p. 110.

8   Historical Manuscripts Commission, *Manuscripts of Lord de L'Isle and Dudley,* III, xxxiii.

9   Digges, *Stratioticos* (1590), p. 265; Garrard, *Arte of Warre,* p. 225.

10 Under Charles I—perhaps even earlier, under Elizabeth and James—the ranks of general and lieutenant general both appear, the latter being second in command to the former. See John Cruso, *Militarie Instructions for the Cavallerie* (1632) for chapters devoted to these two ranks. In May 1587 two different ranks of cavalry generals are listed in the Low Countries: the cornet general and general of the horse. See "A note of such forces as may be drawn into the field," *CSP, Foreign* (April–December 1587), p. 82.

11 Barret, *Theorike,* p. 139. Garrard states that he must be a "personage of singular courage, industry and experience."— *Arte of Warre,* p. 225.

12 Fourquevaux gives a list of cavalry officers for the ideal French army, but although his work, as we have seen in a previous chapter, was translated into English and undoubtedly had in certain areas a definite influence on Elizabeth's army, the list has only a remote relationship to English horse units. See Raimond de Beccarie de Pavie, Sieur de Fourquevaux, *Instructions for the Warres,* tr. Paul Ive (1589), p. 61.

13 Cruso, *Cavallerie,* pp. 1–15, and Robert Ward, *Anima'dversions of Warre* (1639), pp. 277 ff. Digges—and later Garrard, who gets his information in this particular instance, as he does in some others, from Digges—implies that there were other officers and noncommissioned officers among the horse by speaking of "certain of the chief of his [*i.e.,* the captain's] band." See Digges, *Stratioticos* (1590), p. 266, and Garrard, *Arte of Warre,* p. 231. Barret notes the "cornet," which

he states should be carried over the lancers, while the ensign should be carried over the men-at-arms, and the guidon over the shot-on-horseback (*Theorike,* p. 141). Cruso does not make this division. Giles Clayton in *The Approoved Order of Martial Discipline* (1591) mentions the guidon in connection with "lances, light-horse, or carbines" (p. 26).

14 Digges, *Stratioticos* (1590), p. 263; Garrard, *Arte of Warre,* p. 225.

15 Garrard, *Arte of Warre,* p. 227. Barret agrees (*Theorike,* p. 144).

16 Cruso, *Cavallerie,* p. 4.

17 Garrard, *Arte of Warre,* p. 227; Digges, *Stratioticos* (1590), p. 262; Cruso, *Cavallerie,* pp. 3–5.

18 Digges, *Stratioticos* (1590), p. 262; Garrard, *Arte of Warre,* p. 225.

19 Cruso, *Cavallerie,* p. 9.

20 Garrard, *Arte of Warre,* pp. 225–26.

21 *Ibid.,* p. 225. However, some horsemen supplied to the army were "the worst keepers of horses and the worst riders that were ever found out."—*CSP, Ireland* (November 1600— July 1601), p. 182.

22 Barret, *Theorike,* p. 143.

23 Humphrey Barwick, *A Breefe Discourse, Concerning the Force and Effect of All Manuall Weapons of Fire* (1594?), fol. 24 ͬ.

24 Cruso, *Cavallerie,* preface "To the Reader," sig. A3 ͬ.

25 *Ibid.,* Chapters XXVI–XXXII.

26 *Mss. of Lord de L'Isle and Dudley,* III, xxxiv.

27 *CSP, Foreign* (September 1585—May 1586), p. 25.

28 Sir J. W. Fortescue, *History of the British Army* (London: Macmillan and Co., 1910), I, 155.

29 *Calendar of the Carew Manuscripts* (1589–1600), p. 365.

30 Cruso, *Cavallerie,* p. 30.

31 *Shakespeare's England* (Oxford: Clarendon Press, 1917), I, 137; Cruso, *Cavallerie,* p. 29.

32 Barwick, *Manuall Weapons,* fol. 22 ͮ. Cruso suggests it might be wise to have two pistols (*Cavallerie,* p. 29).

33 Barret, *Theorike,* p. 142.

34 *Shakespeare's England,* I, 137.

35 Cruso, *Cavallerie,* pp. 36–37.

36 Mendoza, *Theorique,* p. 55.

37 Cruso, *Cavallerie,* p. 36.
38 Barret, *Theorike,* p. 142.
39 *Ibid.*
40 *Ibid.,* p. 141.
41 Cruso, *Cavallerie,* p. 29.
42 Sir John Smythe, *Certain Discourses Concerning the Formes and Effects of Divers Sorts of Weapons* (1590), fol. 3 ʳ.
43 Barret, *Theorike,* p. 142; see also Sir Roger Williams, *A Briefe Discourse of Warre* (1590), p. 33; Cruso, *Cavallerie,* p. 28.
44 Barwick, *Manuall Weapons,* fol. 22 ʳ.
45 *Ibid.*; Cruso, *Cavallerie,* p. 29.
46 Barwick, *Manuall Weapons,* fol. 22 ʳ.
47 Barret, *Theorike,* p. 143.
48 Cruso, *Cavallerie,* p. 30.
49 Barret, *Theorike,* p. 143.
50 Cruso, *Cavallerie,* p. 29.
51 Williams, *Brief Discourse,* p. 33.
52 Letter from Captain Reade to Cecil, December 10, 1598, *CSP, Ireland* (January 1598—March 1599), p. 403, and letter from Captain Dawtrey to Cecil, February 9, 1601, *CSP, Ireland* (November 1600—July 1601), p. 183. That they were forced to make use of weak and unserviceable horses may explain in part why Elizabethans did not put men-at-arms into the field. Inferior horses could not be barded and carry the weight of fully armed men.
53 Digges, *Stratioticos* (1590), p. 265; Garrard, *Arte of Warre,* p. 227.
54 Barret, *Theorike,* p. 139; Sutcliffe agrees (*Lawes of Armes,* p. 183).
55 Sutcliffe, *Lawes of Armes,* p. 183.
56 Francois de La Noue, *The Politicke and Militarie Discourses of the Lord De La Noue,* tr. E. A[ggas], (1587), p. 185.
57 *Ibid.,* p. 188.
58 *Ibid.,* pp. 185–88; Sir John Smythe, *Instructions, Observations, and Orders Mylitarie* (1595), pp. 160 and 168.
59 La Noue, *Militarie Discourses,* p. 188.
60 Smythe, *Instructions,* p. 168.
61 Williams, *Briefe Discourse,* p. 39.
62 Smythe, *Instructions,* p. 168; Williams, *Briefe Discourse,* p. 38.

63 Williams, *Briefe Discourse,* pp. 38–39.
64 Digges, *Stratioticos* (1590), p. 266.
65 Cruso, *Cavallerie,* p. 97.
66 Sutcliffe, *Lawes of Armes,* p. 182. La Noue feels that attacking the enemy foot by several files of horse rather than by a squadron is the better method, since footmen could then be hit in "sundry places."—*Militarie Discourses,* p. 189.
67 Garrard, *Arte of Warre,* p. 230.
68 *Ibid.*
69 Smythe, *Instructions,* p. 168.
70 Cruso, *Cavallerie,* pp. 95–96.
71 *Ibid.,* p. 97.
72 Digges, *Stratioticos* (1590), p. 266.
73 *Ibid.*
74 Barret, *Theorike,* pp. 143–44. See also Garrard, *Arte of Warre,* p. 230.
75 Garrard, *Arte of Warre,* p. 230; Williams, *Briefe Discourse,* p. 38.
76 Williams, *Briefe Discourse,* p. 34.
77 Cruso, *Cavallerie,* pp. 97–98.
78 Edward Grimestone, *A Generall Historie of the Netherlands* (1609), p. 928. Leicester himself places the number of cavalry at Zutphen at 150 (Letter from Leicester to Burghley, September 24, 1586, *CSP, Foreign* (June 1586—March 1587), p. 165.
79 *CSP, Ireland* (April 1599—February 1600), p. xiii.
80 Williams, *Briefe Discourse,* p. 30.

CHAPTER VI: FIELD ARTILLERY

1 Robert Barret also uses the title "Captain General of Artillery" in *The Theorike and Practike of Moderne Warres* (1598), pp. 136–39.
2 Leonard and Thomas Digges, *An Arithmeticall Militare Treatise, Named Stratioticos* (1590), p. 253; William Garrard, *The Arte of Warre* (1591), pp. 281–82; Thomas Styward, *The Pathwaie to Martiall Discipline* (1581), p. 11.
3 Barret, *Theorike,* p. 139.
4 Barret combines the offices of lieutenant and master gunner. After investigating Elizabeth's campaigns in Ireland, Cyril Falls states that the ordnance master's subordinate in Ire-

land was the master gunner. See *Elizabeth's Irish Wars* (London: Methuen & Co., 1950), p. 36.

5 The captain is not mentioned by Digges.

6 Garrard, *Arte of Warre,* p. 278. Garrard mentions three companies of soldiers. Digges merely says that there shall be "a sufficient band for the guard of the artillery" (*Stratioticos* [1590], p. 255). This statement is repeated by Styward (*Pathwaie to Martiall Discipline,* p. 13). Barret enumerates thirty "Gentlemen of the Artillery," thirty mounted harque-busiers, and eight halberdiers as being in attendance upon the general (*Theorike,* p. 132).

7 Barret, describing an ideal "army Royal," envisions additional personnel consisting of several more subordinate officers as well as two or three interpreters, a minister, a physician, a surgeon (with his servant), a trumpeter, and two or three engineers (*Theorike,* pp. 132–33).

8 Garrard, *Arte of Warre,* pp. 275, 278. Styward says that since the Master of Ordnance "cannot well perform all himself, he may refer the small to those that serve under him, and to execute the great himself."—*Pathwaie to Martiall Discipline,* p. 14.

9 Garrard, *Arte of Warre,* p. 275. Styward, writing ten years before Garrard, gives this job to the Master of Ordnance.

10 Garrard, *Arte of Warre,* pp. 274, 282.

11 *Ibid.*

12 Thomas Smith, *The Arte of Gunnerie* (1600), p. 75.

13 Garrard, *Arte of Warre,* p. 275. The duties of the gunners and fire master here apparently overlap. The probability is that the fire master was a position seldom filled in sixteenth-century English armies or that the fire master directed the gunners in the manufacture of fire works.

14 *Ibid.,* p. 278.

15 *Ibid.*

16 *Ibid.,* p. 239.

17 Digges, *Stratioticos* (1590), p. 255.

18 *The Oppugnation and Fierce Siege of Ostend* (1601), sig. B ͬ.

19 Contemporary accounts agree that the English had six pieces. *A True Relation of the Victorie Atchieved by Count Maurice* (1600) lists the Spanish as possessing "some eight great

pieces" (sig. A4 ʳ), while Edward Grimestone in *A Generall Historie of the Netherlands* (1609) says there were six Spanish pieces besides two more captured from the English at the beginning of the engagement (p. 1248). Barret's ideal "army Royal" would be equipped with 30 double cannon, 20 demi-cannon, 20 culverins, and 15 demi-culverins! See Barret, *Theorike*, p. 134.

20 Historical Manuscripts Commission, *Calendar of the Manuscripts of Lord de L'Isle and Dudley*, III, xxx–xxxvi.

21 *Ibid.,* p. xxxv.

22 For an account of the growing importance of artillery during the period, see Sir Charles Oman, *A History of the Art of War in the Sixteenth Century* (New York: E. P. Dutton, 1937), pp. 20–32.

23 Barret, *Theorike*, sig. ¶2 ʳ.

24 *Ibid.,* p. 136.

25 Smith, in his dedicatory epistle to Lord Willoughby, describes himself as "one of the meanest soldiers in this garrison now under your Lordship's government [*i.e.,* the town and castle of Barwick upon Tweed]" yet one who had been brought up from childhood "under a valiant captain in military profession" (*Arte of Gunnerie*, sigs. Aij ᵛ–Aiij ʳ).

26 Smith, *Arte of Gunnerie*, p. 78.

27 Barret, *Theorike*, p. 136.

28 Cyprian Lucar, *A Treatise Named Lucar Appendix* (1588), p. 48.

29 William Bourne, *The Arte of Shooting in Great Ordnaunce* (1587), p. 61.

30 Edward Grimestone, *A True Historie of the Memorable Siege of Ostend* (1604), pp. 37, 107.

31 Barret, *Theorike*, p. 37.

32 Digges, *Stratioticos* (1590), p. 254.

33 *Ibid.,* p. 255.

34 Lucar, *Treatise,* p. 48.

35 *Ibid.* An examination of the various extant lists of gun weights would indicate that gun foundries varied widely in their casting of cannon. The reader might want to compare these figures with several gun tables gathered by A. R. Hall in *Ballistics in the Seventeenth Century* (Cambridge: Cambridge University Press, 1952), pp. 166–71, and with

those appearing in Brigadier O. F. G. Hogg, "Some Notes on Old Artillery," *The Journal of the Royal Artillery,* LXXXII (1955), 170–91.

36 See various tables in Hogg, "Some Notes on Old Artillery," pp. 180–83, and Lucar, *Treatise,* p. 48.

37 Smith, *Arte of Gunnerie,* pp. 87–88.

38 *A True Discourse of All the Sallyes Which the Soldiers of Grave Have Made* (1602), p. 6.

39 Peter Whitehorne, *Certain Waies for the Orderyng of Souldiers in Battelray* (1562), fols. 27 ᵛ–28 ʳ.

40 *Ibid.,* fol. 33 ʳ.

41 *Ibid.,* fol. 33 ᵛ.

42 Bourne, *Arte of Shooting,* pp. 36–37.

43 Smith, *Arte of Gunnerie,* pp. 51, 67–68.

44 Lucar, *Treatise,* p. 59.

45 See "The brevity and the secret of the art of great ordnance" as reproduced in Hall, *Ballistics,* p. 166. This chart is also reproduced in Hogg, "Some Notes on Old Artillery," p. 181.

46 Humphrey Barwick, *A Breefe Discourse, Concerning the Force and Effect of All Manuall Weapons of Fire* (1594?), fol. 11 ᵛ.

47 Bourne, *Arte of Shooting,* p. 15.

48 *Ibid.*

49 William Bourne, *Inventions or Devises. Very Necessary for All Generalles and Captaines* (1578), p. 33. Bourne borrowed from Tartaglia.

50 Bourne, *Arte of Shooting,* pp. 45–46.

51 See Hall, *Ballistics,* p. 31.

52 Smith, *Arte of Gunnerie,* p. 49.

53 Bourne, *Arte of Shooting,* p. 19.

54 *Ibid.,* sig. Aiv ʳ.

55 *Ibid.,* sig. Aiii ʳ.

56 Smith, *Arte of Gunnerie,* p. 48.

57 Bourne, *Arte of Shooting,* pp. 35–36; Smith, *Arte of Gunnerie,* pp. 51–57.

58 Lucar, *Treatise,* pp. 53–54; Bourne, *Arte of Shooting,* pp. 35–37.

59 Lucar, *Treatise,* pp. 55–56; Bourne, *Arte of Shooting,* pp. 47–51.

60 Smith, *Arte of Gunnerie,* pp. 67–69.

61 Bourne, *Arte of Shooting,* p. 65.

62 *Ibid.,* p. 5.

63 *Ibid.,* p. 6.

64 Although Bourne (*Inventions,* pp. 39–40) describes this device in the late seventies, Hall (*Ballistics,* p. 61) states that it "had been used since at least the mid-sixteenth century."

65 Bourne, *Arte of Shooting,* pp. 10–11.

66 Lucar, *Treatise,* p. 48.

67 Bourne, *Arte of Shooting,* pp. 30–31.

68 *Ibid.,* pp. 61–62; Lucar, *Treatise,* pp. 54–55.

69 Bourne, *Arte of Shooting,* pp. 51–52.

70 *Ibid.,* sig. Aiii ʳ.

71 For instance, during Elizabeth's campaigns in Ireland, "practically no castle could be maintained by the Irish, provided the English could reach the scene with cannon of adequate weight."—Falls, *Elizabeth's Irish Wars,* p. 344.

72 *A True Declaration of the Streight Siedge Laide to the Cytty of Steenwich* (1592), p. 4. Apparently the gunners pulled themselves together after this insult because Steenwijk eventually fell to artillery pounding.

73 Hall, *Ballistics,* pp. 52–53.

74 Oman, *History of the Art of War,* pp. 568 ff.

75 Digges, *Stratioticos* (1590), pp. 255–56.

76 *Ibid.,* pp. 345 ff.

77 Garrard, *Arte of Warre,* p. 193.

78 Niccolò Machiavelli, *The Arte of Warre,* tr. Peter Whitehorne (1560), fol. xlvij ʳ. The *veliti,* who were light infantrymen, would have been armed with bows in Machiavelli's day. By the end of the Elizabethan period, as we have noted in Chapter IV, the bow was supplanted by the caliver, harquebuse, and musket.

79 Bourne, *Arte of Shooting,* sig. Aiii ʳ.

80 See Maurice J. D. Cockle, *A Bibliography of Military Books up to 1642* (London: The Holland Press, 1900; reprinted 1957).

81 Bourne, *Arte of Shooting,* sig. Aiii ʳ.

82 Three interesting evaluations of Machiavelli as a military theorist are Oman, *History of the Art of War,* pp. 93–94; Joseph Kraft, "Truth and Poetry in Machiavelli," *Journal of Modern History,* XXIII (1951), 109–21; and Felix Gilbert, "Machiavelli: The Renaissance of the Art of War," *Makers of*

Modern Strategy, ed. Edward Mead Earle (Princeton: Princeton University Press, 1944), pp. 3–25. Oman points out that all Machiavelli's "recommendations of a practical sort bear no relation whatever to the actual development of tactics," and that his evaluation of artillery was "hopelessly erroneous" (pp. 93–94). Kraft agrees, in much the same words. Gilbert, on the other hand, states that "Machiavelli raised military discussion to a new level and established the principles according to which intellectual comprehension and theoretical analysis of war and military affairs progressed" (p. 20). It might be added, in all fairness to Machiavelli, that his low estimate of the value of artillery certainly seems justified by events in the Italian wars of the twenty-five years before he wrote his *Dell' arte della guerra.*

83 For a general treatment of artillery development in the sixteenth century, see Oman, *History of the Art of War,* especially Chapter 3 and pp. 351–52.

84 Digges, *Stratioticos* (1579), sig. Aij ʳ.

85 Barwick, *Manuall Weapons,* sig. A2 ᵛ.

86 Complete discussions of the impact of Tartaglia on ballistics in the sixteenth and subsequent centuries may be found in Prosper Jules Charbonnier's *Essais sur l'Histoire de la Balistique* (Paris: Société d'Editions Géographiques, Maritimes, et Coloniales, 1928) and Hall, *Ballistics, passim.*

87 Hall, *Ballistics,* p. 42.

88 *Ibid.*

89 *Ibid.,* p. 52.

90 Bourne, *Arte of Shooting,* sigs. Aiii ᵛ–Aiv ᵛ.

91 See Chapters I and VIII.

CHAPTER VII: MILITARY MEDICINE

1 D'Arcy Power, "The Elizabethan Revival of Surgery," *St. Bartholomew's Hospital Journal,* X (1902), 1 ff.

2 Much of the material in this chapter appeared in my article, "English Military Surgery during the Age of Elizabeth," *Bulletin of the History of Medicine,* XV (Baltimore: The Johns Hopkins Press, 1944), 261–75.

3 *Acts of the Privy Council,* New Series, VII (1558–70), 119; XVII (1588–89), 27–28; XVIII (1589–90), 420.

4 "Instructions given 17 July 1559, to Thomas, Earl of Sussex,

Deputy of Ireland," *Calendar of the Carew Manuscripts* (1515–1574), p. 285. These same pays were in effect in 1576 and 1577 (*ibid.* [1575–1588], pp. 44, 111–12). In the previous reign and occasionally during the first few years of Elizabeth's reign, physicians were impressed as privates and kept from serving in their professional capacities. The Privy Council had begun to put an end to this practice by 1562. See *Acts of the Privy Council,* VII, 129.

5 Great Britain, Public Record Office, *Calendar of State Papers, Foreign* (July–December 1588), p. 44.

6 *Acts of the Privy Council,* XVI (1588), 5–6.

7 *Ibid.,* XVII, 27–28. For similar letters, see *ibid.,* XII (1580–81), 216, 232; XVII, 201–2; XVIII, 122, 350; XXI (1590), 22.

8 *CSP, Ireland* (November 1600—July 1601), p. 241.

9 *Ibid.*

10 *Acts of the Privy Council,* XXX (1600) 107–8.

11 C. G. Cruickshank, *Elizabeth's Army* (Oxford: Oxford University Press, 1946), pp. 121–22.

12 *CSP, Ireland* (July 1596—December 1597), pp. 148, 263.

13 *Ibid.* (April 1599—February 1600), p. 143.

14 *Ibid.,* p. 290.

15 Sir John Smythe, *Certain Discourses Concerning the Formes and Effects of Divers Sorts of Weapons* (1590), sig. ***4 ͬ.

16 Letter from Sir Ralph Lane, Muster-Master of Ireland, to Sir Robert Cecil, December 29, 1600, *CSP, Ireland* (November 1600—July 1601), p. 109.

17 *Acts of the Privy Council,* XXX, 107–8.

18 *Dictionary of National Biography,* "Clowes, William."

19 William Clowes, *A Prooved Practise for All Young Chirurgians* (1588), sig. Piiiiiiij2 ͬ.

20 *CSP, Ireland* (March–October 1600), p. 406. Interestingly enough, in the fall of 1598 Nicholas Weston, sometime Mayor of Dublin, proposed the establishment of a military hospital for English soldiers and their Irish allies. As he conceived it, the hospital was to contain fifty beds and every bed was to receive two wounded or sick soldiers. It was to be provided with "sufficient" victuals, bedclothes, and "six old women, that shall keep them clean, and shall wash their clothes, and make their meats." There the soldiers would be

kept until "able to go abroad and shift for themselves for their better relief elsewhere." The argument for providing such a hospital was simple: it would be "no small encouragement and comfort unto the poor soldiers, who, for want of relief . . . do most lamentably starve and die under stalls in the streets, who otherwise might be fit to serve Her Majesty again, whereby others also would be encouraged more willingly to adventure their lives in Her Highness's service."—*CSP, Ireland* (January 1598—March 1599), pp. 296–97.

21 *CSP, Ireland* (November 1600—July 1601), p. 113.

22 *Acts of the Privy Council,* XXX, 122–23.

23 Clowes, *A Prooved Practise,* Epistle to the Reader, sig. [A4] ʳ.

24 *CSP, Foreign* (April–December 1587), p. 145.

25 *CSP, Ireland* (April 1599—February 1600), pp. 383–84.

26 *Ibid.*

27 Quoted in Power, "The Elizabethan Revival of Surgery," p. 3.

28 Clowes, *A Prooved Practise,* commendatory letter by I. G., sig. C ʳ.

29 *Ibid.,* pp. 36–37.

30 Joseph Du Chesne (Josephus Quercetanus), *Sclopotarie of J. Quercetanus, or His Booke Containing the Cure of Woundes Received by Shot of Gunne,* tr. J. Hester (1590), *passim.*

31 The *DNB,* the *Cambridge Bibliography of English Literature,* and several other sources give the date of Baker's death as 1600, but the *Annals of the Barber-Surgeons of London* indicate that Baker was among the "Examiners of Surgeons" as late as July 20, 1607. D'Arcy Power gives his death date as 1609, in "Epoch-Making Books in British Surgery, VI. Johnson's Ambrose Parey," *The British Journal of Surgery,* XVI (1928), 182.

32 *DNB,* "Gale, Thomas." See also Power, "The Elizabethan Revival of Surgery," p. 3.

33 Thomas Gale, *Certaine Workes of Chirurgerie* (1586), p. 38.

34 *Ibid.,* pp. 37, 70.

35 *Ibid.*

36 *Ibid.,* pp. 61–62.

37 Clowes, *A Prooved Practise,* p. 25.

38 Gale, *Certaine Workes of Chirurgerie,* pp. 62–63.

39 *Ibid.*

40 Power, "The Elizabethan Revival of Surgery," p. 4.
41 *Ibid.,* p. 19. Baker was appointed Sergeant Surgeon in 1591 and became Master of the Barber-Surgeons' Company in 1597.
42 Guido's work was originally translated by Robert Copland in 1541.
43 Earlier editions of Vigo's works in English appeared in 1535 (?), 1543, 1550, and 1571.
44 The *Antidotarie* was bound with Baker's translation, *Guydos Questions* (1579).
45 George Baker, *Composition or Making of the Moste Excellent and Pretious Oil Called Oleum Magistrale* (1574), sig. Civ ʳ.
46 *Ibid.,* fols. 1 ʳ–4 ʳ.
47 *Ibid.,* fol. 2 ᵛ.
48 *Ibid.*
49 *Ibid.,* fol. 5 ᵛ.
50 So listed on his title page and discussed in some detail on fols. 6 ʳ⁻ᵛ.
51 *Ibid.,* fols. 3 ʳ–5 ᵛ.
52 *Ibid.,* fol. 7 ʳ.
53 *Ibid.,* fol. 19 ᵛ.
54 *Ibid.,* fol. 26 ʳ.
55 *Ibid.,* fols. 32 ʳ⁻ᵛ.
56 *Ibid.,* fol. 33 ʳ.
57 At the court of the Barber-Surgeons' Company, on March 25, 1577, there was "a great contention and strife spoken of and ended between George Baker and William Clowes, for that they both, . . . misused each other, and fought in the fields together. But the Master, Wardens, and Assistants wishing that they might be and continue loving brothers, pardoned this great offense in hope of amendment."—Power, "The Elizabethan Revival of Surgery," pp. 18 ff.
58 Clowes, *A Prooved Practise, passim.*
59 *Ibid.,* see Dedication.
60 *Ibid.,* p. 8.
61 *Ibid.,* Chapters I and II.
62 *Ibid.,* p. 2.
63 *Ibid.,* pp. 17 ff.
64 *Ibid.,* pp. 21–25.
65 *Ibid.,* pp. 23–24.
66 *Ibid.,* pp. 12–16.

67 *Ibid.,* pp. 25–30.
68 For a reproduction of Clowes' illustration, see John R. Hale, *The Art of War and Renaissance England* (Washington: The Folger Shakespeare Library, 1961), p. 31.
69 Clowes, *A Prooved Practise,* pp. 87–93.

CHAPTER VIII: THE BOOKS AND THE PRACTICE

1 Robert Copland, "The Highway to the Spital-House," *The Elizabethan Underworld,* ed. A. V. Judges (London: George Routledge and Sons, Ltd., 1930), p. 7.
2 John Awdeley, "The Fraternity of Vagabonds," *ibid.,* p. 57.
3 Thomas Harman, *A Caveat or Warening, for Common Cursetors Vulgarely Called Vagabonds,* Early English Text Society, Extra Series, XV (1872), 29.
4 Henry Porter, *The Two Angry Women of Abington* (Malone Society Reprints; Oxford: Oxford University Press, 1912), sig. A2 ʳ.
5 Ben Jonson, "Every Man in His Humor," III, V, 12–30 (*Elizabethan and Stuart Plays,* ed. Charles Read Baskervill, Virgil B. Heltzel, and Arthur H. Nethercot [New York: Henry Holt and Co., 1934], p. 856).
6 Great Britain, Public Record Office, *Calendar of State Papers, Domestic* (1591–1594), p. 120.
7 *Ibid.,* p. 342.
8 *Oxford Historical and Literary Studies* (Oxford, 1913), I, 171.
9 *The Complete Works of George Gascoigne,* ed. John W. Cunliffe, II (Cambridge: The University Press, 1910), 590.
10 *The True Reporte of the Skirmish betwene the States of Flaunders, and Don Joan* (1578), p. 1.
11 Thomas Churchyard, *A Generall Rehearsall of Warres* (1579?), sig. Iii ʳ.
12 Thomas Digges, *A Briefe and True Report of the Proceedings of the Earle of Leycester for the Reliefe of Sluce* (1590), preface "To the Reader," sig. A2 ʳ.
13 *A Particuler of the Yeelding uppe of the Towne of Zutphen* (1591), p. 5.

Glossary

adjutant, the staff officer of a command responsible for certain administrative duties.

ancient, see *ensign.*

angle of elevation, vertical angle between the line from the muzzle of the gun to the target and the axis of the bore when the gun is pointed for range.

angle of site, vertical angle between the horizontal and a line joining the target and the muzzle of a gun.

argoletier, see *harquebusier.*

arquebuse, see *harquebuse.*

assigned, placed permanently in a military organization.

attached, placed temporarily in a military organization for duty, rations, or quarters.

ballista, an engine, often in the form of a crossbow, used in ancient and medieval warfare for hurling large missiles.

bards, armor for a horse's neck, breast, or flank.

bandoleer, a belt from which cases or pouches containing charges for a musket were suspended.

bastion, a projecting part of a fortification.

beaver, bever, or *bevor,* the lower portion of the face-guard of a helmet; in the sixteenth century, confounded with the visor.

217

bill, a weapon consisting of a long staff with a long hook-shaped blade and picks at back and top.

bracketing fire, fire delivered on a target in order to establish range limits over and short of the target, or deflection limits to the right and left of the target.

brigandines, body armor consisting of over-lapping metal plates sewed within canvas, linen, or leather.

burgonet, armor for the head, covering the head and part of the face and cheek.

butt, the end of the stock of an harquebuse, caliver, or musket; or of a lance or pike.

caracole, defensive maneuver by pistoleers against charging shot-on-horseback. The pistoleers, in company formation, divided by the half ranks to permit the enemy to pass part way through their midst. They then turned about and fired upon the enemy by rank or by file. This term also referred to a method of riding up by successive ranks to fire on a formation of enemy infantry or cavalry, then wheeling aside to let the next rank fire.

career, a headlong charge of horse.

casemate, a fortified position or room in a fortress in which ordnance or other guns may be placed to fire through embrasures.

casque, a helmet.

catapult, an ancient military engine for throwing stones, arrows, etc.

chain shot, cannon shot consisting of two balls or half balls united by a short chain; used to clear the field of enemy soldiers.

clive shot, cleft or split bullets.

collar, armor protecting the neck.

cornet, a company of horse.

corn powder, granulated gunpowder worked through sieves.

corselet or *corslet,* armor covering the trunk of the body.

cotton match, a wick of cotton so prepared that when lighted at the end it is not easily extinguished and continues to burn at a uniform rate.

couch, to lower a lance or pike to the position of attack, grasping it in the right hand with the point directed forwards.

creeping fire, a method of getting the range of an enemy position by firing the first set of shots too far, then gradually shortening the range.

cuirass, a piece of armor for the body, reaching down to the waist and consisting of a breast plate and a back plate buckled or otherwise fastened together. (*OED*)

cuish or *cuisse,* armor for the front part of the thighs.

cullion, the part of a bulwark that covers the casemate.

culverin, a piece of ordnance with a caliber of 5.5 inches, weighing approximately 4,500 pounds.

curtain, the part of a wall that connects two bastions.

curtilace, a cutlass; a short, curved sword.

demi-cannon, a piece of ordnance with a caliber of 6.5 inches, weighing approximately 4,000 to 5,000 pounds.

depth, the space from front to rear of any formation or position, including the front and rear units.

dice shot, cubical bullets.

dispart, the difference between the semi-diameter of a gun at the base ring and at the swell of the muzzle, which must be allowed for in taking aim; also, a piece of wax or straw placed on the muzzle of a gun to make the line of sight parallel to the axis of the bore. (*OED*)

double-cannon, a piece of ordnance with a caliber of between 8 and 8.5 inches, weighing between 7,000 and 8,000 pounds.

ensign, the standard-bearer for a company or larger unit.

executive officer, the principal assistant of the commander.

falcon, a piece of ordnance with a caliber of 2.5 inches, weighing approximately 800 pounds.

falconet, a piece of ordnance with a caliber of 2 inches, weighing approximately 500 pounds.

fire master, an officer in charge of preparing wildfire, trunks, etc.

field piece, a field artillery gun; a gun mounted on a carriage for use in the field.

file, a line of persons or things one behind the other. Both *rank* and *file* refer to single lines of troops in formation. *Files* are vertical lines from front to rear; *ranks* are lateral lines from side to side.

flank, the right or left side of a formation of troops.

flanking movement, an offensive maneuver directed against an enemy's flank.

fletcher, one who makes arrows.

flintlock, a gunlock (*i.e.,* the mechanism by which the hammer is driven and the charge is exploded) in which a flint is used to ignite the powder in the pan.

foin, to thrust with a sword, pike, bill, or halberd.

forlorn hope, a body of men detached to the front of a battle formation to begin the attack; a body of skirmishers.

furniture, armor, accoutrements, weapons, munitions.

gabion, a wicker basket of cylindrical form, open at both ends, intended to be filled with earth for use in fortifications. (*OED*)

gorget, armor for the throat.

greave, greeve, or *greve,* armor for the lower part of the leg.

guidon, a forked or pointed pennant.

halberd, a weapon consisting of a battle-ax and pike mounted on a handle about six feet long.

harbinger, a messenger.

hargeletier, see *harquebusier.*

hargulutier, a cavalryman, unarmed, using a caliver with a snaphance.

harquebuse, a wheel lock or flintlock gun fired from the shoulder.

harquebusier, an infantryman or cavalryman who bears a harquebuse.

lance-knight (from *Germ. landsknecht*), a German foot-soldier in foreign service.

lancer, a cavalryman carrying a lance.

lead, the distance ahead of a moving target that a gun must be aimed in order to hit the target; one target length, as it appears to the gunner, used as a unit for measuring lead.

linstock or *lintstock,* a staff with one sharp end to stick in the ground and a forked head to hold a match.

mask, anything that interferes with, or protects from, observation or gunfire.

mine master, an officer in charge of digging mines under fortified walls.

minion, a piece of ordnance with a caliber of 3.5 inches, weighing approximately 1,000 to 1,100 pounds.

morion, a visorless high-crested helmet of Spanish origin worn by foot soldiers.

mortar, an artillery weapon with a short barrel used to reach targets protected or concealed by intervening hills, walls, etc.

musket, a handgun provided with a matchlock. It was fired from the shoulder (or sometimes the breast) with the aid of a forked rest.

musketeer, a soldier armed with a musket.

muster-master, an officer responsible for the accuracy of the muster-roll.

muster-roll, the official list of the officers and men of a command.

ordnance, military materials, stores, or supplies; implements of war; but especially artillery pieces.

pan, the powder cavity in a handgun.

pauldron or *pouldron,* armor which covers the shoulder; a shoulder plate.

petranell or *petronel,* a large pistol used by cavalry. It was usually fired with the butt against the chest.

pike, a weapon consisting of a long wooden shaft with a pointed head of iron or steel.

pioneers, foot-soldiers equipped with tools with which to dig trenches, repair roads, and do other jobs to prepare the way for an army unit.

pistoleer, a cavalry soldier armed with a pistol or petranell.

point-blank range, distance to a target that is so short that the trajectory of a bullet is a straight rather than a curved line. Point-blank range is one for which no elevation is needed.

proof, armor impenetrable to bullets at point-blank range.

provost, an officer in charge of punishing military offenders.

quadrant, an instrument for measuring angles; used to level a piece of ordnance or to mount such a piece to any random.

quarter-cannon, not specifically described in most sources, but apparently a weakly-metaled demi-cannon.

quoin, a wedge-shaped piece of wood, with a handle at the thick end, used to raise or lower a gun. (*OED*)

random, the range of a piece of ordnance; the degree of elevation given to a gun. (*OED*)

rank, see *file.*

saker, a piece of ordnance with a caliber of 3.5 inches, weighing 1,400 to 1,500 pounds.

score, twenty yards or paces.

serpentine powder, gun powder in fine meal.

snaphance, a kind of flintlock used in muskets and pistols.

squadron, a body of soldiers arranged in square formation.

taladros, engines to mount and dismount pieces of ordnance.

tasses, a series of articulated splints or plates depending from the corselet of a suit of armor placed so that each slightly overlaps the one below it, to protect the thighs and the lower part of the trunk. (*OED*)

trench master, an officer in charge of preparing military trenches.

troop, a company of cavalry.

trunks, cylindrical cases for explosives.

vambrace, armor for the fore-arm.

visor, the front part of a helmet, covering the face but provided with openings for seeing and breathing, and capable of being raised and lowered. (*OED*)

Bibliography

This list represents the books related to military science printed before 1640 which were used in the preparation of this study. Not all of them are referred to directly or indirectly, but most of them were helpful in leading me to my conclusions. Titles have been abridged and capitalization has been standardized. The *Short-Title Catalogue* number is given for items which appear in that book. Place of publication is London unless otherwise noted.

A Larum for London, or The Siedge of Antwerpe, 1600. *STC* 16754.

Ascham, Roger. *Toxophilus, The Schole of Shootinge Conteyned in Two Bookes.* 1545. *STC* 837.

———. (Anr. ed.) Newly perused. 1571. *STC* 838.

———. (Anr. ed.) 1589. *STC* 839.

Baker, George. *The Composition or Making of the Moste Excellent and Pretious Oil Called Oleum Magistrale.* 1574. *STC* 1209.

Barret, Robert. *The Theorike and Practike of Moderne Warres.* 1598. *STC* 1500.

Barwick, Humphrey. *A Breefe Discourse, Concerning the Force and Effect of All Manuall Weapons of Fire.* [1594?]. *STC* 1542.

Basille, Theodore (*pseud.* for Thomas Becon). *The New Pollecye of Warre.* 1542. *STC* 1735.

———. (Anr. ed.) *The True Defence of Peace.* 1543. *STC* 1776.

The Besieging of Berghen uppon Zoom by the Prince of Parma. Middelburg, [1589?]. *STC* 331.

Blandy, William. *The Castle, or Picture of Pollicy.* 1581. *STC* 3128.

Blundeville, Thomas. *A Newe Booke, Containing the Arte of Ryding.* (Adapted from the Italian of Federico Grisone.) [1560?]. *STC* 3158.

———. (Anr. ed.) 1597.

Bourne, William. *The Arte of Shooting in Great Ordnaunce.* 1587. *STC* 3420.

———. *Inventions or Devises. Very Necessary for All Generalles and Captaines.* 1578. *STC* 3421.

A Briefe Cronicle and Perfect Rehearsall of All the Memorable Actions Hapned not onelie in the Low-Countries, but also in Germanie, Italy, Fraunce, and Other Countries Since the Yeare 1500. 1598. *STC* 18433.

A Brief Description of the Battles Victories and Triumphs of the Duke of Parma. Tr. E. A[ggas]. Middelburg, [1591]. *STC* 332.

A Briefe Rehersall of the Agreement that the Captaynes and Armie of Middleborow and Armew Have Made. [1574]. *STC* 17865.

Caesar, Caius Julius. *The Eyght Bookes of Caius Julius Caesar Conteyning His Martiall Exploytes in Gallia.* Tr. A. Golding. 1565. *STC* 4335.

———. (Anr. ed.) 1590. *STC* 4336.

———. *Julius Cesars Commentaryes. Newly Translated into Englyshe as much as Concernyth Thys Realm of England.* 1530. *STC* 4337.

Cataneo, Girolamo. *Most Brief Tables to Knowe Redily Howe*

Manye Ranckes of Footemen Go to the Making of a Just Battayle. Tr. H. G[rantham?]. 1574. *STC* 4790.

———. (Anr. ed.) 1588. *STC* 4791.

Certayne Newes of the Whole Description, Ayde, and Helpe of the Princes for Poore Christians in the Low Countries. [1574?]. *STC* 5182.

Churchyard, Thomas. *A Generall Rehearsall of Warres.* [1579]. *STC* 5235.

———. *A Pleasant Discourse of Court and Wars.* 1596. *STC* 5249.

Clayton, Giles. *The Approoved Order of Martiall Discipline.* 1591. *STC* 5376.

———. *A Briefe Discourse of Martial Discipline.* Middelburg, 1587. *STC* 5377.

Clowes, William. *A Prooved Practise for All Young Chirurgians.* 1588. *STC* 5444.

———. (Anr. ed.) 1591. *STC* 5445.

———. (Anr. ed.) *A Profitable and Necessarie Booke of Observations, for All Those That Are Burned with the Flame of Gun Powder.* 1596. *STC* 5442.

Cloynet, Anthony. *The True History of the Civil Wars of France.* 1591.

Corte, Claudio. *The Art of Riding Reduced into English Discourses.* 1584. *STC* 5797.

C[ruso], J[ohn]. *Militarie Instructions for the Cavallerie.* Cambridge, 1632. *STC* 6099.

Digges, Dudley and Thomas. *Foure Paradoxes.* 1604. *STC* 6872.

Digges, Leonard and Thomas. *An Arithmeticall Militare Treatise, Named Stratioticos.* 1579. *STC* 6848.

———. (Anr. ed.) Lately reviewed and corrected. 1590. *STC* 6849.

———. *A Geometrical Practise, Named Pantometria.* 1571. *STC* 6858.

———. (Anr. ed.) Lately reviewed and augmented. 1591. *STC* 6859.

[Digges, Thomas]. *A Breife and True Report of the Proceedings of the Earle of Leycester for the Reliefe of Sluce.* 1590. *STC* 7284.

————. *A Briefe Report of the Militarie Services Done in the Low Countries by the Erle of Leicester.* 1587. *STC* 7285.

A Discourse of the Great Overthrow Given by the French King. 1592. *STC* 11271+.

A Discourse of the Overthrowe Given to the King of Spaines Armie. 1597. *STC* 22993.

A Discourse of the Present State of the Wars in the Lowe Countryes. 1578. *STC* 18438.

Drury, Sir William. *Regulations To Be Observed by the English Army Marching to Besiege Edinburgh Castle.* Edinburgh, 1573. *STC* 8055.

Du Chesne, Joseph (Josephus Quercetanus). *The Sclopotarie of J. Quercetanus, or His Booke Containing the Cure of Woundes Received by Shot of Gunne.* Tr. J. Hester. 1590. *STC* 7277.

Dudley, Robert. *Lawes and Ordinances Set Downe by Robert Earle of Leycester in the Lowe Countries.* [1586]. *STC* 7288.

Du Praissac, *Sieur. The Art of Warre.* Tr. J[ohn] C[ruso]. Cambridge, 1639. *STC* 7366.

E., J. *A Letter from a Souldier of Good Place in Ireland.* 1602. *STC* 7434.

Edmondes, Sir Clement. *Observations upon the Five First Bookes of Caesars Commentaries, Setting Fourth the Practice of the Art Military in the Time of the Roman Empire.* 1600. *STC* 7488.

————. (Anr. ed.) 1604. *STC* 7489.

————. (Anr. ed.) *Observations upon Caesars Commentaries.* 1604. *STC* 7490.

————. (Anr. ed.) 1609. *STC* 7491.

————. (Anr. ed.) [n. p. d.]

Extremeties Urging the Lord General Veare to Offer the Late Anti-Parle with the Arch-Duke Albertus. 1602. *STC* 24651.

Fenne, Thomas. *Fennes Frutes.* 1590. *STC* 10763.

Fourquevaux, Raimond de Beccarie de Pavie, *Sieur de. Instructions for the Warres.* Tr. Paul Ive. 1589. *STC* 7264 (Under Du Bellay).

Frontinus, Sextus Julius. *The Strategemes, Sleyghtes, and Policies of Warre.* Tr. R. Morysine (Morison). 1539. *STC* 11402.

G., C. *A Watch-Worde for Warre.* Cambridge, 1596. *STC* 11492.

Gale, Thomas. *Certaine Workes of Chirurgerie.* 4 pts. 1563. (Also issued with Vigo, *Whole Works.*) *STC* 11529.

———. (Anr. ed.) 1586. *STC* 11529a.

Garrard, William. *The Arte of Warre.* 1591. *STC* 11625.

[Gascoigne, George]. *The Spoyle of Antwerpe.* [1577?]. *STC* 11644.

Gates, Geoffry. *The Defence of Militarie Profession.* 1579. *STC* 11683.

Gheyn, Jacob de. *The Exercise of Armes.* The Hague, 1607. *STC* 11810.

Grassi, Giacomo di. *Giacomo di Grassi His True Arte of Defence.* Tr. I. G. 1594. *STC* 12190.

Grimestone, Edward. *A Generall Historie of the Netherlands.* 1608. *STC* 12374.

———. (Anr. ed.) 1609.

———, tr. *A True Historie of the Memorable Siege of Ostend.* 1604. *STC* 18895.

Grisone, Federico. See Blundeville, Thomas.

Gutierrez de la Vega, Luis. *A Compendious Treatise De Re Militari.* Tr. N. Lichefild. 1582. *STC* 12538.

Heere Foloweth the Ordre or Trayne of Warre. [n. d.]

Hitchcock, Robert. *A General Proportion and Order of Provision to Victuall a Garrison of One Thousande Souldiours.* 1591. (Added to Garrard's *The Arte of Warre,* pp. 353–68.)

Hurault, Jacques, *Sieur de Vieul. Politicke, Moral, and Martial Discourses.* Tr. A. Golding. 1595. *STC* 14000.

Ive, Paul. *The Practise of Fortification.* 1589. (Published with Fourquevaux, *Instructions for the Warres.*) *STC* 14289.

———. (Anr. ed.) 1597. *STC* 14290.

Jonghe, Elbert of. *The True and Perfect Declaration of the Mighty Army by Sea.* 1600. *STC* 14750.

A Journal, or Brief Report of the Late Service in Britaigne. 1591.

A Journall, Wherein is Sette Downe What Was Doone in Both Armies. Tr. E. A[ggas]. 1592. *STC* 14818.

Knyvett, Sir Henry. *The Defence of the Realme.* 1596. Repr. Oxford: The Clarendon Press, 1906.

La Noue, François de. *The Declaration of the Lord de la Noue, upon his Taking Armes.* 1589. *STC* 15213.

————. *A Discourse upon the Declaration Published by the Lord de la Noue.* 1589. *STC* 15214.

————. *The Politicke and Militarie Discourses of the Lord de la Noue.* Tr. E. A[ggas]. 1587. *STC* 15215.

Larke, John. *The Boke of Noblenes.* 1550.

The Late Expedicion in Scotlande, Made by the Kynges Hyghnes Armye. 1544.

Lawes and Orders of Warre. 1599. *STC* 14131.

Le Roy, Louis. *Of the Interchangeable Course of Things in the Whole World.* Tr. R. A[shley]. 1594. *STC* 15488.

Lingham, John. *A True Relation of All English Captains and Lieutenants as Have Been Slain in the Low Countries.* 1584.

Lloyd, Lodowick. *The Stratagems of Jerusalem.* 1602. *STC* 16630.

Loque, Bertrand de. *Discourses of Warre and Single Combat.* Tr. J. Eliot. 2 pts. 1591. *STC* 16810.

Lucar, Cyprian. *A Treatise Named Lucar Appendix.* 1588. *STC* 16890. (Published with Tartaglia, *Three Bookes of Colloquies.*)

Machiavelli, Niccolò. *The Arte of Warre.* Tr. P. Whitehorne. 1560. *STC* 17164.

————. (Anr. ed.) Newly imprinted. 1573. *STC* 17165.

————. (Anr. ed.) 1588. *STC* 17166.

The Mansion of Magnanimitie with a Briefe Table, Shewing, What Munition Ought to be Kept by All Sorts of Her Majesties Subjects. 1599.

Meierus, Albertus. *Certaine Briefe and Speciall Instructions.* Tr. P. Jones. 1589. *STC* 17784.

Mendoza, Don Bernardino de. *Theorique and Practise of Warre.* Tr. Sir E. Hoby. [Middelburg], 1597. *STC* 17819.

Meteren, E. van. *A True Discourse Historicall of the Succeeding*

Governours in the Netherlands. Tr. T. C[hurchyard] and R. Ro[binson]. 1602. *STC* 17846.

Minadoi, Giovanni Tommaso. *The History of the Warres Between the Turkes and the Persians.* Tr. A. Hartwell. 1595. *STC* 17943.

Munday, A., and others. *The First Part of the True and Honorable Historie of the Life of Sir John Oldcastle.* 1600. *STC* 18795.

A Myrrour for English Souldiers; or, An Anatomy of an Accomplished Man at Armes. 1595. *STC* 10418.

Nannini, Remigio. *Civill Considerations upon Many and Sundrie Histories.* Done into French by G. Chappuys and into English by W. T. 1601. *STC* 18348.

Norton, Robert. *The Gunner.* 1628. *STC* 18673.

Nun, Thomas. *A Comfort Against the Spaniard.* 1596. *STC* 18748.

Onosander. *Onosandro Platonico, Of the Generall Captaine and of His Office.* Tr. P. Whitehorne. 1563. *STC* 18815.

The Oppugnation and Fierce Siege of Ostend. Tr. out of Dutch. 1601.

An Oration Militarie to All Naturall Englishmen. 1588.

An Order Whych a Prince in Battayll Muste Observe. [1540?]. *STC* 18842.

Ordonances and Instructions for Musters. [1590]. *STC* 8199.

The Overthrow of an Irish Rebell in a Late Battaile. Dublin, 1608. *STC* 18786.

A Particuler of the Yeeldinge uppe of the Towne of Zutphen. 1591. *STC* 26134.

Patten, William. *The Expedicion into Scotland of Prince Edward.* 1548. *STC* 19479.

A Placarde or Statute Concerning the Musters. [1599?]. *STC* 18469.

Polemon, John. *All the Famous Battels That Have Bene Fought in Our Age.* [1578]. *STC* 20089.

———. *The Second Part of the Booke of Battailes.* 1587. (Published anonymously.) *STC* 20090.

The Politique Taking of Zutphen Skonce. 1591.

Polybius. *The Hystories of Polybius, Discoursing of the Warres Betwixt the Romanes and Carthaginenses.* Tr. C. W[atson]. 1568. *STC* 20097.

Porcia, Jacopo di, Count. *The Preceptes of Warre.* Tr. P. Betham. 1544. *STC* 20116.

P[roctor], T[homas]. *Of the Knowledge and Conducte of Warres.* 1578. *STC* 20403.

Quercetanus. See Du Chesne, Joseph.

Rich, Barnabe. *Allarme to England.* 1578. *STC* 20978.

———. (Anr. ed.) 1578. *STC* 20979.

———. *Faultes Faults, and Nothing Else but Faultes.* 1606. *STC* 20983.

———. *The Fruites of Long Experience.* (Part 2 of *A Souldiers Wishe.*) 1604. *STC* 21001.

———. *The Irish Hubbub or, The English Hue and Cry.* 1617.

———. *A Path-way to Military Practise.* 1587. *STC* 20995.

———. *A Right Exelent and Pleasaunt Dialogue, betwene Mercury and an English Souldier.* 1574. *STC* 20998.

———. *A Souldiers Wishe to Britons Welfare.* 1604. *STC* 21000.

Rutilius Rufus, P. *A View of Valyaunce. Describing the Feates of Romains and Carthaginians for the Possession of Spayne.* (Edited or written by T. Newton.) 1580. *STC* 21469.

S., R. *A Briefe Treatise, to Proove the Necessitie and Excellence of the Use of Archerie.* 1596. *STC* 21512.

Saviolo, Vincentio. *Vincentio Saviolo His Practise.* 1595. *STC* 21788.

———. (Anr. issue with imprint.) 1595. *STC* 21789.

[Segar, Sir William]. *The Booke of Honor and Armes.* 1590. *STC* 22163.

———. *Honor, Military and Civill.* 1602. *STC* 22164.

S[elden], J[ohn]. *The Duello or Single Combat.* 1610. *STC* 22171.

Shute, John. Epistle to his translation of Andrea Cambini, *Two Very Notable Commentaries. The One of the Originall of the Turcks.* 1562. *STC* 4470.

Silver, George. *Paradoxes of Defence.* 1599. *STC* 22554.

Smith, Thomas. *The Arte of Gunnerie*. 1600. *STC* 22855.

Smythe, Sir John. *Certain Discourses Concerning the Formes and Effects of Divers Sorts of Weapons*. 1590. *STC* 22833.

——. (Anr. ed.) 1590.

——. *Instructions, Observations, and Orders Mylitarie*. 1595. *STC* 22885.

Statuts and Ordenaunces of Warre. 1513. *STC* 9333.

——. (Anr. ed.) *Statutes and Ordinances for the Warre*. 1544. *STC* 9334.

Styward, Thomas. *The Pathwaie to Martiall Discipline*. 1581. *STC* 23413.

——. (Anr. ed.) 1582. *STC* 23414.

——. (Anr. ed.) 1585. *STC* 23415.

Sutcliffe, Matthew. *The Practice, Proceedings, and Lawes of Armes*. 1593. *STC* 23468.

Tartaglia, Niccolò. *Three Bookes of Colloquies Concerning the Arte of Shooting*. Tr. C. Lucar. 1588. *STC* 23689.

A True Declaration of the Streight Siedge Laide to the Cytty of Steenwich. Tr. I. T. 1592. *STC* 23241.

A True Declaration of That Which Hapned Since the Enemies First Comming to Brommel. Tr. from Dutch. 1599.

A True Discourse of All the Sallyes Which the Soldiers of Grave Have Made. 1602. *STC* 12197.

A True Discourse of the Armie Which the King of Spain Assembled. Tr. D. Archdeacon. 1588. *STC* 22999.

True Newes from One of Sir Fraunces Veres Companie. 1591. *STC* 24652.

A True Relation of the Victorie Atchieved by Count Maurice. Tr. out of the Dutch copy. 1600. *STC* 17679.

A True Report of the Great Overthrowe Lately Given unto the Spaniards in Their Resolute Assault of Bergen Op Zoom. 1605. *STC* 1900.

The True Reporte of the Service in Britanie, Performed by Sir John Norreys. 1591. *STC* 18655.

The True Reporte of the Skirmish Betwene the States of Flaunders, and Don Joan. 1578. *STC* 11030.

Ubaldini, Petruccio. *A Discourse Concerninge the Spanishe*

Fleete. Tr. R. A[dams]. 1590. *STC* 24481.

Valdes, Francisco de. *The Sergeant Major.* Tr. J. Thorius. 1590. *STC* 24570.

Vegetius Renatus, Flavius. *The Foure Bookes of Martiall Policye.* Tr. J. Sadler. [1572]. *STC* 24631.

Vere, Sir Francis. *The Commentaries of Sir Francis Vere.* (Written *ca.* 1601.) Cambridge, 1657.

Ward, Robert. *Anima'dversions of Warre.* 1639. *STC* 25025.

———. (Anr. issue.) 1639. *STC* 25025a.

Whetstone, George. *The Honorable Reputation of a Souldier.* 1585. *STC* 25339.

———. (Anr. ed.) Eng. and Dutch. 1586. *STC* 25340.

Whitehorne, Peter. *Certain Waies for the Orderying of Souldiers in Battelray.* 1562. (This and later editions published with Machiavelli, *The Arte of Warre.*) *STC* 17164.

———. (Anr. ed.) 1573. *STC* 17165.

———. (Anr. ed.) 1588. *STC* 17166.

Williams, Sir Roger. *A Briefe Discourse of Warre.* 1590. *STC* 25732.

———. (Anr. ed.) 1590. *STC* 25733.

Wilson, Robert. *The Coblers Prophesie.* 1594. *STC* 25781.

Index

Aeneas, 13
Aeneid, 12, 13
Achilles, 13, 181*n29*
Agamemnon, 13
Aiming artillery, methods of, 131–34
Ajax, 181*n29*
Alexander the Great, 8, 12, 19, 56, 181*n27*
Alba y Viamont, Diego de (Spanish scientist), 146, 147
Alphonso, King of Aragon, 35
Alva, Fernando Alvarez de Toledo, 96
Amputation, 158–59, 166–67
Amyot, Jacques, 29
Ancients. *See* Ensigns
Antony, Marc, 49
Antwerp, 34
Archery, 38, 40
Aristotle: *Nicomachean Ethics,* 18; on geometry, 18
Armagh, 83, 102, 202*n106*
Armor: infantry, 89, 90, 199*n58;* of billman, 90–91, 200*n64,* 200*n70;* of musketeer, 97; of lancer, 116–17; of shot-on-horseback, 117; of halberdier, 200*n64,* 202*n70*
Arms. *See* Weapons
Ascham, Roger: *The Scholemaster,* 19; praises captains, 65
Awdeley, John, *The Fraternitie of Vacabondes,* 171

Baker, George (Sergeant Surgeon to Queen Elizabeth): *The Composition or Making of the . . . Oil Called Oleum Magistrale,* 156, 159–62; on military medicine and surgery, 156, 159–62; and Barber-Surgeons' Company, 215*n41,* 215*n57*

Barber-Surgeons' Company, 148, 152, 156, 160, 215*n41,* 215*n57*
Barclay, Alexander: translator of Sallust, *Jugurtha,* 4
Barret, Robert: *The Theorike and Practike of Moderne Warres,* 21, 57, 73, 194*n2;* on selection of officers, 57, 70; on common soldiers, 60; on weapons, 88, 104–5; on tactics of the shot, 100; on cavalry, 110, 112–13, 115–18 *passim;* on artillery equipment, 128–29; service abroad, 128; on artillery officers, 207*n4;* on an ideal army, 208*n7,* 209*n19*
Barwick, Humphrey: *A Breefe Discourse Concerning the Force . . . of All Manuall Weapons of Fire,* 49, 50, 146, 198*n36;* military career, 49, 50; attacks Smythe, 50; attacks Williams, 50; condemns Machiavelli, 50; on weapons, 87, 93–94, 96, 97, 105; on cavalry, 113, 115, 117; mentioned, 146, 147, 170
Baynard, Captain John, 71
Betham, Peter: translator of Porcia, *Preceptes of Warre,* 14, 15
Billmen, 90–91
Biringuccio, Vanoccio (Italian scientist), 146, 147
Blount, Charles. *See* Mountjoy
Bourne, William: on the science of gunnery, 131–35, 141, 146, 147; *The Arte of Shooting in Great Ordnaunce,* 132; *Inventions or Devises . . . ,* 132
Brainworm, character in *Every Man in his Humour,* 172
Brutus, Marcus Junius, 9

233